THE
PLAYBOOK

ALSO BY JAMES SHAPIRO

Shakespeare in a Divided America

The Year of Lear: Shakespeare in 1606

Contested Will: Who Wrote Shakespeare?

1599: A Year in the Life of William Shakespeare

Oberammergau

Shakespeare and the Jews

Rival Playwrights: Marlowe, Jonson, Shakespeare

THE
PLAYBOOK

A Story of Theater, Democracy, and
the Making of a Culture War

JAMES SHAPIRO

PENGUIN PRESS | NEW YORK | 2024

PENGUIN PRESS

An imprint of Penguin Random House LLC

penguinrandomhouse.com

LIBRARY OF CONGRESS CATALOGING-IN-PUBLICATION DATA

Names: Shapiro, James, 1955– author.

Title: The playbook: a story of theater, democracy,
and the making of a culture war / James Shapiro.

Description: First. | New York: Penguin Press, 2024. |
Includes bibliographical references and index.

Identifiers: LCCN 2023048102 (print) | LCCN 2023048103 (ebook) |
ISBN 9780593490204 (hardcover) | ISBN 9780593490211 (ebook)

Subjects: LCSH: Federal Theatre Project (U.S.)—History. | United States.
Congress. House. Special Committee on Un-American Activities (1938–1944) |
Theater and society—United States—History—20th century. | Politics and
literature—United States—History—20th century. | Culture conflict—United States.

Classification: LCC PN2270.F43 S53 2024 (print) |
LCC PN2270.F43 (ebook) | DDC 792.0973—dc23/eng/20240103

LC record available at https://lccn.loc.gov/2023048102

LC ebook record available at https://lccn.loc.gov/2023048103

Printed in the United States of America

1st Printing

Designed by Nerylsa Dijol

For Anne Edelstein

playbook

A book containing the scripts of dramatic plays.

A set of tactics frequently employed by one engaged
in competitive activity.

—*American Heritage Dictionary of the English Language*

Contents

The Federal Theatre's Portable Theatre,
Crotona Park, the Bronx, c. 1936.

Preface

L ike other Americans, I can rely on the federal government to send me a Social Security check once a month when I am old or disabled. And I sleep better thanks to the Federal Deposit Insurance Corporation, knowing that if my bank is the next to fail, my savings are still protected, even as the Securities and Exchange Commission protects my pension's investments. A century ago, these guardrails didn't exist, nor did the Federal National Mortgage Association to secure housing, the National Labor Relations Board to ensure workers' rights, the Soil Conservation Service to help farmers and protect the nation's ecosystems, or the Tennessee Valley Authority to provide natural resource planning and hydroelectric power for communities inadequately served by the private sector. These seven federal programs are the sole survivors of the New Deal legislation of the 1930s, proposed by President Franklin D. Roosevelt, then passed by Congress over the bitter objections of vested interests who to this day keep trying to curtail programs that protect so many. Vestiges of other New Deal projects still surround us, enriching our lives, though I suspect that few Americans are aware when hiking a trail cut on a mountainside in Colorado, or passing a vivid mural in a post office in Mississippi, or thumbing through one of the still-reprinted state guides in a bookstore in Vermont (John Steinbeck called them "the most comprehensive account of the United States ever got together") that these only exist because of the New Deal's Works Progress Administration (WPA).

This book is about a once thriving WPA relief program that did not survive and has left little trace: the Federal Theatre Project, which from 1935 to 1939 staged, for a pittance, over a thousand productions in twenty-nine states seen by thirty million, or roughly one in four Americans, two thirds of whom (according to audience surveys) had never seen a play before. It offered traditional fare, like Shakespeare, mixed in with contemporary plays on issues that mattered to Depression-era audiences, such as slum housing and the threat of fascism, topics largely shunned by Hollywood and the commercial stage. Led by a theater professor, Hallie Flanagan, it employed, at its peak, over twelve thousand struggling artists, some of whom, like Orson Welles and Arthur Miller, would soon be famous, but most of whom were just ordinary people eager to work again at their craft. It was the product of a moment when the arts, no less than industry and agriculture, were thought to be vital to the health of the republic and deserving of its support. The Federal Theatre brought entertainment to the work camps where those hiking trails were being dug. It brought children's plays on touring trucks to kids in crowded cities. It staged works in foreign languages to reach immigrants. It established what it called "Negro Units" from Hartford to Seattle to support Black actors and playwrights. It brought free theater to asylums, orphanages, hospitals, prisons, and veterans' homes. It revived playgoing in rural states where the movies had all but ended it. Ten million listeners a week tuned in to its radio broadcasts. Its popularity, which contributed to its undoing, confirmed that there was a hunger for drama that spoke to the unsettling times.

The Federal Theatre was the first New Deal project to be successfully attacked and abruptly terminated, on the grounds that it promoted un-American activity. When it was shut down, a series of fact-based plays exploring subjects as urgent as war, flood control, food and drugs, tuberculosis, and money, as well as four others on America's racial divide, were in development. Its closing would have a lasting impact on American cultural life, and, inevitably, on the resilience of the nation's democracy, for the health of democracy and theater, twin-born in ancient Greece, has always been mutually dependent. The consequences of the attacks on it, part of a particularly ugly culture war that led to its defunding, are still felt today.

The term "culture war" didn't enter the national vocabulary until the summer of 1992, when Patrick Buchanan, a far-right conservative, declared at the Republican National Convention that there "is a religious war going on in our country for the soul of America. It is a cultural war." Buchanan had lifted the phrase from a groundbreaking book published a year earlier, *Culture Wars: The Struggle to Define America*, by a sociologist of religion, James Davison Hunter. Hunter had argued that "America is in the midst of a culture war," with progressives opposed by an orthodoxy who didn't like where the country was heading. Hunter saw the origins of the conflict as sectarian rather than political, the result of century-long tectonic shifts as a once overwhelmingly Protestant nation fitfully absorbed other religious groups and new coalitions emerged. His book focused on the controversies that followed from these realignments during the 1960s, especially over abortion, the arts, gay and women's rights, and what was taking place in America's classrooms.

The idea that the nation was embroiled in a culture war resonated powerfully, and would be a rallying cry, mostly for those on the right, in the ensuing decades. A slew of books with similar-sounding titles followed—including Andrew Hartman's *A War for the Soul of America: A History of the Culture Wars*, Todd Gitlin's *The Twilight of Common Dreams: Why America Is Wracked by Culture Wars*, Edward P. Lazear's *Culture Wars in America*, Irene Taviss Thomson's *Culture Wars and Enduring American Dilemmas*, and Bill O'Reilly's *Culture Warrior*. While not necessarily sharing Hunter's religion-driven narrative, all these writers, across the political spectrum, were happy to agree with his premise that America's culture wars emerged in the late 1960s.

But to accept that they began as late as that ignores the obvious: culture wars have long divided Americans, as far back as Revolutionary times, when colonists content with life under British rule were opposed by others who fought for independence. In the early decades of the republic fresh ones emerged, between those who favored American expansionism and those who rejected Manifest Destiny, and then, bloodily, in a Civil War between secessionists who fought to perpetuate slavery and abolitionists who opposed them. That war did not put an end to competing worldviews that would lead to fresh culture wars over Reconstruction and citizenship into the 1870s, then over populism in the 1890s, and so on. As the nation changed, so have its culture wars, which have always been with us and rarely serve as precursors to each other.

The culture war that broke out in the late 1930s over the place of the arts and especially of theater in our democracy took place at a time, much like our own, of economic uncertainty, racial tensions, and rising nationalism and fascism, with new technologies transforming how entertainment and news were experienced. But there were fundamental differences too, for it was a time framed by the Depression and the outbreak of World War II, and then a Cold War, in which cultural battles were vastly overshadowed by economic and soon military ones, and never reached their current fever pitch. Crucially, the 1930s were also years in which progressives in America found their voice in both the political and artistic realms, leading their opponents to seek out strategies to halt or reverse what were for them disturbing societal changes. In that respect it anticipated our current divide. A defining legacy of this culture war is how these strategies coalesced into a right-wing playbook, widely used today, for securing power and challenging progressive initiatives.

A central figure in this story is a largely forgotten congressman from East Texas, the charming, bigoted, and ambitious Martin Dies. In 1938 Dies was appointed chairman of the first congressional "un-American" committee—universally known as the Dies Committee—that was expected to look into the rise of Nazism and Communism in America, and seven months later turn in a final report and then disband. Determined to secure a more permanent platform, Dies focused much of his committee's investigations instead on the Federal Theatre and its playbooks (that is, its scripts), generating headlines for months. The political theater riveted the nation, and Dies's popularity soared. The result of this clash between government entities was that the Federal Theatre was killed off in 1939 while the House Un-American Activities Committee survived until 1975.

In the course of waging and winning this battle, Dies assembled that figurative playbook so pervasive it now seems timeless. Long before Joseph McCarthy began naming names of those he deemed "un-American" in his own hearings in the Senate, Martin Dies had instituted the practice. Long before elected officials discovered that informal legislative guardrails could safely be ignored, that journalists rarely followed up on false claims, and that emerging media could easily be exploited, Dies had figured all that out. Long before politicians would galvanize followers by threats of violence against their foes, or brazenly play the race card, Dies would, on the campaign trail, speak of assaulting a Black congressman who dared challenge White supremacy, saying he would have "taken a swing at that nigger's jaw." And long before politicians realized that it was easier to attain power by battling over culture and identity—even if that meant reversing where they stood on specific legislation—Dies had shown how winning a strategy this could be. As forward-looking as Dies was, he was equally gifted at appropriating strategies others had successfully employed in exploiting grievances.

Why Dies went after the Federal Theatre can be explained in part by what Alexis de Tocqueville recognized a century earlier in his *Democracy in America* (1835), where he writes that "the love of the drama is . . . most natural to democratic nations," and where he describes democracy at work in America's theaters: "At the theatre alone the higher ranks mix with the middle and the lower classes; there alone do the former consent to listen to the opinion of the latter, or at least to allow them to give an opinion at all." In a world in which, as Tocqueville put it, the pit makes law for the boxes, those in charge outside the playhouse—the politicians and the wealthy now sitting in America's box seats—had cause to be concerned by what Tocqueville described as theater's power to "lay hold on you in the midst of your prejudices and your ignorance," and educate and rouse people to

change what they believed was unjust. That, at least, is the promise—
or threat—of theater. A century ago, when fewer than one in five
American adults had finished high school and fewer than one in
twenty-five had earned a college degree, schooling didn't serve that
purpose (so didn't provoke the controversy and censorship that America's classrooms now face); but a theater that stretched from coast to
coast, especially one that staged plays on social and political issues,
had the potential to inform and change many minds. Martin Dies,
who believed that the increasingly popular Federal Theatre was
spreading a dangerously progressive as well as a racially integrated
vision of America, decided that it needed to be stopped.

In the face of such an onslaught, the Federal Theatre was unusually vulnerable and soon found itself fighting on two fronts: critics to
its left thought it had not gone far enough in challenging the status
quo, while those on the right accused it of peddling un-American
propaganda. Navigating these narrow straits while buffeted by political winds proved overwhelming, and the Federal Theatre ultimately
foundered. Its loss proved to be a pyrrhic victory for its critics on both
the left and right. Many of the former would soon find themselves
blacklisted and the American theater politically moribund. And conservatives succeeded in eroding the associational life they so highly
prized, for in its brief existence the Federal Theatre had established
ties with hundreds of educational, fraternal, civic, and religious
groups, strengthening communal bonds across the land.

Ten chapters follow. Two recount how the Federal Theatre and the
Dies Committee came into existence; three others explore the consequences of their collision. They frame the intervening chapters which
underscore what was at stake, delving into five Federal Theatre productions that flirted with censorship, confronted the racial divide,

tangled with Congress, tackled issues ignored or sanitized by Hollywood, and expanded the possibilities of what American theater and culture could be. They also land squarely on inflammatory issues that would later inform our current culture wars. These five are a groundbreaking Black production of *Macbeth* in Harlem that toured as far as Texas; an adaptation of Sinclair Lewis's anti-fascist novel *It Can't Happen Here* that opened simultaneously in eighteen cities; White modern dancers performing Black songs of protest in *How Long, Brethren?*; *One Third of a Nation*'s exposé of slum housing, produced nationwide; and a brilliant and bitter history of racism in America that was never staged, *Liberty Deferred*. Taken together, they convey the range of productions that so riled the Dies Committee while capturing the Federal Theatre at its stumbling and self-censoring worst as well as its daringly innovative best.

THE
PLAYBOOK

Martin Dies, chairman, House Un-American
Activities Committee, c. 1938.

CHAPTER ONE

Is Marlowe a Communist?

On December 6, 1938, for the first and perhaps only time in U.S. history, the purpose of theater and its place in American democracy was hotly debated in a congressional hearing. The fraught exchange took place on the second floor of the Old Congressional Building in Washington, D.C., where the recently formed House Un-American Activities Committee questioned its witnesses. The venue, with high ceilings and large chandeliers, its walls lined that day with theater exhibits, resembled a stage set for a courtroom drama. Two long tables had been arranged in the shape of a T. At its foot was a solitary witness chair. An audience of stenographers, reporters, photographers, and cameramen sat behind long tables on each side of the room. They were drawn there in part by the committee's theatrics, vividly described in the *Washington Star*: "Under a blinding glare of spotlights and a bombardment of photographers' bulbs," committee members "shout insults at each other or at witnesses, who retort in kind. Spectators and witnesses exchange taunts. More than once the audience has been permitted to rise and cheer a pronouncement of the chairman."

Sitting at the head of the T that Tuesday morning were five members of the investigative committee: J. Parnell Thomas of New Jersey, John J. Dempsey of New Mexico, Joe Starnes of Alabama, Harold Mosier of Ohio, and its chairman, Martin Dies, a tall and charismatic Texan in his late thirties who worked his way through eight cigars in the course of a day's hearing. While officially known as the Special Committee on Un-American Activities, everyone, including reporters, referred to it as the Dies Committee. Its other members struggled to be more than a supporting cast. The committee, authorized by Congress on May 26, 1938, was due to present its findings in less than a month. Its budget had been a measly $25,000, perhaps half of what it needed to hire enough investigators, signaling Congress's uneasiness with authorizing this special committee, which it hamstrung by underfunding it. This meant that the Dies Committee lacked both the time and manpower to look into its ostensible targets, Nazism and Communism. So it reached for lower-hanging fruit, public relief, which many Americans had grown weary of, focusing its attention on one of the more controversial divisions of the WPA's Federal One, a program that had put to work thousands of unemployed writers, musicians, photographers, painters, and actors. It wasn't easy attacking murals adorning public libraries, or concerts, or photographs, or tourist handbooks. Theater offered a richer target, in part because it had become remarkably popular; in part because it was easy to find and then read aloud incriminating passages from plays that sounded obscene or subversive; and in part—and this is what justified linking it to un-American activities—because it attracted many on the political left who hoped, at a time of massive unemployment, racial division, and income inequality, that plays could expose and help change what they found wrong in America.

Back in August, at the end of its first week of hearings, the Dies Committee had heard from a half dozen or so witnesses who, based on hearsay evidence and unchallenged allegations, had traduced the Federal Theatre as communistic and its plays as subversive of American values. The accusations were front-page news. Subsequent reports of the wild and unpredictable hearings, which Americans seemingly couldn't get enough of, had generated growing public interest. With only weeks left before the committee members had to submit their report to Congress, they had not allowed any officials representing the Federal Theatre to respond to these accusations, despite repeated requests to do so. The previous day the committee finally invited, then grilled, the first of these, the formidable Mississippian and high-ranking WPA administrator Ellen Sullivan Woodward, and that hadn't gone well. Woodward had turned the tables, deriding their biased proceedings as "un-American," and accused them of giving "widespread publicity to testimony given before your committee" by "unqualified, irresponsible, and misinformed" witnesses. She was admonished in turn: "You are not here to ask the committee questions. You are here to answer questions." Dies had made a tactical error in rebuffing Thomas's request to skip Woodward entirely and turn directly to the testimony of a more vulnerable witness who worked under her, forty-eight-year-old Hallie Flanagan, a professor at Vassar College who had risen to national prominence in 1935 when chosen to run the Federal Theatre. From Dies's perspective, Monday's outcome must have been a disappointment, if not a potential disaster, especially after the *New York Times* headline had declared "WPA Plays Upheld at Dies Hearing," and the anti-administration *Chicago Tribune* had not even bothered running a story.

Since August, Flanagan had sought to appear at the hearings to defend the Federal Theatre, but until now the Dies Committee had stonewalled her. The committee couldn't hold off any longer on allowing her to speak; and Roosevelt's administration, having told Flanagan not to respond in public, had reversed course as well, belatedly recognizing the damage already done by this strategy. Flanagan had come prepared, reports and affidavits in hand. Nobody knew the Federal Theatre more intimately or could speak about it with greater passion. She was possessed of considerable poise, but, unlike Woodward, a veteran politician, had never found herself in such a hostile environment. Her mission was to defend the Federal Theatre; Dies's was to trip her up, vilify her program, and, in so doing, make national news and extend the life of his committee. What Flanagan failed to grasp—and it would haunt her to her dying days—was that the hearing room (which to her producer's eye looked "like a badly staged courtroom scene") offered a different sort of drama than she had ever encountered. That shopworn set masked a nascent form of American political theater far more dangerous than the one she had come to defend.

Dies entered the Old Congressional Building that morning bolstered by a successful weekend of politicking in New York City. On Saturday he had spoken at a luncheon at the Hotel Pennsylvania for six hundred members of the nationalist American Defense Society. Before this sympathetic crowd, risking President Roosevelt's wrath, Dies lashed out against Secretary of the Interior Harold Ickes and Secretary of Labor Frances Perkins for having "gone to great lengths to 'ridicule and destroy' his investigation." His strategy was to play the victim while wrapping himself in the flag: "The enemies of this country . . . have been stupid. Their tactics of ridicule, misrepresentation, lies, abuse, etc., have done more to arouse the patriotism of this country to the seriousness of the situation than all the testimony we have heard." Dies's hosts were furious that no radio station had covered the popular congressman's speech (though Dies had not asked any station to do so, and he had been on NBC radio alone seven times since April). Arnold Davis, cochair of the society, wondered aloud, "Who had the power to do that?"—intimating that Roosevelt's administration was conspiring to subvert Dies's investigation. National papers jumped on the conspiracy theory, several running a version of the headline that appeared in the *Los Angeles Times* the next day: "Six Radio Stations Refuse Time to Dies." The press also reported that those at the luncheon voted unanimously to urge "Congress to appropriate sufficient funds for continuation of the investigation." While this was a vote of confidence, the need for one was a sign of how vulnerable Dies's committee now was. Dies told the crowd that "long before he undertook the investigation . . . he was advised by a friend not to begin it because a concerted attempt would be made to 'smear' it," hinting at an even deeper and long-standing conspiracy to silence him.

Buoyed by this response, on Sunday he spoke to an admiring crowd of over three thousand at the Brooklyn Academy of Music, where he declared (in a barely veiled attack on Communists in the country) that anyone "who advocates class hatred is plainly un-American." He was still struggling to find effective ways to attack the Communist threat, since there was nothing illegal about being a member of the Communist Party in America. So he had to find a better way to persuade people that Communist values were fundamentally un-American, and at the same time quietly absolve fascism, which he had been far less keen on investigating. That evening Dies tried out a fresh argument, suggesting, as the *New York Herald Tribune* reported, that "property rights were closely linked to human rights," and that history has shown "if you lose one you lose the other." By this logic, to oppose private corporations and to advocate for public programs—socialized medicine, say, or state ownership of utilities—was by default un-American, as well as against human rights. This crowd, too, adopted a resolution "asking Congress to increase the appropriation of the Dies committee." His fellow speakers at the event praised Dies, and one of them, George Harvey, the Queens borough president, even "suggested him for the Presidency."

Heading back to the nation's capital either late that night or very early the next morning, what did Dies think was more likely: his nomination to succeed Roosevelt in the Oval Office or his failure to secure his committee's future? At that moment it was anyone's guess. The newly established Gallup poll was at this very moment tabulating its findings about what Americans thought about his committee; the results of that survey were as yet unknown.

Flanagan came prepared to share with the committee how much the Federal Theatre had accomplished in its short life as well as to defend it from accusations that it was promoting Communism. She was progressive in her worldview and believed that theater should be "a thorn in the flesh of the body politic," but she had never imposed an ideological agenda on the Federal Theatre, and had pushed back against radicalism in her organization. The overwhelming majority of the hundreds of productions she had approved were unobjectionable—classical and modern drama, religious plays, vaudeville acts, marionette shows—though a few contemporary plays had not shied away from controversy (and had angered those across the political spectrum, from the Roosevelt administration to its foes in Congress, the latter far more often). The cost to American citizens for all this was negligible: less than 1 percent of money allocated for all federal work relief. The price tag over the past three years or so had amounted to—as Flanagan herself would put it—the cost of building one battleship.

The committee made Flanagan wait. Before allowing her to testify, there was a warm-up act: they first wanted to hear from Howard Stone Anderson, minister of the First Congregational Church in Washington, D.C., who was invited to speak about "the best ways and means to promote Americanism." Anderson spoke uninterrupted and interminably about "the spiritual lethargy and moral indifference" threatening America, and recommended that radicals should be dealt with "by force or persuasion, by confinement, or deportation." If Flanagan thought she was going to be treated with similar courtesy, she was in for a surprise. She, too, had planned to read from a prepared statement, but the committee had other ideas. J. Parnell Thomas and Joe Starnes, either out of impatience or to see whether they could rattle her, began peppering her immediately with questions as soon as she was sworn in. *The New York Times* reported that they "heckled" Flanagan and "interrupted each other in their eagerness to question her": "Their questions tumbled out so fast that she had to juggle with two or three at a time and was continually cut off from completing her sentences." They were ill-equipped to deal with the hard-earned authority of professional women like Woodward and Flanagan who refused to defer to them. Dies, who allowed this spectacle to go on for too long, at last intervened, started things over, asking Flanagan what her duties were as head of the Federal Theatre.

Unwilling to cede to the committee members who defined what was American, or for that matter un-American, Flanagan in her reply flipped the script, a bit too wittily: "Since August 29, 1935, I have been concerned with combating un-American inactivity." Dies misheard her and replied: "No. We will get to that in a minute." Flanagan had to repeat herself: "Please listen. I said I am combating un-American inactivity." A confused Dies responded, "Inactivity?" Flanagan explained: "I refer to the inactivity of professional men and women; people who, at that time when I took office, were on the relief rolls; and it was my job to expend the appropriation laid aside by congressional vote for the relief of the unemployed as it related to the field of the theater." Starnes, impatient, jumped back in, cherry-picking Flanagan's official correspondence, trying to drive a wedge between the two goals of her project that had always been in tension with each other: providing relief to thousands of unemployed actors and staging first-rate productions. Flanagan, despite his interruptions, held her ground, repeatedly placing the snippets he was quoting within larger and inoffensive contexts. She just as deftly refuted Starnes's accusation that her goal was creating a *national* theater.

There were a few reasons why she had to do so. The first was that the name was taken. On July 5, 1935, a bill authorizing the "non-political, non-sectarian" and not-for-profit American National Theatre and Academy (assigning "sole and exclusive rights" to the name) had been signed into law. The new organization asked for no financial support; it was simply dedicated to stimulating public interest in theater, securing the best actors and plays "at a minimal cost," and encouraging the study of drama. Having wealthy donors spend their own money to support drama was something Congress had no trouble rubber-stamping, and it was only "national" in the sense that it was intended to benefit the entire country. After the Federal Theatre was created later that summer, Flanagan was visited by one of its members, who warned her "that the expression 'national theatre' had been pre-empted." Flanagan replied that she "had no intention of using what would be an inaccurate title." Though she hoped that the two organizations might collaborate, they wanted nothing to do with her project, and since then little had been heard from the American National Theatre.

The term "national" for Flanagan was also inaccurate insofar as it conjured up images of, as she put it, "a national theatre in the European sense of a group of artists chosen to represent the government." There really wasn't much difference, practically speaking, between a federal and national theater in an American context, once it was clear that the Federal Theatre bore no resemblance to French or German models. When Burns Mantle, the theater critic for the *New York Daily News*, toured theaters across the country in the spring of 1938, he concluded that he looked forward to the day "when we quit thinking vaguely of a national theatre as a marble building housing a golden-voiced stock company, and begin to think of it, as we should, in terms of a circuit of national theatre units." That's fairly close to what Flanagan aspired to, though she was also careful to avoid the term "national" because it conjured up—especially for Southern congressmen like Starnes of Alabama and Dies of Texas—the threat of a centralized government encroaching on states' rights. A civil war had in part been fought over this in living memory.

Once that line of attack sputtered, Starnes began another and more serious one: painting Flanagan as a Communist. He began with her background, referring to the months she had spent as a Guggenheim fellow studying theater in Europe and especially Russia, though interrupting her so often that his colleagues on the committee had to intercede. An overmatched Starnes, not yet done with proving a Russian connection, came at it a fresh way, asking whether she thought theater "was a weapon." He again tried turning Flanagan's words against her, this time reciting passages from her 1928 book, *Shifting Scenes of the Modern European Theatre*, as well as "A Theater Is Born," a report she had written in 1931 for *Theatre Arts Monthly* about workers' theater in America. But that attack was easily parried, as Flanagan explained the difference between reporting on something and advocating it; a workers' theater had, of late, been born in America, she told him, but it "was not born through me." Starnes grew increasingly agitated as Flanagan pointed out time and again that while he was quoting from her article accurately, he was merely quoting information that she was reporting and not her own views (silently passing over her obvious sympathy for them). Flanagan, like everyone else in the room, saw where his line of questioning was heading: Was the Federal Theatre promoting propaganda? Since it was impossible to deny that a small number of the Federal Theatre plays, especially the fact-checked Living Newspaper dramas, were committed to political and social advocacy, Flanagan, while acknowledging that these were propagandistic, insisted that they were propaganda for democracy. Propaganda for the elimination of slum dwellings. For better health care. For fairer labor practices. She concluded that that "propaganda, after all, is education," to which Starnes had no answer. For the reporters in the room it looked like a repeat of the previous day's tepid headlines.

It was time again for Dies, who had been silently watching this unfold, to take over. He began by asking Flanagan about the audiences that the Federal Theatre reached. That twenty-five million Americans had by then seen at least one of its productions was, for Flanagan, a mark of its success; for Dies, it was evidence of how influential the Federal Theatre had become, and if some of its plays were truly un-American, how dangerous an institution. Flanagan then refuted the accusation made by an earlier committee witness that the Federal Theatre "couldn't get any audiences for anything except Communistic plays," pointing out its affiliation with hundreds of mainstream organizations across the land: "Note gentlemen that every religious shade is covered and every political affiliation and every type of education and civic body in the support of our theater. It is the widest and most American base that any theater has ever built upon."

Starnes was not yet done. Failing to see the web Dies was slowly weaving to trap Flanagan, and still sure that she had confessed to Communist sympathies in her article, he forced his way back into the conversation, reading aloud what he believed to be the most incriminating quotation from Flanagan's writing:

> Unlike any art form existing in America today, the workers' theatres intend to shape the life of this country, socially, politically, and industrially. They intend to remake a social structure without the help of money—and this ambition alone invests their undertaking with a certain Marlowesque madness.

Confident that this was damning evidence of socialist sympathies, he demanded to know: "You are quoting from this Marlowe. Is he a Communist?" It was a question Starnes would regret asking for the rest of his life. The *New York Herald Tribune* called it the "high comedy relief of the day," and it would be quoted in his obituary a quarter century later. After "the loud laughter" (as *The New York Times* described it) subsided, Flanagan, who had abandoned her usual self-restraint and joined in, even, as one reporter observed, rolling her eyes, apologized for her rude response. She then explained: "I was quoting from Christopher Marlowe." But Starnes still didn't get it: "Tell us who Marlowe is, so we can get the proper reference, because that is all that we want to do." To which Flanagan replied, "Put in the record that he was the greatest dramatist in the period of Shakespeare, immediately preceding Shakespeare."

A "reddened" Starnes salvaged what he could, asking whether all drama, since its origins in ancient Greece, is fundamentally about social conflict, and so, by extension, Communist? Surely "Mr. Euripides was guilty of teaching class consciousness." His choice of classical dramatist hit close to home; three months earlier, in a fiery radio address, J. Parnell Thomas had singled out *Trojan Incident*, a recent modern-dress version of Euripides's tragedy by the Federal Theatre that dramatized the aftermath of the Trojan War, "wherein the people are shown the way to revolution." The adaptation of the play for that controversial Broadway production, in which the defeated women of Troy confront the Greek men who had conquered them, was the work of Flanagan's husband, Philip Davis, a Vassar professor of Greek and Latin, and Flanagan herself had advised the show. She was not going to back down about Euripides. Drama, dating back to the Greeks, had always been about social conflict and questioning the status quo. Flanagan might have added that this helped account for why millions of Americans, in the midst of a Depression, were flocking to see Federal Theatre productions. But how could she explain that—without further incriminating the Federal Theatre in promoting class conflict—to a committee that found any questioning of the way things were so threatening? Euripides, Marlowe, Shakespeare, Molière, it didn't make much of a difference to the committee members; if theater advocated social change, it was by default subversive and communistic, and therefore "un-American," and not something that the U.S. government should be funding.

Flanagan also found herself in a bind when it came to accusations that there were Communists within the Federal Theatre. The American Communist Party, which had initially opposed the New Deal, would pivot in 1935 from a rigidly oppositional to a more flexible "popular front" strategy of infiltrating labor unions, arts organizations, and the government itself. But as far as the Communist Party's efforts to bankroll radical American theater went, there has rarely been a poorer return on investment. Flanagan knew that there must have been card-carrying Communists in her ranks; the total number of party members nationally, which was never substantial, swelled from twenty thousand Americans in 1933 to sixty-six thousand by 1939. Yet she was forbidden by law from asking about the political or religious affiliation of those on relief, and certainly couldn't fire anyone on these grounds. She also knew, and had repeatedly pushed back against, "fellow travelers" sympathetic to Communism who pressed their views in a handful of productions, mostly in New York's units. She had no choice but to negotiate with the Workers Alliance of America, a union founded in March 1935 and run by Socialists and Communists, since it was WPA policy to meet with union representatives. You couldn't get a show off the ground without haggling with at least a dozen unions, and those same Workers Alliance representatives also met with her superiors in Washington. While she couldn't prevent some of its members from circulating strike notices or other flyers before the start of the workday, she should have come down more forcefully when they illegally circumvented that arrangement. But they were a nuisance, not a threat, and had never attained positions of leadership in her project or shaped its policies. Flanagan personally found the "whole thing . . . infuriating," and in July 1936 wrote to her husband that between "the fascists and communists" the Federal Theatre "will not have much chance." But she was wise not to explain all this to the Dies Committee, which would have seized on her testimony as a headline-generating admission of guilt, as it would do with the conciliatory explanations of Henry Alsberg, head of the Federal Writers' Project, who testified right after her.

Thomas then took over the questioning, steering the conversation toward specific plays. He failed spectacularly to make inroads against a children's play, *Revolt of the Beavers*, which he tried to label as Communist (and which *The New York Times* had called "Mother Goose Marx"). It didn't help that neither he nor any other member of the committee had ever seen a Federal Theatre production. Once again Flanagan was prepared and devastatingly read aloud from questionnaires that children had filled out after seeing this show. "The play teaches us never to be selfish," one wrote. Another, that "it is better to be good than bad." This line of attack was heading nowhere, so Thomas turned to an example that had especially infuriated him, how the New Jersey legislature—at a time when he was serving in it—was maligned in a play called *Injunction Granted*. What he failed to understand was that the offending lines he quoted from the play were spoken verbatim by those legislators, having been reported in newspapers. Flanagan made that clear. How could he object, she asked, to what had actually been said?

A fundamental problem, Flanagan realized, was that these congressmen didn't quite grasp how plays worked or how dramatists, through their characters and dialogue, pitted competing points of view against each other, so that it was misguided to quote any single speech and conclude that it somehow represented a play's message. She managed to make that point during Mosier's more civil questioning: "We would be on very dangerous ground if we denominated and denounced as subversive any play in which any character opposing our own political faith appeared. For instance, you might as well say that Marlowe that we discussed a while ago, because he introduced the devil into the play had sold his soul to the devil. You might as well say *The March of Time*, because it quotes from Stalin, is Communistic, or because it quotes from Hitler, is Fascist."

It was now midmorning, and it was left to Martin Dies to reverse what was at this point going quite badly for the committee. Once again he began disarmingly, asking Flanagan whether the purpose of the Federal Theatre was "amusement or . . . the teaching of a particular idea, or the presentation of facts or material in a way to leave a definite impression?" The question seemed innocuous enough, one that had been debated by writers and critics since the Roman poet Horace had asked two thousand years earlier whether the point of literature was to delight or to instruct. Dies kept returning to it, rephrasing his question, as he patiently and inexorably approached what both he and Flanagan knew was being centrally contested: Should the Federal Theatre be used to convey "ideas along social, economic, or political lines"? Sensing a trap, Flanagan asked Dies to exclude "political," and he graciously did so, only to ask her once again whether she believed "it is correct to use the Federal Theatre to educate people, audiences, along social or economic lines?" Flanagan grudgingly admitted, "Among other things, yes." That was all Dies needed to hear, and he spent the next hour delving into exactly how the various Federal Theatre plays were leftist propaganda, intended to foment class struggle and undermine what for him were essential American values. The only moment that he dropped his folksy courtroom manner and turned icy was when, discussing a Federal Theatre musical currently in rehearsal, *Sing for Your Supper*, he couldn't resist reminding Flanagan of the power he wielded; the show might well reach the stage, he said, "unless you are interrupted by lack of funds, or some action of Congress."

Having set aside for the moment the loaded term "Communist," Dies steadily, and with increasing success, forced Flanagan to acknowledge that Federal Theatre plays did indeed raise issues pertaining to social class, and he asked her whether taxpayers should pay for plays "that portray the interest of one class to the disadvantage of another class," even though what those plays have to say might be accurate. When Flanagan insisted that "we are not doing plays to stir up class hatred," he pointedly replied, "That is a question of opinion." And he then succeeded in getting Flanagan to concede that a play called *Power*—about how the New Deal's Tennessee Valley Authority established a publicly owned utility that provided inexpensive electricity to the underserved—had advocated public ownership of utilities. Too late, Flanagan saw where this was going, saying "that is a very clever move on your part to maneuver me into a certain position." Dies, having succeeded in doing exactly that, came right back at her: "I would not undertake to match my cleverness with you on this subject because you are so thoroughly acquainted with it."

Dies then asked her where the Federal Theatre drew a line on advocacy. At public ownership of utilities? At public appropriation of private property? Flanagan knew that heading down this path would eventually lead, as she put it, to "recommending the overthrow of the

United States Government, and I do not want that, gentlemen, whatever some of the witnesses may have intimated." But Dies was relentless, insisting that she specify what sort of advocacy went too far, or alternatively, concede that she wanted theater to change America's political and economic order incrementally. It must have been enthralling to witness this pointed exchange, their dialogue reproduced in newspapers the next day as if it were lifted from a play. The more Flanagan tried to explain how theater that questioned the status quo worked, the closer Dies got to the headlines he so badly needed.

Flanagan was cornered, and knew it. She tried to extricate herself by declaring that Dies was now asking hypothetical questions, and demanded that she at last be entitled to share her prepared statement: "I came up here under the distinct understanding that I was to refute testimony by witnesses before your committee." But Dies was too shrewd to allow that to happen, since so much of what those witnesses had said—and which had gone unchallenged by his committee—was, as Woodward had pointed out, untrue, or biased, or not credible. The back-and-forth on this was tense. Flanagan managed to trip up Dies when he confused the Federal Theatre Project with the Federal Writers' Project; Dies, in turn, insisted, with a bit of sophistry, that because she was not in a position to repudiate Communist activities that took place without her *direct* knowledge, anything she had to say on the subject was hearsay, so that witness testimony must stand unchallenged.

Dies was almost done now, and, shifting gears, he read aloud provocative lines from a 1934 play, *Stevedore*, that had been a hit off-Broadway and was subsequently revived by the Federal Theatre. Here's how *The Baltimore Sun* described his exaggerated performance: "The recital began with a blasphemy and went on from there until the committee chairman, with an apparent shudder, halted himself: '*God damn dem, anyhow. What dey thin I am? Do I look like some kind of animal? Do I look like somebody who'd jump over a back fence and rape a woman?*'" "Absolutely vulgar lines," Dies "almost hissed." The lines he reproduces (and probably the voice he mimics) are those of a Black laborer, Lonnie, spoken when defending himself from a false accusation that he raped a White woman. But that storyline, at a time when Black men were still being lynched in America (which explains why an outraged and terrified Lonnie is cursing), is not what concerned Dies. For him, the passage was about the blasphemy and obscenity that the Federal Theatre was peddling—salacious language that the press, he knew, would report on. But this was as close as Dies would venture that day to the volatile issue of race, which was just below the surface of so much of the testimony about the Federal Theatre. He was well aware that over the past three years the Federal Theatre had broken many long-standing racial barriers, allowing Whites and Blacks to perform together, staging all-Black productions before integrated audiences in Jim Crow states, including Texas, that had previously outlawed such productions, and pouring federal dollars into "Negro Units" across America. But Dies, as staunch a foe of Black equality as one was likely to find in Congress, knew better than to risk alienating the Northern press, and knew as well that by law the Federal Theatre was required to be nondiscriminatory.

After Dies's performance, Thomas tried once again to get back into the fray, failing to understand that the show was over. Dies cut him off, asked what the hour was, and when told that it was already a quarter after one, called for an adjournment, to be followed by a fresh witness. Flanagan was stunned: "Just a minute, gentlemen. Do I understand that this concludes my testimony?" When Dies replied,

"We will see about it after lunch," she insisted on making a final statement. To which Dies, who had no intention of allowing such a formidable adversary any more time to make her case, said once more, "We will see about it after lunch." As the hearing broke up, Congressman Thomas approached Flanagan, she recalled, looking "jovial," and told her: "You don't look like a Communist. You look like a Republican." She told him that she wanted to continue testifying after lunch. Thomas laughed, then told her: "We don't want you back. You're a tough witness and we're all worn out." Flanagan approached the secretary of the committee, Robert Stripling, and asked that her written brief be included in the *Congressional Record*. She handed it to him and he assured her that it would be. It never was.

Hallie Flanagan, c. 1937.

CHAPTER TWO

The Creation of
the Federal Theatre

I t's almost impossible to grasp how deeply theater was woven into the fabric of American life, from coastal cities to frontier towns, before the rise of Hollywood. It helps to see this through the eyes of a young woman, born in 1873, who grew up in Red Cloud, Nebraska, went to college in the state capitol, Lincoln, and as an undergraduate began reviewing local productions for the *Nebraska State Journal*. Lincoln had fallen on hard times in the 1890s, its population dropping sharply from fifty-five thousand to forty thousand in the course of that decade due to an extended drought and a nationwide economic depression. Despite financial hardship, a great many people in Lincoln continued to flock to the theater, frequenting the Funke Opera House as well as the newer Lansing Theatre. The two houses could hold well over three thousand playgoers, and there were smaller venues in town as well. Remarkably, for a rural and mostly agricultural state with just over a million inhabitants, Nebraska had more than fifty playhouses in 1890, with new ones being built as rail service made transportation faster and more dependable, enabling some of the finest talent in the country to tour the state.

That young theater reviewer in Lincoln was the future novelist Willa Cather, later celebrated for her portrayal of frontier life. In the course of one especially busy week in April 1894, Cather reviewed five plays: *Black Crook* (one of America's earliest musicals), *The Fencing Master* (another New York transfer, which played to "uttermost capacity"), *Panjandrum* ("the best comic opera of this or of many seasons," that also played to "a packed" house), *Brother John* (by Martha Morton, one of America's first women playwrights), and *Police Patrol* (a "ponderous and patriotic" melodrama). On top of that she took in a minstrel show at the Lyceum Hall. Cather reports that the run of plays seems to have lifted spirits in town: "Despite the sleepiness which is a necessary result of attending five good plays in one week everyone seems more cheerful for the dissipation."

Twenty-five hundred playgoers could cram into the Lansing for a standing-room-only show, paying from twenty-five cents to a dollar. With at least two packed shows and three at half capacity, it's likely that eight thousand tickets were sold that week at the Lansing (the aging Funke, which would soon be refurbished, was dark). If you subtract the third of the population not yet fifteen years old, so likely too young to spend an evening at the theater, and subtract as well those too old or infirm, you are left with roughly thirty thousand adults who could go to the theater (and many, like Cather, went more than once). So it's likely that as many as one in four adults in Lincoln went to a play that week, a percentage approaching a theatergoing intensity not seen since London in Shakespeare's day.

Lincoln was not exceptional; playgoing was a national pastime. In 1896 Julius Cahn published the first of his annual *Official Theatrical*

Guide: Containing Information of the Leading Theatres and Attractions in America. Cahn listed every town in every state that had a playhouse, and provided information on train schedules, hotel accommodations, stage dimensions, admission charges, and much else. Cather's reflections on the recent season in Lincoln in 1894, in which dozens of companies had passed through town, convey the effect of this touring on rural America: "There were poor companies here, but there were also good ones," and she writes excitedly about the international stars of the stage, including Sarah Bernhardt, who reportedly "will play in all the smaller cities of America and will, of course, include Lincoln in her dates." A local historian recalled that a "list of the names of the players who came to Lincoln in those days reads like a Who's Who of the American stage." Acting companies touring Nebraska knew that even small towns had their own theaters; Red Cloud, where Cather grew up, with a population of two thousand, had its own opera house that could seat eight hundred. Looking back years later, Cather recalled how her town's "opera house was dark for most of the year, but that made its events only the more exciting. Half a dozen times each winter—in the larger towns more oftener—a traveling stock company settled down at the local hotel and thrilled and entertained us for a week." Theater connected Americans, and Cather took care to keep her readers abreast of the latest news about actors and plays from California and Texas to Chicago and New York. For Cather, "the people of this century have a right to demand something that is close to them, something that touches their everyday life," and touring companies provided that.

Cather, who kept one eye fixed on the stage, the other on the audience, provides a rich sense of the social cohesion that theater was forging, which rival forms of entertainment (including college football, then in its infancy in Nebraska) could not match. Those of different social classes mingled and interacted, often noisily, in the playhouse. She describes nights when "the sons and daughters of toil greatly predominated," the "kind of people who know how to enjoy themselves and who are thoroughly uncorrupted by any suspicion of taste," who felt "at liberty at any time to call out the approval or disapproval in not unmistakable terms." For those born abroad (and at this time perhaps a quarter of those living in Nebraska were European immigrants, for many of whom English was not their native language), theater helped overcome this barrier. There weren't many Black people living in Lincoln at this time, but Cather's reviews—in one of which she describes the reaction of "a big happy negro" sitting in the front row of the Lansing balcony—confirm that casual racism persisted, and that its theaters were integrated. Cather also describes amateur performances, including one by members of the Nebraska National Guard, the Lincoln Light Infantry. And the wall between town and gown was breached when a "full standing capacity" crowd at the Lansing came to see students from the university perform plays by Plautus and Sophocles in the original Latin and Greek. It's hard not to feel the infectiousness of playgoing in Lincoln at this time, across the social spectrum, captured by Cather in her description of those who came to see a song-and-dance revue, *Devil's Action*, at the Lansing in late September 1894. It was, she wrote, "one of the happiest crowds ever gathered in Lincoln. It was of course top-heavy, the gallery element predominating. The gallery was full, so full it could not contain itself. . . . It was a glorious audience, downstairs and up . . . the kind that can't stand a specialty performance without something elevating and classical, something Shakespearean. . . . It was a wildly enthusiastic audience; it enjoyed itself and it got its money's worth."

Even as automobiles were replacing the horse and buggy, movies were displacing theatrical performances across America. In 1900, nearly four hundred acting companies crisscrossed the country; two decades later that figure had dropped to forty-two, and by 1935, half that. One of the most knowledgeable writers on theater at the turn of the century, William Winter, recalled that in 1880 there had been as many as five thousand theaters in 3,500 locales. If Winter's estimate is accurate, roughly a third of American towns and cities had hosted theaters, quite a few of them, like Lincoln, more than one. Close to half these theaters had resident stock companies, a cohort of local actors who were a bedrock of the local arts community. While there had been roughly 2,000 permanent stock companies in 1910, by 1923 only 133 remained, a hollowing out of local culture. By 1925, according to *Billboard*, the number of playhouses outside major cities had dropped to 674. Many had been turned into cinemas. A decade later, Thomas Gale Moore writes in *The Economics of the American Theater*, "the total of stock, repertory and tent theaters had dwindled to 110." Outside of big cities, playgoing was fast disappearing, and part of the decline was self-inflicted, grounded in the conviction that theater, as Alfred L. Bernheim writes at the time in *The Business of the Theatre*, is "necessarily commercial," so it was natural for there to be a drive to consolidate control of the industry in the hands of the few, in this case the powerful Theatrical Syndicate, established in 1896, a monopolization of power and profit that rendered the entire system vulnerable.

The bottom seems to have fallen out in 1910 or so, the year in which Julius Cahn stopped publishing his annual guides. That year nearly 30 million Americans were going to the movies every week; admission was seven cents, a fraction of what a theater ticket cost. Those attendance numbers doubled by 1927 and nearly doubled again to 110 million in 1929 after talkies were introduced (at which point admission, now that serious competition from plays was gone, had risen to a quarter). It meant that on the eve of the Depression, on average, nearly every American—the population in 1930 was 123 million—went to the movies once a week. Even during the depths of the Depression that figure only dipped to 80 million or so. Hollywood soon elbowed its way onto Broadway, bankrolling shows at a loss, using theaters to try out plots and talent-hunt for actors, writers, and directors. In 1929, reflecting on how film "has put an end to the old-fashioned road companies which used to tour about in country towns," Cather lamented what was lost. Having witnessed these changes, and having been so marked by theater herself, she was sensitive to the cost of Hollywood's triumph. For her, film didn't quite measure up: "Only a living human being in some sort of rapport with us, speaking the lines, can make us forget who we are and where we are, can make us (especially children) actually live in the story that is going on before us, can make the dangers of that heroine and the desperation of that hero much more important to us, for the time much dearer to us, than our own lives." Cinematic "pictures of them, no matter how dazzling, do not make us feel anything more than interest or curiosity or astonishment."

It was the touring actors who embodied for Cather "the old glory of the drama in its great days," and "why its power was more searching than that of printed books or paintings because a story of human experience was given to us alive, given to us, not only by voice and attitude, but by all those unnamed ways in which an animal of any species makes known its terror or misery to other animals of its kind." She would find herself studying the audiences who went to the movies, even as she had once watched fellow playgoers, and put her finger on the difference: "I see easy, careless attention, amusement, occasionally a curiosity that amounts to mild excitement; but never that breathless, rapt attention and deep feeling that the old barnstorming companies were able to command. . . . Only real people speaking the lines can give us that feeling of living along with them, of participating in their existence." When, in 1936, the Federal Theatre "brought the theatre back to the people" of Nebraska and, as the *Omaha World-Herald* added, "filled, to some extent, the gap that was made when the movies took over," it was for many something new and strange: "Our actors" in Nebraska, Hallie Flanagan writes, "found that 90 per cent of their audience had never seen a play and could not believe that the actors were not moving pictures. After each performance they would wait in the doorway to see 'whether the people are real.'"

It's hard to determine how many Americans still earned a living in theater in the early decades of the twentieth century or how many had drifted away into other jobs before the Depression hit. Even in the best of times, there were always actors looking for work. In 1920, the U.S. Census counted 48,172 "actors and showmen," of which 28,361 were actors, including, presumably, those employed in film. No unemployment figures were given. A decade later, the 1930 census lumped together "actors and showmen," reporting that there were over 75,000, with 64,695 currently employed. If the proportion of actors and showmen remained the same, that meant there were roughly 38,000 actors. In 1932, more than 22,000 of them, hungry for work, had registered with Hollywood casting bureaus, though few would find employment, almost all as extras.

It wasn't just actors who had depended on theater for their livelihood; there were also playwrights, prop makers, musicians, prompters, stagehands, producers, ushers, designers, managers, carpenters, bill posters, advertising agents, scenic artists, electricians, dancers, and costume makers. Thirty-five separate unions represented these and other workers, from the Ushers, Doormen and Cashier's Union to Actors' Equity. With theater in decline, many no doubt used their skills to seek employment in other fields, including film and radio, which was still possible when the national unemployment rate remained, on the average, around 5 percent from 1900 to 1929. But when that percentage spiked to nearly 16 percent in 1931, and then climbed to an unprecedented 25 percent in 1933, there were very few jobs of any kind available. In New York City that year, impoverished actors lined up for clothing, cash, and the three hundred thousand meals dispensed by the Stage Relief Fund and the Actors' Dinner Club.

Several things, all of them unprecedented, had to fall into place before this crisis would lead to the creation of the Federal Theatre. The first was a radical shift in relief policy, providing jobs for the unemployed rather than, as in the past, putting them "on the dole." "Work relief," an oxymoron for many, was a new concept, driven largely by the emerging influence of social workers whose experience of the early years of the Depression had convinced them, as one put it, that if you give "a man a dole and you save his body and destroy his soul," but "give him a job and pay him an assured wage, and you save both the body and the spirit." But, since work relief cost more than handouts, there had to be political will to legislate it, and a leader and a political party bold enough to dispense funds, given the entrenched hostility to such policies by business interests fearful of their impact on the labor market. Taxpayers and legislators then had to be convinced of the value of giving a paycheck to unemployed violinists to perform concerts and actors to stage plays, rather than, as one unnamed congressman put it, handing them shovels and expecting them to dig ditches. Concerns about the government getting into the theater business—especially from unions worried about lower salaries and those who ran commercial theaters opposed to subsidized competition—also had to be allayed. The only time in American history that all these factors aligned, briefly, was the mid-1930s.

✦

It could never have happened without the vision and savvy of Harry Hopkins, an Iowan who, after graduating from Grinnell College, moved to New York City in 1912, where he became a social worker. In the two decades that would pass before the newly inaugurated President Roosevelt called him to Washington to head up national relief efforts, Hopkins, a workaholic with a genius for organization, developed a wealth of experience working with the destitute, from his early years in New York with the Association for Improving the Condition of the Poor, as well as the Board of Child Welfare, to his time with the Red Cross in the South. Given his expertise at large-scale relief efforts, when the Depression hit, Hopkins was asked by then governor of New York Franklin Roosevelt to serve as executive director of the Temporary Emergency Relief Administration. It would be the start of a long and consequential relationship.

In 1934, now president Roosevelt appointed Hopkins head of the newly formed Federal Emergency Relief Administration (FERA), which Congress authorized to spend $500 million for unemployment relief. Within two hours of settling in at his desk Hopkins had dispensed $5 million of it. FERA accomplished a great deal in the next eighteen months, employing over twenty million, including painters and writers, and supporting acting companies in seventeen states, whose plays were seen by five million spectators. Many of the features that would come to define the Federal Theatre were first tried out through FERA's programs, including performances at Civilian Conservation Corps sites and portable theaters in New York City. Its scale was small, and arts funding limited, but it confirmed for Hopkins that work relief, as he had put it, could save both the body and the spirit of the unemployed, including those of artists.

The midterm Democratic landslide of 1934 led Roosevelt to pursue more progressive policies. In January 1935, with unemployment still at a frighteningly high 20 percent, he proposed a massive $5 billion public program that would employ three and a half million jobless Americans, leading to the Emergency Relief Appropriations Act, the largest appropriations bill Congress had ever authorized. At its heart was the Works Progress Administration, which replaced the short-fix Civil Works Administration (CWA) that Hopkins had also overseen. Hopkins, who deftly outmaneuvered political rivals for control of WPA funds, understood how fleeting such opportunities were and told his staff: "This is our hour. We've got to get everything we want—a works program, social security, wages and hours, everything—now or never." The clock was ticking. Only five years would pass between Roosevelt's inauguration in 1933 and his final New Deal measure, the Fair Labor Standards Act of 1938. Hopkins recognized that "with the first flush of recovery, many of those who enjoy its benefits find themselves weary of their contingent responsibilities" and are "bored with the poor, the unemployed, and the insecure." And with Hitler's and Mussolini's rise to power in Europe, international commitments threatened to derail domestic ones.

A centerpiece of the WPA, and while only a small fraction of its budget its most controversial set of projects, was Federal One, which included the Federal Theatre Project, the Federal Writers' Project, the Federal Music Project, the Federal Art Project, and the Historical Records Survey. Twenty-seven million dollars was set aside for its programs in 1935, a little under $7 million of that for the Federal Theatre. Unlike FERA and the CWA, these would be run out of Washington rather than by state or local authorities. There had been calls for a national theater in America since its early years. The first was likely by William Dunlap, born in 1766, a playwright and theater manager in New York City. In his 1833 *History of American Theatre*, Dunlap wondered whether it was "visionary to suppose a free government, a government of the people, regulating and making more perfect and even more attractive an amusement which the people love." He anticipated objections, many of which would be repeated a century later: "This plan may appear chimerical, and perhaps may be opposed, at first view, by players and managers, as well as by all the enemies of the theatre, who are such from the various motives of blind prejudice, or honest belief that it is a promoter of evil."

Dunlap would not be the last to call for an American national theater; by August 1934, Edith J. R. Isaacs, editor of *Theatre Arts Monthly*, would write that "half the pigeonholes in Washington are said to be full, today, of schemes for a national theatre": there "are plans for building a national theatre in New York, for building it in Washington, for building it in Los Angeles." But, as with Dunlap's fantasy a century earlier, plans hadn't been fully thought through. Vast obstacles remained: what "repertory there will be, what standards, method, central idea, seem to be nobody's concern." It would take time to resolve these many issues, and Isaacs thought this process shouldn't be rushed: a national theater "may—should, in fact—wait to inaugurate performances; can wait for years, if necessary." The challenge confronting Hopkins five months later, on January 21, 1935, when Congress allocated funds for the Federal Theatre, was that there was no time; in retrospect, it was already a year or so too late to introduce a New Deal initiative of this sort. Once the plight of unemployed artists was leveraged to justify the creation of what amounted to a national theater, it had to be put in the right hands quickly, fully imagined overnight, and then begin staging plays soon after, from coast to coast, with productions good enough to justify the expense and quiet critics.

In his search for the right director, Hopkins interviewed leading figures from the noncommercial theater, including Isaacs, Frank Gilmore (a founder of Actors' Equity), and Eva Le Gallienne (who had established the Civic Repertory Theatre Company). Le Gallienne claimed to have turned the job down, and later that year published an essay in *The New York Times* questioning the direction of the Federal Theatre, urging the government to fund instead an elite theater employing the best talent available, the sort of national theater that "exists in many European countries." Hopkins was unimpressed by what he had heard, and complained that these ostensible leaders "are driving me crazy": "When I talk about plans for an American theatre, each one talks about his own little problem."

In late April the playwright Elmer Rice traveled to Washington in an unsuccessful attempt to secure FERA funding for the Theatre Alliance, a nonprofit repertory company. While there he was invited to speak with Hopkins, who asked him "pointblank whether he had any plan for a Federal theatre project," and Rice, who had not given the subject much thought, subsequently did so, writing a long letter in

which he urged Hopkins to bring back much of what had disappeared since the turn of the century, reestablishing theaters in a hundred communities across the country that would put thousands of
people back to work through local stock companies. These would
stage high-quality productions for low prices in renovated theaters,
supplemented by visits from touring stars. Rice himself wasn't interested in overseeing it, and when asked by Hopkins who could do the
job, he suggested Hallie Flanagan.

◆

Flanagan was born in Redfield, South Dakota, in 1890; her family
moved to Omaha, Nebraska, and then to various other Midwestern
towns and cities before settling in Grinnell, Iowa, at the turn of the
century. As a child, Flanagan recalled, she and her siblings "wrote
plays and acted them" for their parents. Her father was a traveling
salesman who had a hard time finding employment; her mother contributed to the family income as a dressmaker. During the economic
downturn of the 1890s her father "lost one job after another." She
never spoke or wrote about this, and we know of it only because of
what her stepdaughter Joanne Bentley, in researching Flanagan's life,
was able to uncover. Her father's struggles to find work made a powerful impression on Flanagan, though even close friends didn't know
why she uncharacteristically wept, in later years, after seeing *Death of
a Salesman*.

In 1907 she enrolled in Grinnell College, where Harry Hopkins
was a classmate. She was an excellent student and acted in the Dramatic Club. She also met the man she would marry not long after

graduation, Murray Flanagan. In 1916, four years after they wed, her young husband died of tuberculosis, leaving her to raise their two young boys by herself. Needing to support her family, Flanagan took a job teaching high school in Grinnell; she "did not choose work," she later said, "but had to earn a living." Had her husband survived, she would likely have remained a frustrated homemaker who, like her mother, worked on occasion. In 1920, at the age of thirty, she began teaching freshman English at her old college, the year Grinnell introduced playwriting and production into its curriculum. Flanagan herself began writing plays at this time and won the Iowa State Playwriting contest for her autobiographical and moralistic *The Curtain*, which was soon published and staged. Two years later disaster struck again when her older son, Jack, at age seven, died of spinal meningitis.

When her mentor at Grinnell resigned, she took over theater courses there, and then, in 1923, on the strength of her playwriting, was admitted to Harvard for the academic year to participate in the leading graduate theater program in the country, George Pierce Baker's "47 Workshop." Flanagan thrived in the program, and when she returned to Grinnell began to put into practice what she had learned at Harvard. Her talents soon recognized, she was offered—and accepted—a teaching position at Vassar College, in Poughkeepsie, New York, and, at Baker's urging and with his support, won a Guggenheim Fellowship in 1926 to spend a year studying theater in Europe. It would prove to be a life-altering experience.

Her travels took her from Ireland, England, and Scandinavia to France, Germany, Austria, Hungary, Italy, and, for the bulk of her time, the Soviet Union. She had the chance to discuss theater with many of the leading practitioners of the day, including William Butler Yeats, Lady Gregory, Sean O'Casey, Gordon Craig, Luigi Pirandello, Konstantin Stanislavsky, and Vsevolod Meyerhold. Flanagan was underwhelmed by what she saw in England, but found livelier productions in Scandinavia, and filled her notebooks with fresh ideas about design, lighting, acting, and directing that broke with the conservative realism that characterized most American productions at the time. She was especially excited by what she encountered in the Soviet Union: an intellectually rigorous theater committed to education and propaganda.

Flanagan brought back to Vassar many of the practices she had witnessed and rechristened her theater program the "Experimental Theatre." The program was notable for its range: her students were required to stage historical dramas, new works by classmates, and plays that employed new stagecraft techniques, as well as plays concerned with "modern problems." Not everyone was thrilled; Flanagan recalled how one faculty member walked out of her racy production of Shakespeare's *Antony and Cleopatra*, complaining that she "felt as if she were in a brothel." Others chafed at her insistence that performance mattered as much as literary analysis. It turned out to be very hard to say no to Hallie Flanagan, whether you were the president of Vassar (soon enlisted to perform in her shows) or the devoted students she attracted and then trained to realize that vision. Flanagan established a national reputation when she published a book about her encounters in Europe, *Shifting Scenes of the Modern European Theatre*. At Vassar she continued to oversee campus productions, though felt her ambitions cramped, writing wistfully at the time, "God help me to be able to do something more vivid in life than adding to the number of Vassar girls in the world."

In March 1931 Flanagan wrote her best known and most influential play: *Can You Hear Their Voices?* A former student, Margaret Ellen

Clifford, asked Flanagan whether she had read Whittaker Chambers's short story about the terrible drought faced by Midwestern farmers, "Can You Make Out Their Voices," which had appeared in that month's edition of the *New Masses*. Chambers, after reading a disturbing account that ran nationally, including in *The New York Times* on January 4, 1931—"500 Farmers Storm Arkansas Town Demanding Food for Their Children"—turned the news story into a parable of how small-town farmers armed themselves and turned to Communism to save their lives and livelihood. (This was the same Whittaker Chambers who later repudiated his days as a Communist and whose testimony to the House Un-American Activities Committee would land his fellow traveler Alger Hiss in federal prison.)

After reading the short story, Flanagan suggested to Clifford that they collaborate on a dramatization of it. They secured Chambers's permission to do so and researched and wrote the play in ten days, with the support of Vassar students who helped with the research. Flanagan maintained that it wasn't "radical" or "subversive"—though conservative playgoers may have flinched when hearing a desperate farmer say "Some people come into communism through their minds and some though their bellies, but I guess most of 'em come in because they can't stand seeing the folks they care about go hungry." The play substituted for Chambers's party-line Communist message a more tempered one, a change made explicit in their new title. Chambers's story ends with a mother asking her husband if he can still hear their departing sons in the distance, heading off to be protected by Communist comrades back East, while they remain to battle capitalist forces with their neighbors at home. In their play—staged less than two months after Chambers's short story was published—the line speaks to whether audiences can hear the plight of America's farmers confronting a terrible Depression, while the farmers who agitated for food, and for change, patiently await their arrest by state troopers on Christmas Day.

Can You Hear Their Voices? was a call for governmental support for farm relief, an appeal made directly on the screen projection with which the play ends: "These boys are symbols of thousands of our people who are turning somewhere for leaders. Will it be to the educated minority? CAN YOU HEAR THEIR VOICES?" Whether that leadership will come from a more progressive president than Herbert Hoover or from the Communist Party, or whether the message is that only strong national leadership can prevent destitute Americans from turning to Communism, is left unresolved. Anticipating similar work by John Steinbeck, Dorothea Lange, and other artists who were turning their attention to the plight of destitute American farmers, the play was, for Flanagan, a breakthrough moment. It was published and translated, and productions of it mounted on campuses and in regional theaters across America, as well as overseas, as far as Japan, Australia, France, Greece, and Russia. The play was still being revived three years later when it was staged off-Broadway. Reviewers admired it, with *Theatre Guild Magazine* noting that the "frankly propagandist play . . . deeply moved its audiences," and *The New York Times* praising it as "a searing, biting, smashing piece of propaganda." The most hostile review appeared in the Communist *Workers Theatre*, which complained, accurately, that "Flanagan and Clifford mutilated the class line of the story and adapted it into a play form with a clear liberal ideology."

Six months after the opening of *Can You Hear Their Voices?*, Flanagan published a long essay, "A Theatre Is Born," in *Theatre Arts Monthly*, which began with a vision of the future of American theater:

"At a time when Broadway is offering alibis for a disastrous season, during a period when art and community theatres are closing in many cities, . . . at this confused time, a new theatre, unknown in spite of the fact that it has been smouldering for ten years, leaps into life." The "theatre being born in America today is a theatre of workers" whose "object is to create a national culture by and for the working class of America. Admittedly a weapon in the class struggle, this theatre is being forged in the factories and mines. Its mouthpiece is the *Workers Theatre*."

Anyone reading this opening paragraph might be excused for thinking that Flanagan was promoting her own views. It turns out that she is reporting on those of others, after attending a conference of 224 "workers' cultural societies" in New York City on June 13, 1931, sponsored by the Communist John Reed Club and the *New Masses*. Flanagan is at pains in her essay to distinguish the American scene from the Soviet one: as "the meeting progressed, a number of speakers emphasized the fact that the problems of America are not the problems of the U.S.S.R., and that they must work out their own ideas and their own style." While ambivalent about the aesthetic merits of much of this agitprop drama, she concludes that there are only two kinds "of theatres in this country that are clear as to aim: one is the commercial theatre which wants to make money; the other is the workers' theatre which wants to make a new social order." She admired the latter's commitment to improving American lives, in a passage that would later be cited by the House Un-American Activities Committee: "Unlike any art form existing in America today, the workers' theatres intend to shape the life of this country, socially, politically, and industrially."

The essay's claims came back to haunt her, as she struggled to walk a fine line—in her campus productions, her playwriting, as well as in her journalism—between a progressive and a more radical politics. It is impossible to know whether her unwillingness to step over that line, or step over it very far, was grounded in pragmatism, Midwestern caution, or an ideological aversion to doing so. And that line, in the early 1930s, with the deepening Depression and the troubling rise of fascism, was constantly shifting; only a card-carrying member of the Communist Party could be certain of ideological purity. For those at the opposite end of the political spectrum, already suspicious of artists and professors, any such distinction was little more than hairsplitting.

In the decade or so since, as a young widow, she had begun to support herself and her sons teaching freshman English, Flanagan—as a scholar, director, producer, and playwright—had emerged as one of the more promising voices in American theater. As the Depression worsened in 1932 she would stage a pair of radical plays, *Miners on Strike* and *We Demand*, which led to pushback on campus for their Communist sympathies. She balanced these productions with classics like Shakespeare and modernist plays across the political spectrum, including those by T. S. Eliot and W. H. Auden. Despite the success of many of these productions, and the attention they drew in the theater world, her ambitions were increasingly frustrated. She was overworked and hungry for new challenges. She tried pitching short stories and a book idea through an agent, but *The New Yorker* and other magazines and publishers passed on her writing. If she were honest with herself about her talents, Flanagan must have known that she was a capable though not exceptionally gifted playwright, essayist, and fiction writer. Her directing was solid enough, though it relied heavily on the styles and techniques she had picked up in Europe

39

rather than something distinctively her own. There wasn't much call for what she really excelled at: collaboratively producing timely shows, getting more than anyone could possibly have expected out of limited budgets and modestly talented actors and designers, using her determination and quiet charisma to inspire others.

Flanagan had another sabbatical in 1934 but failed to secure a second Guggenheim Fellowship. She managed to return to Europe when invited to visit Dartington Hall in England, an experimental arts center that was looking to hire an artistic director. Shortly before that she had become close to Philip Davis, a Vassar professor who had recently lost his wife and was now a single father to three young children. She was offered the job, and they would have hired Davis too, but she wasn't prepared to leave America. She left for Greece to meet up with Davis and, though torn about the impact that remarriage and raising his young children would have on her professional life, agreed to marry him, and they returned to teach at Vassar and moved their families into a large house there. Other than a more prestigious academic posting, there were few jobs to which, in 1935, at age forty-five, Flanagan could aspire. Had President Roosevelt not created the WPA and not put Hopkins in charge of it, there is every likelihood that she would have settled into a career out of the spotlight, as a tenured critic and director, writing, staging plays, meeting with international directors and playwrights, and training the next generation of Vassar theater students.

On May 16, 1935, Flanagan received a call from Hopkins inviting her to Washington to discuss the Federal Theatre. Before leaving Poughkeepsie she sent telegrams to influential figures in the theater world seeking their advice. Only Elmer Rice responded, and Flanagan met with him in New York on her way to Washington, exchanging ideas and soon "plagiarizing each other," as she put it. When interviewed by Hopkins, Flanagan was asked whether she thought people would come to see shows staged by relief workers. She was confident they would. Hopkins asked her to draw up a plan, then led her to a garden party at the White House, where she consulted with Eleanor Roosevelt, then spent an evening with the leaders of the other Federal One programs, who had by now all been chosen, at the end of which Hopkins asked Flanagan when she could get to work. The job was hers.

The obstacles Flanagan faced were daunting. Establishing dozens of local units at sites across the country presumed that enough actors and stagehands, as well as local directors, could be found in each region. Yet until unemployed actors applied for work relief (and they had until mid-November 1935 to do so), nobody knew how many of them there were or how unevenly they were distributed across the country. Applicants would then have to audition to determine if they were stageworthy. Rice's suggestion that stars might also tour was now out of the question, since they were ineligible for relief. Other pressing questions would have to wait: What plays would be performed? How many would be original works that spoke to local interests? Would audiences be asked to pay a modest admission fee? Would some regional actors be allowed to tour across state lines, redistributing talent from major cities to rural areas where theater had all but disappeared? Mounting a single show was challenging enough; putting together a season more so. Nobody had ever attempted to stage several hundred productions a year—from circus shows to vaudeville to classics to new American plays—in scores of locations, relying on mostly untried or rusty performers.

And all this didn't begin to address challenges unique to a federally run relief program. Since it was decided that funding would flow through states' coffers, what sort of political and logistical bottlenecks might that give rise to? Given the decision by Congress that 90 percent of funds had to be spent on labor, how would money be found for everything else involved in staging a play, from lighting to costumes to sets to renting a space in which to perform? And how was Flanagan to persuade top directors and producers to quit their current jobs to work for the Federal Theatre for far less money? When she tried cajoling a talented young Broadway producer to run the Hartford, Connecticut, office and he asked how he could afford to do so for only $200 a week, Flanagan had to explain that he had misunderstood her; the salary was $200 a *month*. Flanagan herself had taken a 40 percent pay cut from her $10,000 a year Vassar salary to head up the Federal Theatre. Again and again, the desire to establish the foundations of a nationwide theater kept running into the constraints imposed by its source of funding: a relief project.

In setting her plans in motion, Flanagan relied heavily on the counsel of a farsighted theater veteran, E. C. Mabie, who had given considerable thought to reviving playgoing nationally while creating the theater program at the University of Iowa. Mabie agreed to head the Midwest division and drafted for her "A Plan for the Organization of Regional Theatres in the Unites States." He also organized the National Theatre Conference that was held at his university in late July 1935, attended by many of those who would go on to lead the Federal Theatre. Recognizing the importance of this gathering, Harry Hopkins, arguably the busiest man in Washington, decided to show up himself, accompanying Flanagan on the long train ride to Iowa City. At the conference, Hopkins, who believed that "a vital new American drama" would emerge from this enterprise, formally introduced Flanagan as his choice for national director of the Federal Theatre, then told those gathered there, many of whom had doubts about the project, what they needed to hear from the head of the WPA: "I am asked whether a theatre subsidized by the government can be kept free from censorship, and I say, yes, it is going to be kept free from censorship. What we want is a free, adult, uncensored theatre."

Flanagan was formally sworn in on August 28, 1935, and as summer turned to autumn, she scrambled to recruit first-rate regional directors, then invited them all to Washington for an inaugural meeting on October 8. It was held at the McLean Mansion, the Federal Theatre's new headquarters, with its extravagant chandeliers and gold faucets, and Flanagan began the meeting by juxtaposing the building's outmoded "conception of art as a commodity to be purchased" with their own mission, which was to address "the problem of thousands of artists, no longer able to live in America, except on charity." Their goal was "to form a plan whereby people will again become enough interested in the work of artists to make such a work a salable commodity." She made clear that she had no interest in going back to the good old days of nineteenth-century theater, "temporarily reviving a corpse." If they failed to create a theater that was "conscious of the implications of the changing social order," that "changing social order will ignore, and rightly, the implications of the theatre." She challenged those in the room to focus on "rethinking rather than on remembering" what theater could do, for they now had to compete with the movies, whose "kaleidoscopic speed and juxtapositions of external objects and internal emotions" were finding "visible and audible expression for the tempo and the psychology of our time." The stage, too, she insisted, "must experiment." And she set a timetable for all this to happen: in three months, "I should like to turn in a report to Mr. Hopkins saying that all employable people from relief rolls are at work on the theater projects as intelligent, as vital, as varied as the imaginations, around this table." Later that month, when Flanagan sent out "Instructions" for the Federal Theatre, she did her best to elide the official and undeclared aims of the project: while its "primary aim . . . is the reemployment of theatre workers now on public relief rolls," its "far reaching purpose is the establishment of theatres so vital to community life that they will continue to function after the program of this Federal Project is completed."

It would prove to be the high-water mark of the aspirations for the Federal Theatre. Flanagan described it in a letter to her husband as "a thrilling and significant day for all of us"—the moment before collective hopes collided with the soul-crushing day-to-day of battling red tape, local politicians, censorship of various kinds, opposition from powerful unions used to dictating terms of employment, and requisitions on the WPA's dreaded Form 320, as every penny spent had to flow through the Treasury Department's procurement division, then through "the finance division of the WPA state offices." Before six months had passed, two thirds of the twenty-four regional directors who had gathered at the McLean Mansion had quit. In many cases, including Mabie's, the reason was simple enough: dealing with state and local authorities proved to be a nightmare (Iowa's administrator kept trying to staff Mabie's office with friends, including one who came recommended for having done a "good job" of "counting hog carcasses" for a farm program).

Yet a resolute Flanagan carried on and by year's end managed to establish offices in eleven cities: New York, Los Angeles, San Francisco, Chicago, Detroit, Milwaukee, Hartford, Boston, Philadelphia, New Orleans, and Denver. There would soon be others, in Seattle,

Portland, Jacksonville, Oklahoma City, Miami, Atlanta, Chapel Hill, Raleigh, Pittsburgh, and elsewhere, but much of the work would be centered in the three major cities—New York, Chicago, and Los Angeles—in which theater was still deeply rooted. As Jane De Hart neatly puts it in *The Federal Theatre, 1935–1939*, the "foundation stones for a regionally centered national theatre had, in short, been dumped in three large piles with a few pebbles scattered about elsewhere." This distribution would have dire political consequences, as members of Congress from Southern and rural states had little investment in supporting what they saw as a mostly Northern and urban enterprise.

As 1935 drew to a close, the Federal Theatre, at least on paper, had been in existence for eight months yet had not staged a single production. Hopkins and others in Washington were growing impatient. Critics—and among the most vocal was the trade magazine *Variety*, which described the "practically complete collapse of the highly-ballyhooed Federal actor-relief program"—found the project in "a state of confusion and uncertainty" when it came to how many actors were employed, whether any would tour, what would be staged, and whether admission fees would be charged. In an essay that ran in *The New York Times* on January 5, 1936, Elmer Rice half jokingly wrote that before one of its shows had even opened, the Federal Theatre "has been variously characterized as a super boondoggle, a sinecure for the faithful, an attempt to supplant the professional theatre by the amateur, and a plot to overthrow the government of the United States." By then progress was at last visible, with thousands on the payroll working on shows in twenty states, and by March the Federal Theatre was employing 11,000 workers and could boast of a weekly audience of 150,000. But it had yet to produce anything very good. Its inaugural New York show, a production in Brooklyn of Shakespeare's *The Comedy of Errors* on January 13, 1936, didn't even merit a review.

But an ambitious production slated to open soon after, at the Biltmore Theatre on Broadway, undoubtedly would. Called *Ethiopia*, it was the first of the Living Newspapers, a theatrical form that combined the immediacy of cinematic newsreels with the political urgency of revolutionary European theater. It resembled newspaper accounts in aspiring to be factual, carefully researched, and focused on current events or policies. Dramaturgically, it relied on flexible staging, few props, and large casts. Looking back twenty years later on his time with the Federal Theatre, Arthur Miller identifies as well as anyone what was so distinctive about the Living Newspaper, which he calls "the only new form that was ever introduced into the American theatre." It was a product of a particular historical moment in an America badly shaken by the Depression that tried "to join in one theatrical presentation a picture of the social background and causation, for the disasters around us, on an epic scale." The plays' emphasis on cause and effect, whether the subject was racism, syphilis, or slum housing, was key. Miller was acutely conscious of a sea change in sensibility that subsequently took place with the outbreak of World War II and then living in an age of the atom bomb, so was attuned to how these large-scale dramas—"history plays in a new context"— spoke to prewar Americans in ways that would no longer be as meaningful, for it "was news, in those days that we were creatures of our own environment. It was a great discovery for many people."

Ethiopia was everything Flanagan had dreamed of for the Federal Theatre: experimental, collaborative, and politically engaged, with an interracial cast that wasn't reliant on star turns. Its scale also helped solve the problem of putting enough of the unemployed to work: by the end of 1935, in New York City's unit, nearly four hundred actors, researchers, playwrights, and journalists were involved in producing Living Newspapers. *Ethiopia* dramatized Mussolini's recent and brutal invasion of that African nation, about which the U.S. government had officially remained neutral. What made the show possible was the availability of a company of Black actors and dancers, led by Asadata Dafora and Abdul Assen. In 1934 Dafora, from Sierra Leone, and Assen, a Nigerian, had collaborated on a sensational dance drama called *Kykunkor.* Dafora wrote, choreographed, and performed in it, and Assen starred as lead drummer and "Witch Doctor." The New York production, which ran for months in various houses, drew national coverage and was one of "the top ten productions of the season." By the time it was briefly revived on Broadway in early 1935, just a few months before the creation of the Federal Theatre, the show had drawn "celebrities from the worlds of theatre, music, and dance." Hallie Flanagan had seen it, and when plans for touring *Kykunkor,* as well as Dafora's next show, *Zunguru,* fizzled out, she invited Dafora and his Shogola Oloba troupe, made up of both African and African American performers, to join the Federal Theatre, then made them available to *Ethiopia.*

Arthur Arent, the young dramatist who assembled and wrote *Ethiopia,* injected their music, dance, and drumming into what was otherwise a news story, opening the play with an idyllic scene of Ethiopian soldiers at midday rest, playing instruments, and then singing "a sad, keening sort of air," before those sounds are interrupted by "the sharp rat-a-tat-tat of a machine gun," as the Italian forces attack them on the Somaliland frontier. The dance and drumming troupe would be even more central to the play's climactic fifth scene, Arent's Orien-

talist fantasy (and a replay of *Kykunkor*) set at the emperor's palace in
Addis Ababa:

> As the curtain rises, there is an intense, electric atmosphere.
> Suddenly, a single clear voice rings out, singing one of the
> psalms of David. The melody is taken up by the musicians,
> and then the entire multitude. At the topmost note, the mel-
> ody suddenly stops dead. There is a pause, and then a witch
> doctor steps forward, fantastically dressed. She emits weird,
> blasting cries, starting a dance of incantation. The tomtoms
> beat more furiously, the voices become hysterical. The entire
> scene becomes a saturnalia. . . . At this point the warrior on
> the balcony pounds his tomtom, signalling the entrance of
> the Emperor! Immediately everybody freezes. Slowly Haille
> Selassie appears on the balcony.

Eager to make the production as newslike as possible, Morris Watson, head of the Newspaper Guild, whose unemployed journalists
worked on the project, had reached out to an old friend, Roosevelt's
press secretary Steven Early, hoping to secure a recording of one of
Roosevelt's speeches to use in *Ethiopia*—with disastrous consequences.
Hopkins, having caught wind of this, dispatched his assistant Jacob
Baker to New York. After Baker reported back, Hopkins informed
the White House, then instructed Baker to tell Flanagan to let Elmer
Rice know that it was "not wise to go ahead with this project." The
State Department then got involved, calling the production "danger-
ous" and informed Flanagan that "no one impersonating a ruler . . .
shall actually appear on the stage." This was not the "free, adult, un-

censored" theater that Hopkins had so recently promised. Flanagan tried and failed to negotiate a solution acceptable to all, then confided in a letter to her husband that she despaired over this "political censorship" and feared that working under such constraints, "we are never going to be able to operate anything worth doing."

Rice, outraged at this censorship, felt that he had no choice but to quit (and Baker had already typed out Rice's resignation letter). In a defiant last act, Rice invited reviewers to a preview on January 24, staged with only a few props and costumes. Brooks Atkinson of *The New York Times* was there and, while acknowledging that it was "no masterpiece," found *Ethiopia* "sobering and impressive—even frightening." Atkinson also thought that "the Negro scenes were particularly stirring." But "we all know now," he concluded, "that a free theatre cannot be a government enterprise." It would be *Ethiopia*'s first and last performance.

Stuck with a now dark Broadway house, Flanagan and her staff made the ill-advised decision to offer a different preview at the Biltmore, showcasing John McGee's *Jefferson Davis* shortly before its planned tour of forty-four cities down South (where McGee, deputy director of the Federal Theatre, also served as regional director for the South). Even a local Daughter of the Confederacy conceded that the show—which celebrated the president of the Confederacy and included a scene in which one of Davis's slaves begs his master to keep him enslaved—"might better be confined to below the Mason-Dixon line." Flanagan herself admitted in a letter to her husband, after sitting through a dress rehearsal, "When I think this is our first Broadway show . . . I am ill. . . . If I were any reporter I would pan the life out of it." *The Daily Worker* wondered why "a government project should produce a play that is dedicated to the purpose of whitewashing a dictator who upheld the institution of slavery." On March 3, Flanagan confided in her husband that, so far, the Federal Theatre had "not one single distinguishing thing to point to." After this stumbling start, the fledgling Federal Theatre had to do better, and badly needed a hit.

Opening night of *Macbeth*, Lafayette Theatre, April 14, 1936.

CHAPTER THREE

Macbeth: The First Hit

H ad *Ethiopia* not been censored, Asadata Dafora and his troupe would likely have entertained audiences on Broadway from late January through early spring, if not longer. But after that show's abrupt cancellation, they were transferred to the Negro Unit up in Harlem, where they were featured in a Shakespeare production that opened on April 14, 1936, after eleven weeks of rehearsals. Over the next six months this so-called Voodoo *Macbeth* (set in nineteenth-century Haiti, with voodoo replacing Scottish witchcraft) was seen by nearly 120,000 playgoers, first in Harlem, then on Broadway, and after that on a national tour that took the all-Black cast to parts of the country where Jim Crow still ruled. It was the Federal Theatre's first and arguably greatest hit, one that quickly erased memories of the project's shaky start. The production also launched the careers of Orson Welles, who directed it, and John Houseman, its producer, neither of whom was keen on crediting Dafora and his troupe for its success.

An anecdote that can be traced to both Welles and Houseman, then circulated widely by others, weaves together several of the myths generated by the celebrated production. It recounts the fate of Percy Hammond, a critic who reviewed *Macbeth* harshly then supposedly died as a result, the victim of a powerful voodoo curse. Houseman retells the story at length in his 1972 memoir, *Run-Through*:

> Early in the afternoon of April 15th, the day of the *Macbeth* reviews, Orson and I were formally visited in my office by Asadata Dafora Horton and his corps of African drummers, including Abdul, the authentic witch doctor. They looked serious. Asadata was their spokesman. They were perplexed, he said, and desired guidance. He then produced a sheaf of clippings from which he detached the *Herald Tribune* review. He had read it to his men, he declared, and it was their opinion, and his, that the piece was an evil one.

They asked Houseman whether its author was "an enemy" and a "bad man," and he agreed, at which point, he writes, a grim-faced "Asadata nodded," then "turned to his troupe, to Abdul in particular, and repeated what I had said. The men nodded, then silently withdrew." Houseman then adds:

> It was reported to us by our disturbed house manager when we arrived at the theatre around noon the next day that the basement had been filled, during the night, with unusual drumming and with chants more weird and horrible than anything that had been heard upon the stage. Orson and I looked at each other for an instant, then quickly away, for in

the afternoon paper which we had picked up on our way uptown was a brief item announcing the sudden illness of the
well known critic Percy Hammond. He died some days
later—of pneumonia, it was said.

Welles had previously shared his version of the story on television
in 1955, characterizing their Black colleagues as primitives who spoke
in the broken English of extras in a Hollywood film set in darkest
Africa. The performer he refers to as "Jazbo"—Houseman's "Abdul"—
was Abdul Assen:

> Critics were very kind to us, except . . . for Mr. Percy Ham-
> mond. . . . I was approached by Jazbo, who said to me, "This
> critic bad man." And I said, "Yes, he's a bad man." To which
> Jazbo replied: "You want we make *beri-beri* on this bad man?"
> All this dialogue's very much like the native bearers in *Tar-
> zan* and so on, I apologize for it, but it's really what went on. I
> said, "Yes, go right ahead and make all the *beri-beri* you want
> to." . . . Woke up next morning, proceeded on ordinary course
> of work, and bought the afternoon paper to discover that Mr.
> Percy Hammond for unknown causes had dropped dead in
> his apartment. I know this story is a little hard to believe, but
> it is circumstantially true.

The actual circumstances of Hammond's death were sadder and
less dramatic. A few months earlier, his wife of thirty-nine years, to
whom he was devoted, died of a heart attack. Disconsolate, Hammond moved from their Long Island home into a hotel room, fell ill,
and, according to his friends, lost the desire to live. Eleven days after

reviewing *Macbeth* he died of pneumonia. But no matter; the anecdote was too good, and stuck. Actors had long associated *Macbeth* with a curse, and every modern production of *Macbeth* had struggled to make its witchcraft believable. Perhaps the powers of darkness *were* real. The anecdote suited the play and production so perfectly that even the habitually careful Hallie Flanagan repeated it.

What had really irritated Percy Hammond was the show's late start: "*Macbeth* could not get its curtain up until 9:30 o'clock last night—an hour later than advertised. So I, as a punctual reporter, had to desert the performance before Miss Thomas, as Lady Macbeth, walked and talked in her sleep." Hammond failed to grasp that the pre-performance excitement outside the Lafayette Theatre on opening night, where thousands of Harlemites had joyously gathered, and then the orchestra playing within (further delaying the start of the play) were part of the show, essential to the experience of everybody at the theater that evening, except perhaps a sick and depressed critic working on a tight deadline.

In 1936 both Welles and Houseman were struggling to get noticed; Asadata Dafora and Abdul Assen were far better known and widely admired. Dafora had studied opera in Italy and could speak French, Spanish, German, and Italian, in addition to English and various African languages, and was far better educated than either Welles or Houseman would acknowledge. In later years Welles, who strenuously downplayed the contribution of *all* of his collaborators on *Macbeth*, including Houseman, remembered things differently:

> Witch doctors were specially imported from Africa because the governments in the West Indies took the view that there was no such thing as voodoo. So we had to go all the way to

the Gold Coast and import a troupe. And they were quite a troupe, headed by a fellow whose name was Asadata Dafora. The only other member of the coven who had any English was a dwarf with gold teeth by the name of Jazbo. At least we called him Jazbo up in Harlem; I don't know what his African name was. He had a diamond in each one of those gold teeth.

The story of how *Macbeth* in Harlem took shape is sharply at odds with these self-aggrandizing recollections. In late August 1935, Flanagan announced that Negro Units were planned for Harlem and for the South (though that unit never materialized). But until a suitable playhouse in Harlem could be found, New York's Negro Unit had to work out of offices on Madison Avenue, which were soon jammed with hundreds of applicants. Houseman recalled that when the move uptown at last took place in October, "we began to take down the rotting boards which had long covered the doors and windows of the old Lafayette Theatre on Seventh Avenue between 132nd and 133rd Streets. The Lafayette was a sordid, icy cavern when we moved in—with peeling plaster, a thick accumulation of grime, burst bulbs, rotting carpets, and broken seats in the hairy recesses of which lurked rats, lice and other horrors."

Houseman's recollection of the Lafayette as derelict until their arrival is another myth. Just a few months earlier a Black company was staging *Sailor, Beware!* there, starring, among others, Canada Lee, who would soon play Banquo in *Macbeth*. The Black press was keenly interested in the fate of this historic playhouse, and its reopening in May 1935 after periodic closures prompted the *Baltimore Afro-American* to hope that this "may have far-reaching effect and influence on the Harlem theatre situation" at a time when most "of the other houses here are content with cabaret presentations." But that reopening was short-lived. After three weeks the company "gave up." The reason, explained a disappointed actor, "is that there are no Negro audiences of sufficient size to support a theatre in Harlem." The fate of Black performers on Broadway was no better. By the early Thirties the door that had seemed to crack open more widely in the Twenties turned out to be a revolving one. As Dewey Roscoe Jones put it in *The Chicago Defender*: "Plays with a Race theme and with a Race cast in full or in part, marched upon the street called Broadway, said their little piece and marched off again with the regularity of trained soldiers. Few of them managed to stay there longer than a month."

The Lafayette, built in 1912, was owned by two White men, Leo Brecher and his business partner Frank Schiffman, who two years earlier had also bought Harlem's Apollo Theatre. They also owned other neighborhood theaters and were known in the community for not segregating theatergoers and for supporting Black and Latino talent. But like theater owners across the country, they faced stiff competition from movies. In the spring of 1935 Brecher and Schiffman were desperate enough to offer the house rent-free to Black theater companies, in what newspapers described as an effort to bring the "serious stage . . . back into popular favor." It must have come as a godsend when in the autumn of 1935 the Federal Theatre agreed to rent the Lafayette on a long-term basis for $1,800 a month, then installed cutting-edge electrical and lighting systems for free, using skilled Black electricians and carpenters long denied admission to the all-white Stagehands Union (when the union threatened to take action, Houseman told them to try their luck picketing "a Negro theatre in Harlem for hiring Negroes").

As important as it was for the Negro Unit to have a home in

Harlem, it still needed a leader, and a plan. The Urban League insisted on having a say in how it would be run. So did those in the Black theater community, who had long been running small acting companies and saw no need for White administrators. It was soon clear that the only candidate competing interest groups could agree upon was Rose McClendon, "the First Lady of the Negro Stage," familiar to both White and Black audiences for her leading roles in Broadway shows that delved into racial issues, including *In Abraham's Bosom* (1926) and *Porgy* (1927). McClendon was deeply involved in Black community theater. She also wrote and directed plays, and in 1935 cofounded the Negro People's Theatre, which began promisingly with a benefit production she codirected of Clifford Odets's *Waiting for Lefty* on June 1, 1935, seen by over four thousand people, probably the largest number of playgoers to attend a modern drama in Harlem. McClendon referred to its success in a long letter she published in *The New York Times* later that month calling for support for the new company, arguing that it showed "that a Negro theatre operated by Negroes as a cultural experiment and based on a program of social realism could be established on a permanent basis."

Flanagan undoubtedly recognized how closely McClendon's vision for a Black theater suited her own project's needs and could serve as a template for it. In the midst of what must have been a tremendous workload getting the Federal Theatre up and running, Flanagan called on McClendon, more than once, to persuade her to head the Negro Unit, recalling that at "the first meeting in McClendon's house I asked her whether it would not be advisable to have the direction and designing of their project by members of their own race." According to Flanagan, McClendon declined to take on the job alone: "Miss McClendon felt that since Negroes had always been performers and had no previous means of learning direction and design, they would prefer to start under more experienced direction"—that is to say, someone White. Houseman writes erroneously in *Run-Through* that McClendon was "a performer, not an administrator or director," and describes her "one condition": that "a suitable white associate be found that would work with her, on the basis of complete equality, as her artistic and executive partner." And her choice, he writes, was Houseman himself, who accepted the position as "joint head."

McClendon's account of these conversations doesn't survive. But it seems clear that her desire to bring a White administrator on board was also driven by her failing health as well as an acting commitment she had already made: the lead role in Langston Hughes's new Broadway play about race relations in the South, *Mulatto*, a part that Hughes had written for her. McClendon's involvement in that production had likely begun by August, before Flanagan approached her, for it had a summer tryout in Dobbs Ferry before opening in New York on October 24, 1935. It was a huge hit, running for nearly a year. But McClendon fell seriously ill and had to leave the play in early December, replaced by a White actor. She died of cancer seven months later at the age of fifty-one. Welles later told a biographer that McClendon had been slated to play the part of Lady Macbeth.

There had been no report of her failing health in the story about the Negro Unit that ran in the *Amsterdam News* in late November, in which she was identified as the unit's director. McClendon made clear that her commitment was to more than employment; her goal was "to establish a community theatre in every sense of the word . . . so that in time a permanent theatre by and for Negroes will become a lasting theatre institution in Harlem." And "Executive Director Houseman" confirmed in that article "that the project for a Negro Theatre was organized around what seemed to be the most significant Negro theatrical group, 'The Negro People's Theatre,' founded several years ago by Miss McClendon." The Federal Theatre's Harlem Unit was effectively McClendon's Negro People's Theatre, federally funded. The mission and leadership were identical; all that had changed were the name and the addition of a few White administrators. Houseman acknowledged in that article that his role would be temporary, part of the start-up: the "few non-Negroes who are aiding in its formation are lending their services at the request of Miss McClendon and her group."

Contemporary reporting serves as a corrective to later histories of the Negro Unit, which rely heavily on Houseman's and Flanagan's accounts and inaccurately suggest that from the outset McClendon and Houseman were equal partners and that McClendon had wanted it that way. Houseman's appointment did not go unquestioned in the national Black press. The *Baltimore Afro-American* quoted critics who noted that "the short experience of Houseman would not put him in the same class with colored directors who have had from ten to twenty-five years' experience directing shows." Nonetheless, Houseman took over from McClendon when she became seriously ill. How he came to serve in the Negro Unit and then brought Orson Welles aboard, and how that led to the Negro Unit staging *Macbeth*, gives some sense of how much about the production depended on random encounters, timing, and luck.

As the nearly three months of rehearsals stretched on, there was growing concern in Harlem that *Macbeth* was going to be yet another instance of exploitative blackface, a "farcical sketch," rather than, as the *Amsterdam News* put it shortly before the play opened, what the community badly needed: "a milestone in the cultural life of the

American Negro," a production that will "disprove for all time the palpably common belief that Negro actors are adapted only for special character parts or for dialectical bits." Houseman felt that he had to respond to "the prevalent, erroneous impression that the Negro theatre's version of *Macbeth* will turn out to be a blackface comedy or a satirical skit" and tried reassuring the community that this was not the case. Assuming that the production was going to insult Blacks, an unnamed assailant accosted Welles in the lobby of the Lafayette and tried slashing him with a razor; Canada Lee, a former boxer, fortunately intervened. Given the inexperience of everyone involved— from administrators who had never tackled anything on this scale, to a director staging his first professional show, to actors for the most part with limited experience acting in Shakespeare's plays, performing in a community badly scarred by a recent race riot—the success of *Macbeth* in Harlem was unexpected, extraordinary, and never to be repeated.

A riot had shaken Harlem the previous spring, on March 19, 1935. Cheryl Greenberg's *"Or Does It Explode?,"* the best account of the conditions that led to the riot, summarizes its toll: "By the end of the night 697 plate glass windows in some 300 business establishments were shattered at a cost to insurance companies of $147,315, the police had detained 121 people, and 57 civilians and 7 police had been injured. And most tragically, Lloyd Hobbs, a black schoolboy on his way home from the cinema, had been shot and killed by the police." Mayor Fiorello La Guardia called for an investigation, but the police, who had acted brutally, wouldn't testify. The report wasn't submitted for a year and it was then quietly shelved, its unsettling findings finally leaked to the Black press.

Given the dire conditions in Harlem, where unemployment rates were staggering, it didn't take much to trigger a riot. Alain Locke had this to say at the time: "the Harlem riot" is "variously diagnosed as a depression spasm, a Ghetto mutiny, a radical plot and dress rehearsal of proletarian revolution." For Locke and many other Black observers the root cause of the riot was economic exploitation, especially by White-owned stores that would sell to African Americans but not hire one: "Its immediate causes were trivial—the theft of a ten-cent pocket-knife by a Negro lad of sixteen in Kresge's department store on 125 Street. . . . As a matter of fact the boy had given back the stolen knife and had been released through the basement door. But it must be remembered that this store, though the bulk of its trade was with Negroes, has always discriminated against Negroes in employment." The riot, Locke concluded, "was an attack upon property rather than persons, and resentment against whites who, while exploiting Negroes, denied them an opportunity to work."

The New York Times belatedly acknowledged that it "took the recent riot to awake New York generally to deplorable conditions" in Harlem, which has "suffered the impact of depression first and most." The *Times* went on to describe "tenements where squalor was unbelievable," and provided figures, including those gathered by the Urban League, which had surveyed a representative crowded Harlem block, where "70 per cent of the tenants were jobless, 18 per cent ill, 60 per cent behind in their rent and 33 per cent receiving public or private aid." Whites, meanwhile, had taken advantage of the Depression to buy up Harlem: in 1929, the *Times* reported, they "controlled 65 per cent of Harlem real estate"; six years later Whites owned all but 5 percent of the neighborhood. Also galling was "white man's Harlem," where "expensively dressed [White] women and their escorts visit the various 'hot spots'" that "are almost all run by whites"—and excluded most Blacks. Little wonder, then, that there were concerns within Harlem that the Federal Theatre would prove to be yet one more White-run enterprise.

Houseman, bizarrely, compared the explosive rioting to the catharsis offered by a successful production: if it proved to be a hit, he later wrote, *Macbeth* "promised the Harlem community an emotional release such as they had not known since the riots of 1935." Until the stock market crashed in 1929, Houseman—then Jacques Haussmann, a Romanian-born British subject—had been making good money as a speculator in international grain markets. After the business collapsed, he cast about for a new career, writing a couple of forgettable comedies, then directing an experimental opera, *Four Saints in Three Acts*, for which Gertrude Stein had written the libretto. Searching for a place in New York's battered theater world, Houseman saw an opportunity for producing limited-run shows that were experimental and subscription-based. He teamed up with Nathan Zatkin and formed the Phoenix Theatre, which would appeal to a "very limited, very cultured audience."

Houseman fabricated a fresh version of his past, telling the press that he had been "a cowboy in Argentina after his graduation from Cambridge," and a journalist as well. The truth was that he never enrolled at Cambridge, to which he had been admitted, sailing to Argentina instead to study the grain trade; he later wrote a few pieces for the *New Statesman*. But it sounded like a better résumé for someone now trying to make his way in not-for-profit theater. A charitable way of explaining these falsehoods is to acknowledge that at age thirty-four and as an undocumented immigrant using a false name, Houseman was a talented but not so young man in search of success, and discovering that the theater world of the 1930s was even more precarious than speculating in commodities. In March 1935 he produced a verse drama by Archibald MacLeish called *Panic*. Its interracial cast was unusually large: a mixed chorus of twenty-three as well as twenty-five actors, including Rose McClendon. Also cast was a young White actor in his first professional performance as a lead. Houseman had seen him recently as Tybalt in a production of *Romeo and Juliet* and was thrilled by his audition. His name was Orson Welles. The plan, Houseman told the *New York Herald Tribune*, was to open with *Panic* and then stage a modern version of *Medea* by the Black playwright Countee Cullen, with McClendon in the title role. *Panic* ran for three scheduled performances. But lacking wealthy backers, that was the end of the Phoenix Theatre. After this, Houseman writes in *Run-Through*, his "savings gone," he resumed his "life of plots and maneuvers, of watching and waiting for my next chance."

If not for the timely creation of the Federal Theatre that summer, one wonders whether Houseman would have had much of a future in the theater. Even with his appointment as McClendon's executive director, Houseman kept looking for work, perhaps because he expected his job as a White administrator in the Negro Unit to be temporary. In December 1935 the *Amsterdam News* ran a story about the dissatisfaction within the Harlem community with White leadership in WPA programs, adding that it "is rumored that Houseman will resign his position in the near future to appear in *Hamlet* with Leslie Howard." The report, not covered in the White press, was half true: Houseman seems to have had no intention at this point of resigning, but he would moonlight, working simultaneously on *Hamlet*, which he would go on to codirect with Howard, in a Broadway production slated to go into previews in April 1936, the very month that *Macbeth* opened in Harlem. In the end, *Hamlet* was postponed until the autumn of 1936, then panned by the critics.

It was Houseman's good fortune to have befriended McClendon. When Flanagan hired her, she brought him along to assist her, and he, in turn, brought along an actor whom he had found so prodigiously talented and with whom he would partner for the next five years, Orson Welles. When McClendon became seriously ill, Houseman took control of the Negro Unit and split it in two, with one part devoted to staging what McClendon had always wanted: plays written by Black dramatists performed by Black actors. The other division would stage the classics, and its first would be *Macbeth*. If McClendon had been more fully engaged, she might have asked Ralf Coleman to direct it, for Coleman was an experienced Black director who had just staged *Macbeth* in Boston with an all-Black cast (and had recently acted alongside her in the Broadway production of Paul Green's *Roll Sweet Chariot*). But it was now Houseman's call, and he chose the twenty-year-old Welles, who had never directed a professional production of anything.

Looking back on *Macbeth*'s success, the Black poet and scholar Sterling A. Brown ruefully noted that it "was the only Negro production for which white audiences stood in queues," then quoted an unnamed source on the obstacles it had to overcome: "Harlem had lost its tourist trade, *Macbeth* its attraction for theatregoers, and the revival of both together was no mean accomplishment." It's an astute observation, for its setting in Harlem as well as its role in reversing *Macbeth*'s declining appeal proved crucial to its success. Perhaps no play had been revived in America more often in the early twentieth century; since 1900 *Macbeth* had returned to one New York City theater or another nearly every year. None of these productions had been especially memorable. Yet another revival arrived in town in October 1935, shortly before Houseman and Welles decided to stage it. It had bored the *New York Times* reviewer Brooks Atkinson, and left him wondering how the play had managed to appeal to playgoers in Shakespeare's day. Directed by an Englishman, with English actors in the lead roles, this latest *Macbeth* had all the familiar trappings: Scottish costumes and setting, "metal roofing thunder and witches' cauldrons." While the actors spoke Shakespeare's verse well enough, the production failed to hold Atkinson's interest: "The gory events of *Macbeth* call for ferocity of feeling and action," and these were absent. The problem, as he saw it, was that the world had changed, and theater too, since *Macbeth* was written. Shakespeare, Atkinson decided, was "not a good modern dramatist." It didn't help that witchcraft, so essential to the plot, was now robbed of its once "terrible plausibility." "If we are to have *Macbeth* on the stage," he concluded, "it must be charged with some sort of vitality," though what that might be he stopped short of imagining.

The tradition that Atkinson found so wearyingly familiar—with the cast in tartan and the sets depicting medieval Scotland—had been radical when introduced to the London stage by Charles Macklin in 1773. Macklin broke with a long-standing modern-dress tradition that originated at Shakespeare's Globe Theatre in 1606 and ran in an uninterrupted line through William Davenant's Restoration revival, up to the 1744 production of Macklin's archrival, David Garrick. Macklin turned *Macbeth* into "the Scottish play," and his innovations were picked up a decade later by John Philip Kemble, starring opposite one of the greatest Lady Macbeths, Sarah Siddons, in a wildly popular production. They in turn also established a long tradition of the play as a two-hander, with audiences in both Britain and America flocking to see a pair of stars play the most fascinating married couple in Shakespeare.

It wasn't until 1928 that a heretical director bucked tradition and restored modern dress. When Barry Jackson did so at London's Royal Court Theatre, playgoers jeered and critics pounced. His setting was still Scotland—but post–world war. Castles were now country houses. Men wore khaki army uniforms, and Lady Macbeth appeared in a "short-skirted evening dress." There were machine-gun bursts and shellfire in the battlefield scenes. It was at once familiar and strange for playgoers, who needed more distance from the play's horrors: "The khaki," as one critic put it, "has associations too recent and too intense." Modern dress also seemed to knock audience identification off-kilter, diminishing sympathy for the Macbeths and shifting it to their victims. And the Witches, one critic concluded, "will not do," and provoked laughter. Word traveled, as the failure of this modern-dress *Macbeth* was international news.

While the traditional way of staging the play seemed exhausted, modern playgoers were not quite ready for modern dress. Welles would claim that his wife, Virginia Nicholson, came up with the idea of a third way: setting the play in early-nineteenth-century Haiti, with Macbeth loosely modeled on the Black slave-turned-king Henry Christophe. It was a brilliant idea, one that solved many of the challenges facing the Negro Unit at one go, and an excited Welles recalled how he called Houseman at two in the morning to share it. But this, too, seems to have been another bit of retrospective mythmaking, for it would have been impossible to have realized this concept without knowing that Dafora's popular troupe was available, and that wasn't the case until January 1936, when rehearsals on the show began.

Welles's later claim that he "had to go all the way to the Gold Coast and import a troupe" to realize his conception of *Macbeth* got things exactly backward.

Aside from being well suited to an all-Black cast—that would not be seen as impersonating White characters—the Haitian setting was also timely. A year earlier the United States had ended its two-decade military occupation of Haiti. A critique of that invasion had in part inspired one of the finer American plays written for a Black lead in the 1920s, Eugene O'Neill's *The Emperor Jones*, and many reviewers of the *Macbeth* in Harlem noted how aligned the two tragedies were. Those familiar with W. W. Harvey's influential *Sketches of Hayti* (1827) would have recognized how directly the gorgeous costuming of *Macbeth* was lifted from its pages, the dazzling military uniforms "bedecked with gold and lace," their shoulders "burdened with epaulets of an enormous size," and their caps "adorned with feathers nearly equalling their own height," which "rendered their appearance supremely fantastical."

Setting the play in Haiti also helped solve several of the problems Atkinson had identified, from a lack of "ferocity of feeling and action" to how medieval Scottish witches were no longer disturbing; exotic voodoo practitioners were, especially to curious Whites drawn to lurid accounts of "the ritual orgies of these transplanted primitives" peddled in works like the 1935 bestseller *Voodoo Fire in Haiti*. Setting the play in nineteenth-century Haiti also tilted the production to the left politically; in *Macbeth*, as Richard France put it, "Welles played on his audience's current paranoia—the threat . . . of fascism and impending war," and the "impression left in the theatre was that of a world steadily being consumed by the powers of darkness." Ira Katznelson, in *Fear Itself*, an outstanding study of what drove American political culture in the 1930s, speaks of the three predominant fears: fear of fascism, fear of racial equality, and fear of global violence. *Macbeth* ticked all three boxes.

The Federal Theatre was now the largest employer in Harlem, and with hundreds on its payroll, jobs needed to be found for as many people as possible. The Haitian *Macbeth* would accommodate a cast of 137, in addition to a small army of costumers, prop makers, and stagehands. But resituating the play came at a price. Its emphasis on voodoo upended the careful balance in the play between fate and free will. Productions had long struggled to get this tension right: if *Macbeth* is a story of a potential tyrant waiting for the right moment to seize power, the supernatural forces become superfluous; but if the Witches are all-powerful and drive a helpless Macbeth to commit one murder after another, his tragic stature is diminished. Finding the right balance didn't interest Welles, who went all in on having Hecate and the Witches, from first to last, control Macbeth's fate. When Welles came upon moments in the text that suggested redemption or reflection, he cut them. Welles also expanded the role of Hecate (who rules the Witches), who had appeared in only a pair of late scenes in Shakespeare's original, turning it into a male role, then casting the strongest classical actor in the company, Eric Burroughs, who had trained at the Kammerspiele theater in Hamburg, assigning to him as well the role of the Third Murderer, and giving him the show's ominous final words, lifted from earlier in the play—"The charm's wound up!"—suggesting that the power Hecate exercised over Macbeth would now be turned on his successor, Malcolm, in an ongoing cycle of violence.

A generous take on why Welles turned the tragedy into a crowd-pleasing melodrama, privileging drumming and spectacle over introspection, is that it took pressure off of the actors playing the Macbeths, neither of whom had classical training or experience speaking blank verse. A more cynical one is that productions of *Macbeth* were usually known by their stars: we speak of such celebrated pairings as John Philip Kemble and Sarah Siddons, Laurence Olivier and Vivien Leigh, Ian McKellen and Judi Dench, and more recently Denzel Washington and Frances McDormand. But once Hecate and the Witches predominate, the focus of the audience shifts. Which is why almost nobody remembers the names of the leads of the *Macbeth* in Harlem, Jack Carter and Edna Thomas. It would come to be known, instead, as Orson Welles's Voodoo *Macbeth*.

While Welles had barely turned twenty when he was invited to stage *Macbeth*, no untried director had a greater working knowledge of Shakespeare's plays. Welles was sent, at age eleven, to the Todd School for Boys outside Chicago, where he immersed himself in designing, directing, and acting in student productions, including one-hour versions of *Twelfth Night* and *Richard III*. At sixteen, while on holiday abroad, he found employment painting scenery at the Gate Theatre in Dublin, where his working knowledge of professional theater deepened considerably. Upon his return to America his headmaster at the Todd School, Roger Hill, asked the precocious seventeen-year-old to collaborate on a collection of the plays he was putting together, *Everybody's Shakespeare*. At eighteen, Welles was invited to tour nationally with Katharine Cornell's repertory company. He was cast as Mercutio in *Romeo and Juliet* but was shifted to a lesser role when he briefly left the company to run a summer repertory with Hill; it was after he rejoined the tour that Houseman saw him play Tybalt and tied his fortunes to Welles's.

Welles was a charismatic and tyrannical director who insisted on controlling every aspect of *Macbeth*, from how actors spoke and moved, to sound, lighting, and design. The title page of his working script sums this up nicely: "*Macbeth* by William Shakespeare, Negro Version, Conceived, Arranged, Staged by Orson Welles." The eleven weeks of rehearsal that Welles and his cast were allowed—unheard of in the commercial theater—gave him time to sharpen every aspect of the show. Rehearsals were tumultuous; a visitor described them as "absolute pandemonium." Because Welles was earning good money doing radio programs during the day, rehearsals typically began in the evening and ran through the night. He drove the actors hard, telling a biographer that at one point he kept them rehearsing for seventy-two hours straight, with breaks only for napping. Houseman, who guessed that Welles was now working twenty out of twenty-four hours in the day, estimated that a quarter of what he earned was spent on food and taxis, a quarter on handouts or loans to company members, another quarter on props (including Macbeth's severed head), and the rest entertaining his male lead, Jack Carter (after rehearsals the two would frequent Harlem's clubs and brothels).

Welles would shout instructions to his large cast through a megaphone. His notes for the company, which he had his wife type up, were precise about blocking and timing, and were often brutal. At times he went too far. Edna Thomas, who thought him "a genius of a director," recalled a moment in rehearsals when "Orson began to get very abusive, until, finally, he said to me, 'Darling, come down here. I'm not going to have you standing there all this time while these dumbbells aren't catching on.'" She came down, took him aside, and told him, "'Orson, don't do that; these people will take your head off.' And they would have."

However inspired his concept, Welles could not have pulled it off without an extraordinarily talented team of Asadata Dafora, Virgil Thomson (who provided incidental music), designer Nat Karson, and Abe Feder, widely regarded as the creator of modern theatrical lighting design. Feder never forgave Welles for constantly berating him and thought he was mad. Karson worked his magic with both the stage design—a castle surrounded by a jungle—and costuming, his team in the basement of the Lafayette outfitting the large cast, as well as the set, for only $2,000. Costuming and lighting chosen by designers with White actors in mind wouldn't work for this production. So Karson and Feder "devised light-friendly make-up and a series of gels" designed specifically for Black actors, and Karson ordered that scene painting absorb rather than reflect lighting, and discovered that "a light touch of color at the wrist and at the collar" helped show the Black cast to better effect. Together they somehow met Welles's demand that the "scenery should at all times have an eerie, luminescent quality" that suited the play's voodoo world.

Harlem's Negro Unit would be one of the first to mount a Federal Theatre production. Houseman had pressed for a provocative play by Zora Neale Hurston, *Lysistrata*, but was opposed, he writes, "by both the Left and Right." So the unit led instead with Frank Wilson's *Walk Together, Chillun*, a social drama about Black workers, opening at the Lafayette on February 2, 1936, followed there on March 11 by Rudolph Fisher's mystery-farce *Conjur Man Dies*. Neither was much of a commercial or critical success. The critics tried to be kind, Atkinson writing in *The New York Times* that by "Broadway standards" *Walk Together, Chillun* "is artless and sometimes unintelligible," but allowed that "there is obviously more to it than any white man is likely to understand." But the two shows proved helpful to *Macbeth*, for by April,

Harlem had begun to take notice of what was happening at the Lafayette.

Some clever promotion, underscoring how closely this *Macbeth* was
identified with Harlem, helped. While the Federal Theatre was not
permitted to spend money on advertising, three days before the show's
opening workers were sent out to stencil "Macbeth" in luminous paint
on street corners from 125th to 140th Street, and from Lexington Avenue to Broadway, and "garlands and bright colored ribbons" were placed
a block south of the Lafayette on what remained of the Tree of Hope,
long seen as a good-luck charm in the community. The elm tree had
been cut down two years earlier when Seventh Avenue was widened,
but its three-foot stump was soon "polished smooth by the touch of
hands." A free preview for the community on April 11 drew three thousand playgoers, far more than the Lafayette could hold, and the police
had to disperse the crowd. By then, the opening had already sold out
and tickets were being scalped.

Opening-night festivities began with the Improved Benevolent
and Protective Order of Elks of the World Band, dressed in light
blue, scarlet, and gold, marching through the neighborhood behind
a pair of crimson banners that read *"Macbeth* by William Shakespeare." They continued to play at the Tree of Hope, as ten thousand
Harlemites gathered around the Lafayette, halting traffic, a scene me-
morialized in photographs that capture the palpable excitement as
the lights, cameras, and arriving celebrities rival the drama soon to
take place within the theater. *The New York Times* reported that
mounted police struggled to clear a path to the theater's lobby, and
the *New York World-Telegram* described the crowd, both Black and
White, arriving in their respective outfits: "Harlemites in ermine,
orchids and gardenias, Broadwayites in mufti." This was about far

more than a play. The festivities continued inside the Lafayette, where the curtain was long delayed, as the Negro Unit orchestra entertained ticketholders with several planned pieces, including James P. Johnson's *Yamekraw*, a "Negro rhapsody" of "spiritual, syncopated, and blues melodies." When the curtain fell at the end of the show, the applause and ovations went on for fifteen minutes, and then, Welles recalled, "the audience came up on the stage to congratulate the actors. And that was, that was magical."

Macbeth, like all great productions, struck a nerve. It confronted playgoers and the culture at large with questions about what happens when Black actors play Shakespeare. Reactions to the production, many of which are impossible to read without wincing, offer a snapshot of how Americans imagined racial difference in 1936. This, in turn, raised other questions: Having exposed cultural fault lines, could the Federal Theatre do anything to bridge them? And who, ultimately, benefited from *Macbeth*? For many in the Black community, the show signaled an unequivocal victory, something that erased the stigma of Harlem's recent and violent past: "This unusual play will be remembered," the *Norfolk New Journal and Guide* declared, "long after the less uplifting news of the half year is forgotten." An editorial devoted to the show in the *Baltimore Afro-American* was defensive about some of the criticism in the White press that had questioned "whether colored actors were capable of 'doing' Shakespeare," and reassured readers that when "a whole lot of people say something is good, it IS good": "The play may go down in history as the greatest thing that colored actors have ever accomplished in the theatre." The editorial urged every Harlemite "with forty cents to spare to go and see the play," and ended on a prescient note: "Ten years from now they will be talking about the *Macbeth* which was put on at the Lafayette."

The closest that any Black critic came to suggesting that it was not much of an improvement on blackface was Lew Amster, who wrote in the *Sunday Worker* that *Macbeth* was "a white man's play done for whites by Negroes," one that fails to capture "the Negroes' consciousness of their miserable state." The novelist Richard Wright shared with Amster a preference for Black plays by Black playwrights, in the hope of solving what he saw as the main problem: to "create a Negro theatre literature and at the same time create and organize an audience for itself." But Wright also saw signs of progress in *Macbeth*: "The long evolution of the Negro actor from the clowning minstrel type to Edna Thomas' lofty portrayal of Lady Macbeth represents a span of years crowded with abortive efforts." As such, *Macbeth*, in which "talent long stifled rose to the surface and compelled public attention . . . presented a compromise," providing "Negro actors a wide scope for their talent" while dealing "with a theme which was acceptable to a white theatre-going audience."

Carl Van Vechten (a patron of the Harlem Renaissance) wrote excitedly to his friend Langston Hughes that he had seen "*Macbeth* last night for the third time. Again crowds, again cheers, again all sorts of excitement! I've found out at last what Harlem really likes." Hughes did not write back to his enthusiastic White friend. When interviewed by a Black newspaper, Hughes diplomatically replied that it was a "magnificent production," one that created opportunities "for Negro talent." But four years later he would write more darkly about it in his poem "Note on Commercial Theatre," lamenting: "You put me in Macbeth and Carmen Jones / And all kinds of Swing Mikados / And in everything but what's about me." For Hughes something crucial in Black culture was used up and lost when channeled through plays that had little to do with the lived experience of Blacks. It's hard not to feel the residual impact of *Macbeth* on the volume he would publish in 1942, *Shakespeare in Harlem*, in which the title poem suggests that what is essential in Shakespeare only truly lives in contemporary America through Black culture.

The most visceral response by a Black critic was by Roi Ottley, who wrote in *New Theatre* that the "Negro has become weary of carrying the white man's blackface burden in the theatre," and that in "*Macbeth* he has been given the opportunity to discard the bandana and burnt-cork casting to play a universal character." For Ottley, from "the point of view of the community, Harlem witnessed a production in which the Negro was not lampooned or made the brunt of laughter," and for that reason *Macbeth* "was an eminent success." As for himself, he "attended the *Macbeth* showing, happy in the thought he wouldn't again be reminded, with all its vicious implications, that he was 'a nigger.'"

But Ottley was unhappy about the many White playgoers heading uptown to see it, bringing with them offensive ideas about Black actors. He called out several White critics for using *Macbeth* to belittle Black capability and accomplishment: Percy Hammond, who wrote in the *New York Herald Tribune* that Blacks "seemed to be afraid of the Bard, though they were playing him on their home grounds"; Arthur Pollack, in the Brooklyn *Daily Eagle*, for whom Blacks "play Shakespeare as if they were apt children who had just discovered him and adored the old man"; and Burns Mantle, for reporting in the *New York Daily News* that Black playgoers "applauded because of their natural gaiety." Mantle adds that he knew "something was wrong" when "the colored actors begin to read the text of *Macbeth*": "This is not the speech of the Negroes, nor within their grasp," and the play, for him, became "a charade and little more," the cast "overwhelmed and frightened by the magnitude of what they had undertaken." These and other White critics, Ottley wrote, had "journeyed to Harlem with the idea of seeing a mixture of Emperor Jones and Stepin Fetchit, with burlesque thrown in," and responded accordingly in reviews that showed how ignorant they were "of what the production meant to Harlem." No review by a major critic in a national newspaper was entirely free of prejudice, though some might have insisted that their attacks were grounded on aesthetic principles, not racial bias. Even when departing from the consensus and condemning the production for its "blackface attitude," the young journalist Edward R. Murrow couldn't help resorting to stereotypes about the "'truer emotional roots' of the Negro people" and of the "frustration, humor, and, yes, victories" of that "deeply emotional race."

Black and White playgoers mingled during the sold-out Lafayette run, and this integration was, for a number of White reviewers, itself worthy of comment. Some were clearly uncomfortable with mixed seating, such as the unnamed reviewer who, Houseman writes, asked that he and his wife not be placed next to Blacks. Before her career as a famed war reporter, a young Martha Gellhorn found herself scrambling for one of the last remaining tickets to see *Macbeth*, which she reviewed for the British *Spectator*. She secured a seat in the second-tier box next to "an enormous black lady . . . vast-bosomed and wearing a splendid dress of red poppies on yellow," who talked to her "in a soft voice about the negro theatre and how, of course, as anybody knew, Shakespeare had always intended his plays to be acted by negroes. She herself had seen this production of *Macbeth* four times and hoped to see it four more times." The mix of condescension and astonishment is typical of many White reviewers, and Gellhorn, who would enjoy and praise the production, slyly mocks the woman's conviction that the plays of Shakespeare could be intended for Black actors. Gellhorn's fascination with Black bodies extended to those onstage, as she describes the actor playing Macbeth as "one of the finest looking men in the theatre," a "negro the color of rich coffee, taller than one expects, put together perfectly." And when she glanced down at the orchestra section she was struck by how the "audience stretched beneath us, blonde heads and black wool," resembling "a checker board." A similar reaction can be found in Robert Littell's sympathetic review in *Vogue*, titled "Everyone Likes Chocolate." Littell found "the audience at the Lafayette Theater was almost as interesting as the show itself": "Next to a Harlem poet who makes his living as a Pullman porter one might see a blond broker with his Junior League wife, who normally would no more think of going to a play by Shakespeare than he would think of reading Proust." Littell suggests that the show's popularity stems from what he imagines to be deep-seated racial differences and desires: "We palefaces go to the Negro because the Negro has something we have not, never will have, and dreadfully want. In watching them we recapture briefly what once we were, long centuries ago before our ancestors suffered the blights of thought, worry and the printed word."

After eleven weeks at the Lafayette, *Macbeth* had to make way for the next Negro Unit play, *Turpentine*, about Black workers at a Southern labor camp. After a brief transfer to Broadway's Adelphi Theatre, *Macbeth* then went on a three-month national tour, the largest Shakespeare production to ever tour America. The 180-person company traveled for four thousand miles in a special six-car train, first to Bridgeport and Hartford, then to Dallas, before returning to Brooklyn's Majestic Theatre with stops in Indianapolis, Cleveland, and Detroit (where "comparatively few Negroes were on hand to witness it," even though, the local reviewer added, it marked "a departure from the stereotyped 'nigger' roles generally placed upon the shoulders of dark actors"). The shows in Indianapolis broke the color line, for this was the first time Black playgoers could sit "downstairs"; but that line held fast in Cincinnati, where the tour stop had to be canceled when local officials refused to allow Black playgoers to sit next to White ones.

The ten-day run at the Texas Centennial in Dallas was the most groundbreaking stop on the tour. Jesse O. Thomas, in charge of Black participation at the Centennial, proudly reported: "We had the play *Macbeth* with a Negro cast, in the Band Shell. Whites and Negroes sat on the same floor. This was not true of any theatre in the City of Dallas in which Negroes and whites both attend." The integration seems to have been more symbolic than substantive, and restrooms were still segregated. *The Philadelphia Tribune* reported that White Texans "found an all-Negro cast in a Shakespeare play something they couldn't stomach and remained away from the 6,000-seat house in large numbers," though the special "Negro night" attracted a good crowd. *Variety* similarly reported that "southerners are understood to have felt that colored players in a colored play is one thing, but colored players in Shakespeare is another." John Rosenfield, Jr., who reviewed it for *The Dallas Morning News*, remembered the production as "something to be seen if only to be despised." The company faced a small crisis departing Dallas when Chandos Sweet, the White company manager and a Texan, put up a sign saying that the first ten seats in their special railway car were reserved for Whites only (meaning himself and a few stage technicians and electricians). Sweet said he was only following Texas law. That sat poorly with the rest of the company, who thought that Sweet "took advantage of the situation to embarrass the colored members of the cast." Sweet would be fired. What might have been a longer tour closed soon after; the expense and the challenges of staging a road show of this size, including finding housing for so many Black performers in a segregated America, proved too daunting.

Looking back on *Macbeth* in 1982, Orson Welles told an interviewer that "By all odds my great success in my life was that play." He claimed, though no newspaper or member of the cast ever confirmed it, that he stepped in and played the role of Macbeth one night in Indianapolis, in blackface (as he would later play Othello), when the lead and understudy both fell ill. He also told a biographer, "I was really the King of Harlem! I really was." If so, then like Macbeth, he wasn't king for long. He and Houseman talked about staging *Romeo and Juliet* with the Negro Unit, with White Capulets and Black Montagues, but nothing came of it. Perhaps they thought that the success of *Macbeth* in Harlem couldn't easily be repeated. In any case, they didn't try. They were given permission to run their own Classical Unit, then left the Federal Theatre after their all-White musical *The Cradle Will Rock* was ordered closed, an act of censorship driven by discomfort over the show's pro-union advocacy. It famously ran for one night anyway. They were soon mounting shows commercially at the Mercury Theatre, before going on, separately, to long and illustrious careers on stage and in film. Asadata Dafora and his troupe continued to perform for another quarter century, but never again to such acclaim; once they faded from the scene there was no obstacle to Welles and Houseman rewriting the history of *Macbeth* in Harlem. With its classics division now abandoned, the Negro Unit staged a half dozen or so more Black plays at the Lafayette, none of them hits, and none toured. Cutbacks forced the Negro Unit to abandon the

Lafayette in 1938. After the demise of the Federal Theatre, trained Black stagehands from the Negro Units struggled for nearly twenty years before they would be admitted as equals in the all-White union, Local No. 1. Canada Lee, Edna Thomas, Jack Carter, Eric Burroughs, and others who had acted in *Macbeth* in Harlem all struggled, with meager success, to find significant roles in theater or film in the years, then decades, that followed.

Censored poster, Detroit production
of *It Can't Happen Here*, 1936.

CHAPTER FOUR

It Can't Happen Here:
Going National

In September 1935, a month before the novel was even published, MGM bought the film rights to Sinclair Lewis's *It Can't Happen Here* for $200,000 (in today's dollars a staggering $4 million). Sidney Howard, who had won a Pulitzer Prize for Drama and had already adapted for the screen a pair of Lewis's novels, *Arrowsmith* and *Dodsworth*, was hired to write the script for a fee of $22,500, plus $3,000 a week. The huge investment was worth it to MGM, for the pair of earlier films of Lewis's novels had brought in close to $3 million at the box office.

Howard didn't flinch from showing the horrors of the fascist take-over of America so powerfully imagined by Lewis in *It Can't Happen Here*. His script, according to David Platt, a journalist with whom Howard shared it, "shows the sadistic outrages of the fascist concentration camps, the burning of the books, the invasion of homes, the blood purges, and the beginning of the underground movement against the reign of terror." Howard even included a scene reported in the novel, one that eerily anticipated Nazi exterminationist practices, in which "a country schoolhouse crowded with women and children" is surrounded by stormtroopers who pump carbon dioxide into the schoolhouse, gassing to death those trapped inside. Howard's script, Platt concluded, was "dynamite against fascism," and "if produced exactly as written would create a vast wave of alarm at the danger of fascism in the United States among many millions of Americans." Star actors were cast, including Lionel Barrymore, Wallace Beery, Walter Connolly, Virginia Bruce, Basil Rathbone, and Jimmy Stewart.

Sinclair Lewis had begun writing *It Can't Happen Here* in a white heat that May up in Barnard, Vermont, where there were few distractions. Working on it every day, twelve hours a day, he was done by mid-August. The idea for it can be traced back to 1931, when Lewis's wife, Dorothy Thompson, one of the nation's leading journalists, had interviewed Hitler and was among the first to alert the world to the dangers of Nazism. The Lewis and Thompson household was soon flooded with visitors eager to talk about the growing danger of fascism in America, and Lewis began grilling anyone who had firsthand knowledge of totalitarian leaders.

The leading candidates for protofascists who threatened American democracy were Huey Long, the demagogic senator from Louisiana, and the no-less-charismatic radio personality Father Charles Coughlin, populists who were skilled at demonizing those they identified as enemies of the people—bankers, plutocrats, Communists, and, in Coughlin's case, Jews. By 1935 both were on the verge of consolidating national political platforms: Long's "Share Our Wealth" movement and Coughlin's "National Union for Social Justice." A year later Coughlin told a reporter that America was at a crossroads: "One road leads to communism, the other to fascism." When pressed about which road he would take, Coughlin replied, "I take the road to fascism." In retrospect, contemporary fears of where Long's and Coughlin's fascist tendencies might lead strike modern historians as overblown, but at the time alarm bells were ringing and the pages of magazines from *The Nation* to *Modern Monthly* filled with articles about this danger. A few months before Lewis began writing *It Can't Happen Here*, Thompson, after interviewing Long, wrote to her husband, "If things move in the present tempo I think we may very easily have a Republican-fascist dictatorship in 1940."

He may not have been the most dazzling stylist or original thinker, and readers today may find his characters two-dimensional and his work too hastily written, but few authors have taken America's pulse—at least White America's—more accurately than Sinclair Lewis. It was his great gift to turn what journalists and cultural critics were discussing into bestsellers read by hundreds of thousands of Americans. Benjamin Stolberg, reviewing the new novel in the *New York Herald Tribune*, made the same point in a backhanded way, writing that Lewis "has successfully plagiarized our social atmosphere." Clifton Fadiman wrote more generously in *The New Yorker* that it was "one of the most important books ever produced in this country" and a "public duty" to read it.

It Can't Happen Here takes place in the near future in the imaginary Vermont town of Fort Beulah. The story centers on Doremus Jessup, a sixty-year-old editor of the local newspaper, *The Daily Informer*, who is married to Emma, involved extramaritally with a widow, Lorinda Pike, and is father to three children: Mary (who is married to a local doctor, and has a son, David), Philip (a politically acquiescent lawyer), and Cecelia (Sissy). Jessup is also an employer of a resentful French Canadian handyman, Shad Ledue. Their lives are upended when President Roosevelt is edged out for renomination by Senator Berzelius "Buzz" Windrip (modeled on Huey Long), who secures the endorsement of Bishop Prang (a stand-in for Father Coughlin) and goes on to defeat the Republican nominee, Senator Walt Trowbridge, in the November election. He had campaigned on a platform of "5 Points of Victory for the Forgotten Men," that disenfranchised Blacks, banned Jews from public life, forced women out of the workplace, urged the imprisonment of all Communists, and called for a constitutional amendment granting the president dictatorial emergency powers. On assuming office, Windrip declares martial law, strips Congress of its authority, arrests Supreme Court justices, empowers a loyal paramilitary force, co-opts industrial leaders, and herds those deemed enemies of the state into concentration camps. Women, Blacks, and Jews are all—as promised—oppressed. Most Americans at first go along with these changes, out of passivity, self-interest, the conviction that they are necessary to maintain America's strength, or because they felt that while Windrip has "got a few faults, he's on the side of the plain people." Trowbridge flees to Canada, which becomes the seat of political resistance to Windrip's authoritarian regime.

Over time, and in response to violence in his own community (including the murder of his son-in-law by the paramilitary), Jessup, a cautious liberal who is at first slow to respond, becomes radicalized. He is arrested after circulating an anti-Windrip editorial, then forced to publish government propaganda. He and his family try and fail to escape to Canada. Jessup then quits his job, secretly joins the resistance, and produces a mimeographed sheet—the *Vermont Vigilance*—attacking Windrip's regime. He is eventually caught by Ledue (who has risen in the ranks of the paramilitary Corpos) and sent to a concentration camp, Trianon, where he is tortured. Ledue subsequently attempts to seduce Sissy, is exposed by her, and is himself sent to Trianon, where he is killed by fellow inmates. Jessup's daughter Mary, whose husband had been murdered, becomes radicalized as well and dies in a suicide mission. Back in Washington, President Windrip is deposed by his secretary of state, Lee Sarason, who is himself brutally overthrown in a power grab by the military, led by General Haik, who tries to consolidate his eroding power by conscripting forces to invade Mexico. Lorinda helps Jessup escape from the concentration camp, and they flee to Canada to join the resistance, as the country grows increasingly disaffected with its totalitarian government.

Jessup has as little patience with zealous Communists as he does with defenders of fascism. A mouthpiece for Lewis's own political views, Jessup concludes: "The world struggle today was not of Communism against Fascism, but of tolerance against the bigotry that was preached equally by Communism and Fascism." The end of the novel finds Jessup in Minnesota organizing local resistance. His hard-earned knowledge has taught him that "everything that is worth while in the world has been accomplished by the free, inquiring, critical spirit." The battle to restore democracy in America has yet to be won, but armed resistance is growing.

At first, Sidney Howard didn't think there was enough in the novel to work with, but he eventually found a way forward, letting an MGM executive know that with this film the company was "going to carry the American screen into the field of living controversy." He sent the finished draft to Lewis, who wrote back, expressing "the greatest admiration" for the adaptation, and made a few suggestions for changing the ending, which Howard ignored. All that remained was for the studio to run the final version past the Hays Office. A

veteran screenwriter, Howard was familiar with the censorship guidelines set out by the Motion Picture Production Code of 1930, under
the jurisdiction of Will H. Hays and the direct oversight of censor in
chief Joseph Breen, which had become rigidly enforced after 1934.
His script would include no profanity, nudity, or miscegenation, no
clergy would be ridiculed, or race or creed willfully offended. He
omitted the homosexuality of the sinister secretary of state, Lee Sarason, left out as well Ledue's threatened sexual assault of Jessup's
daughter Sissy, and made a schoolhouse rather than a synagogue the
site where stormtroopers gassed their victims, for all these would
have violated the code. Everyone knew the game: the scriptwriter and
studio would carefully self-censor, Breen would make a half dozen
or so suggestions for what should be changed or cut, those instructions would be followed, and a certificate of approval granted.

But that's not what happened. The problem was not that the film
was immoral; it wasn't. But it was politically inflammatory. After
reviewing the script Breen told Hays that "it is hardly more than a
story portraying the Hitlerization of the United States of America."
Stepping beyond his role as moral censor, he then pointed out to Hays
that the film, if released, would hurt foreign-market sales. When
Breen then asked Hays "whether industry policy should permit such
a picture to be made," Hays chose not to intervene. What happened
next was out of the ordinary. On December 18, Breen wrote directly
to Louis Mayer of MGM, telling him that Hays was reviewing the
case. Weeks passed. Mayer didn't hear from Hays, assumed there was
no problem, and the film went into production, with shooting scheduled to begin in late March 1936.

At the end of January, Mayer received a seven-page letter from

Breen, urging him to kill the film: "This story," Breen wrote, "is of so inflammatory a nature, and so filled with dangerous material that only *the greatest possible care* will save it from being rejected on all sides." He then demanded that an outrageous number of cuts be made—sixty in all—which if the studio failed to make would subject the film to "the most minute criticism on all sides," adding, ominously, that "this criticism may result in enormous difficulty to your studio." Breen here hints at objections that will come from the German and Italian fascist regimes that dictated terms to Hollywood studios. By this time only three major American film studios remained in the German market: MGM, Paramount, and Twentieth Century Fox. All the others—including Warner Bros., RKO, Disney, Universal Pictures, and Columbia Pictures—had already pulled out. These last three companies continued to accommodate Nazi censors, who rejected all films in which Jews were employed (to get around this, credits were changed and German music dubbed over that written by Jewish composers). Lewis's novel had itself been translated and published in Germany, before it was promptly banned. Things worsened after Kristallnacht, when the Germans produced a blacklist of Hollywood Jews whose films could not be seen in Germany. Non-Jews, including Ernest Hemingway, who had participated in an anti-Nazi film, as well as Bing Crosby and Joan Crawford, were blacklisted. Even then, the three studios, including MGM, kept selling their films for German distribution, carefully avoiding banned artists. Yet MGM was determined to make *It Can't Happen Here* and turned to outside lawyers, who pored over the script and found thirteen potential instances that might lead to litigation or were in bad taste, and could be easily remedied. Mayer decided to push ahead, telling Sidney

Howard "not to pull punches." Howard spent two weeks responding to all sixty of Breen's suggestions and resubmitted the script in early February. Lionel Barrymore grew a beard for the part of Jessup.

Then, unexpectedly, a fresh obstacle emerged, only revealed long after by Ben Urwand in *The Collaboration: Hollywood's Pact with Hitler* (2013). A Philadelphia real estate agent named Albert Lieberman was deeply disturbed when he heard about the making of the film and wrote anxiously to his rabbi, William Fineshriber, who happened to chair the film committee of the Central Conference of American Rabbis. Rabbi Fineshriber, who had spent time in Hollywood and knew the key players there, wrote to Mayer on February 7, 1936, warning that the film would have a negative impact on "the Jewish problem." Fineshriber also wrote to Hays, saying that the "only wise method to pursue in these days of virulent anti-Semitism is to have no picture in which the Jewish problem is ventilated." A few days later, armed with this request, Hays spoke with Mayer.

It's hard to know what tipped the scales—pressure from Hays and Breen, fear of losing business in Germany, the intervention of Georg Gyssling (the German consul in Los Angeles, who a few years earlier had personally expelled Warner Bros. from the German market), the timidity of an influential rabbi, or most likely the accumulation of these and other unknown concerns. On February 13, 1936, MGM canceled the film. A movie depicting the erosion of democracy through official censorship was itself censored. Hays immediately denied responsibility, claiming MGM had acted independently. Mayer said in an official statement that the film "was abandoned because it would cost too much." Samuel Goldwyn weighed in as well, suggesting that it was probably "casting difficulties" that led to the film's cancellation, since "it is well known that the Hays organization does not ban films." It was national news. Ten days after the film was canceled, an angry Sidney Howard told the *New York Herald Tribune* that the "industry policy is determined to keep motion pictures out of anything that matters to the public, any controversial interest." "I was forbidden," he said, "to use the word 'Fascism' but I could say 'Democracy is no good,'" before adding that he had heard Breen say: "'Things like freedom of speech and freedom of press are all right to talk about, but do they belong on the screen?'"

Sinclair Lewis was furious and, not knowing the backstory, publicly blamed Hays: "Mr. Hays actually says that a film cannot be made showing the horrors of fascism and extolling the advantages of liberal democracy because Hitler and Mussolini might ban other Hollywood films from their countries if we were so rash." He believed that domestic politics was behind the decision as well, telling the *New York Herald Tribune* that he was told that Hays barred it because he "didn't know which way the election might go, and he certainly didn't want to offend the Republicans." The day after Lewis railed against Hollywood, German and Italian spokespersons weighed in, applauding MGM's decision. Lewis responded by placing ads in newspapers saying "Hollywood can censor every motion picture theatre in the country, *but it cannot yet censor your bookseller!*" In the aftermath of the MGM controversy, sales of the novel doubled, eventually totaling more than 320,000 copies.

A few months later, on July 22, 1936, the heads of production for the Federal Theatre gathered to discuss their upcoming season. They wanted provocative American plays and were unhappy with the choices they were offered, heavy on Viennese and French farce, Russian comedy, African dance-drama, and Irish melodrama. Francis Bosworth, director of the project's Play Bureau, suggested obtaining the rights to *It Can't Happen Here* and having Lewis himself adapt it for the theater, then staging "it all over the country." Flanagan's deputy director, Bill Farnsworth, thought that if they could pull this off, the productions could "open everywhere the same night"—the largest opening for a play in the history of theater.

Everyone involved in these discussions knew that movies, more than radio, even more than the Depression itself, had gutted the theater industry. Hollywood had not only lured away their audiences but had also swept up the best talent, richly rewarding former playwrights like Sidney Howard while leaving many others in the theater world out of work. What could be better than turning the tables, taking a timely story censored by Hollywood and not only bringing it to theaters from coast to coast but also showing that, like a film, a play could open on the same day everywhere? Better yet, unlike the movies, which were uniform, these productions could be tailored to America's great ethnic and regional diversity: there could be productions in different languages and by different races, even multiracial ones. A production in Huey Long's Louisiana would land a lot differently than a Yiddish one in New York City. And it would alert all Americans to the totalitarian dangers that film censors preferred to keep from them.

When Hallie Flanagan called this idea "the logical next step in the development of the Federal Theatre," she was quietly suggesting that the Federal Theatre was on the verge of providing Americans with something approaching a truly national theater. She and her staff had no illusions that they could ever compete with Hollywood, but staging productions of Lewis's novel across the land could remind Americans that a nationwide theater could again happen here. It would, at the same time, restore something vital to democracy that only serious theater could provide. Flanagan and Bosworth acted quickly. They arranged to meet in New York with Lewis, who came down from Vermont to hear their pitch. According to Pierre de Rohan, who recounted these details in the *Federal Theatre Bulletin*, having a "national audience" proved to be the "deciding factor" for Lewis, who had told *Variety* that "no Broadway producer appeared interested in his book's stage possibilities." The deal was signed on August 21, 1936, with Lewis telling the press that "I prefer to give it to the Federal Theatre for two reasons: first, because of my tremendous enthusiasm for its work, and, second, because I know I can depend on the Federal Theatre for a non-partisan point of view."

By this time Lewis had been "working night and day" on the playscript and was confident that he could turn it in by mid-August. The Federal Theatre had committed itself to a nationwide opening night of October 27, 1936, which meant that it had just over two months to turn the sprawling novel into a viable show, find as many regional companies as possible capable of staging it, book theaters, design and construct as many as a dozen sets for each production (for which every scrap of wood and canvas had to be requisitioned through the federal government), and, crucially, get playscripts into the hands of directors and actors with enough time to rehearse before opening night.

It was a quixotic plan. And in the wake of the MGM controversy those running the Federal Theatre knew that they would face intense scrutiny, especially from the fiercely anti–New Deal Hearst papers. William Randolph Hearst made his own political views clear, declaring in an editorial a few days before Lewis's novel was published that "whenever you hear a prominent American called a 'Fascist,' you can usually make up your mind that the man is simply a LOYAL CITIZEN WHO STANDS FOR AMERICANISM." A reporter from his

Los Angeles Examiner tipped off Federal Theatre officials that the paper had been told "to launch a vigorous campaign against the Project and its National Director" in October 1936. While the Federal Theatre was not permitted to publicize its productions, by the time that *It Can't Happen Here* opened nationwide it had been widely discussed in the press. The fact that opening night was a week before Election Day only intensified speculation. As Flanagan herself later put it, "There were stories and editorials for and against from one end of the country to another. Some people thought the play was designed to re-elect Mr. Roosevelt; others thought it was planned in order to defeat him. Some thought that it proved Federal Theatre was communistic; others that it was New Deal; others that it was subconsciously fascist." Its mercurial politics perfectly suited the Federal Theatre, which was anxious to avoid being seen as partisan. Lewis himself refused to be embraced by any faction, including the Communists, who were the most eager to claim him, declaring at a press conference on September 14: "Is the play propaganda for a party? The answer: No. It is not. It is propaganda for an American system of Democracy. Very definitely propaganda for that."

Given the tight deadline and the play's explosive subject matter, much could go wrong, and it's surprising that not more did. Lewis seems to have finished an early draft by late August. It's unclear why or when John C. Moffitt, a former journalist who was working for Paramount Pictures in Hollywood, was brought in to help with revisions. Moffitt first went to join Lewis in Vermont, before they relocated to Lewis's house in Bronxville, New York. But Moffitt moved out after their relationship soured. Flanagan booked space for each of them to write in Essex House on Central Park South—with Moffitt on the thirty-eighth floor and Lewis on the twenty-second—and acted as intermediary, shuttling between them, along with Bosworth. She captures the tensions in her subsequent history of the Federal Theatre, *Arena*, as they all raced against the clock:

> The play was produced by polygenesis. It was partially created by Mr. Moffitt who paced up and down in his apartment at the Essex House and threatened, if Mr. Lewis did not omit certain scenes and include others, various unusual reprisals; it was simultaneously springing almost visibly from the brain of Sinclair Lewis, who, in another apartment at the Essex House, composed and acted every part differently every day. "Let's change the whole scene to an interior and have the Corpos beat Doremus almost to death—Bosworth, take the typewriter in the other room and pound out a rough draft and Hallie and I will just sketch through the details." At this point a note would be slipped under the door saying that Mr. Moffitt would appreciate it if I would communicate certain things to Mr. Lewis. Mr. Lewis would then communicate certain things to Mr. Moffitt, and since by that time I was the only acceptable medium of communication between the embattled collaborators, I would on the way up to Mr. Moffitt with the message, communicate certain things to the Almighty, the only being in whom I could safely confide.

Her breezy account masks how serious the friction was between the coauthors. *Variety* reported that Flanagan herself "disliked the first act as originally submitted and she is said to have told Moffitt to do the rewriting on his own." By then, he and Lewis were not speaking; separately, both sent their revised work to the WPA to be typed, where a stenographer placed a scene written by Moffitt in Lewis's script by error. Lewis then threatened to withdraw the play completely. The collaboration fell apart. Moffitt returned to Hollywood and was replaced by Vincent Sherman, who was directing the Broadway production at the Adelphi Theatre. A *New Yorker* reporter who observed their final rushed revising wrote that "Lewis made an effort to rewrite the whole show again, and had to be suppressed. . . . Some of the scenes," he added, "weren't in the hands of the directors until the week before the opening."

It would be a three-Act play with a cast of twenty-seven, not counting extras. The Federal Music Project would loan musicians. To make the play feel more local, regional productions were encouraged to alter the original Vermont setting. Jessup was now five years younger and a widower, and his mistress, Lucinda, a "devoted spinster" rather than the spirited and financially independent widow of the novel. Jessup's son, Philip, and younger daughter, Sissy, were cut, while his daughter Mary was turned into an embodiment of heroic American motherhood. Much of the political commentary, including that concerning President Windrip, was cut as well, effectively nudging *It Can't Happen Here* toward domestic melodrama. Stealing a page from Howard's screenplay, it opens on the eve of Windrip's nomination with an autumn picnic, where we learn that Jessup initially supports Windrip and is sure that a dictatorship *"can't happen here!"*

The second Act picks up several months later, in winter. Things in Fort Beulah have become considerably grimmer. We learn that congressmen and Supreme Court justices are being arrested. Jessup prepares an antigovernment editorial and is accused of treason. His son-in-law tries to intervene and is summarily executed. His former handyman, Ledue, takes over Jessup's old desk at the newspaper and

Jessup is forced to write fascist propaganda. Visited by a member of the resistance, Jessup commits to joining it, along with his family and friends, who secretly produce and distribute an antigovernment newsletter. He is exposed when Ledue, searching for volumes for a book burning (including the novels of that "Communist" Charles Dickens), discovers the newsletters. The curtain falls as Jessup is sent to a concentration camp.

In the first of the final Act's three scenes, an emboldened Ledue has moved into Jessup's home and threatens to rape Mary. The second scene shifts to the grim concentration camp where Jessup is imprisoned, and the final one to the Canadian border. Lorinda, who has helped Jessup flee the concentration camp, tries escaping with him, disguised, to Canada. They are waved through the border crossing, but Mary and her young son, David, who are also trying to leave, are stopped and interrogated by a border official who recognizes her. We learn that Mary had killed Ledue when he tried to rape her. When the official is about to send troops to arrest Jessup and Lorinda before they can reach freedom, Mary grabs a rifle and points it at him. She then sends David across the border to join his grandfather, telling him to *remember America.* At this point, Lewis and his collaborators couldn't quite figure out how to end the play, and each director was given license to bring the play to a close in a way that worked best locally. So, for example, in Cincinnati, Tacoma, and Seattle the play ended with Mary shooting the official, while in Omaha she raised the gun to her shoulder as the curtain fell to the rousing sounds of "America." In San Francisco, Mary fired the gun and was then shot to death.

As opening night approached, a couple of planned productions fell by the wayside: New Orleans pulled out because of sensitivities over

Huey Long's recent assassination. A Brooklyn production had to be postponed when six of the major actors landed commercial jobs. Flanagan canceled the Missouri run after the "authorities wished to change the script as to intent and meaning." And the production in Kansas City was pulled, *Variety* reported, when state officials refused to allow a modest admission to be charged. Planned productions in San Bernadino, San Antonio, Raleigh, and Manchester never materialized. Elsewhere it was a mad dash to opening night. Revised versions of Acts 2 and 3 were still being mailed across the country on October 10, leaving actors less than a week to learn their new parts and exasperating those translating the play. The cast in the Spanish production in Tampa only received a translation less than two weeks before opening night. The script was still far too long—three and a half hours—so directors were urged to make cuts. Five days before opening night, telegrams went out from the Washington office instructing all companies to eliminate a scene set in the White House (though it was acceptable to stage it *if* there was no explicit mention of the White House itself) and to cut an inflammatory line about those "billygoats of the Supreme Court." Lewis, who was closely involved with the Broadway production at the Adelphi Theatre (even handpicking the cast), called Flanagan in despair forty-eight hours before opening, demanding that she delay opening night, as the set was a disaster. Flanagan jumped on a train from Poughkeepsie and, drawing on her experience at Vassar, managed with a small team to find new "furniture and draperies and lamps and pictures" and, with no time to spare, repaired the sets that "had been bungled."

A declassified folder in the National Archives details the Federal Theatre's plans to ensure that the production would not be derailed by accusations of partisanship. E. E. McCleish, director of promotion for the play, distributed a nine-page directive forbidding any reference in the play or promotional materials to any political figures, foreign governments, or even fascism itself. Those writing press releases were told to "Toss your purple passages into the waste basket. There must be no references in news release of . . . Dictatorships, pro or con. There can be no political discussions, comment, or speculation." Mc-Cleish's instructions extended to what took place onstage: no bayonets or cannons should be used as props, and no effigies of political figures should appear. Some of the directors were flirting with the idea of dressing ushers in paramilitary garb, as Corpos, but that, too, was forbidden.

Perhaps because so much of the politics of the novel had been excised in the script, it was initially proposed that handbills be circulated in various theaters detailing Windrip's authoritarian platform—his notorious Fifteen Points—including them in the program, and then, between the second and third Acts distributing copies of Jessup's samizdat newsletter, *The People's Party Underground*, detailing the brutality of the regime (e.g., Windrip's "Corpos are marching throughout the land. When you hear their feet at your door, pray they pass, for if they stop it means torture and death for someone you love"). The Federal Theatre's Living Newspaper Unit got to work printing them. When they were sent to Flanagan, who had not seen drafts of them in advance, she admitted to being "very disturbed" and instructed regional productions to destroy every copy.

McCleish even vetted posters for the production, rejecting one produced in Detroit in which an allusion to Hitler was unmistakable. He sent a telegram instructing those in Detroit to "DESTROY THESE POSTERS," "RECALL ALL THAT ARE OUT," and "PLEASE WIRE THAT THIS HAS BEEN DONE." The Federal Theatre was walking a fine line, promoting itself, in contrast with Hollywood, as offering uncensored fare. But at the same time, Flanagan and her staff knew how vulnerable they were to controversy that might result in the cancellation of the show (as *Ethiopia* had been nine months earlier). *Variety* reported a week before opening night that Chicago's mayor, Edward Kelly—who insisted on the right to close any show he pleased, had recently canceled the commercial run of *Tobacco Road* on the grounds of indecency, then blocked the Federal Theatre's production of *Model Tenement*, seemingly because it was communistic—was "antagonistic to *It Can't Happen Here* and may ban it." If he canceled it, a chain reaction leading to further censorship nationwide might compromise the entire enterprise. The Federal Theatre risked seeing its funding cut; all the ammunition its enemies needed would be an improper prop or poster, or evidence that it was somehow, by opposing dictatorship, promoting Communism.

It was an enormous relief to Flanagan and the many actors, designers, directors, and stagehands who were involved when the Federal Theatre opened twenty-one productions of *It Can't Happen Here* in eighteen cities on the evening of October 27, 1936. Crowds packed houses in Omaha, Indianapolis, Los Angeles, Chicago, Miami, Birmingham, Seattle, San Francisco, Cleveland, Denver, Detroit, New York City, and a half dozen other cities. When the first performance ended on Broadway and was met with great applause, Sinclair Lewis, who was in the audience, was asked to speak after the curtain came down at 11:30. He kept it short, saying, "I have been making a speech since seven minutes to 9." Flanagan writes in *Arena* that the exiled German playwright Ernst Toller saw the opening-night performance and said at the celebratory party after, that "I sat on the edge of my seat and a cold sweat broke out all over me. That's the way it ought to affect all of you, for you, too, will be in this war long before it ends."

It was staged in Seattle by a Black troupe that cast White actors as the malevolent Windrip and Sarason. On opening night in Cleveland there were nine curtain calls. Boston's opening night, like many, was sold out, disappointing hundreds of others who showed up to see it. In the Yiddish production in New York, seen by over 25,000 play-goers in all, the future film director Sidney Lumet played young David, and several playgoers, perhaps refugees from Nazi persecution, fainted during the concentration camp scene. In the touring Suitcase production that began its run in Tomkinsville Community Center on Long Island, "half-grown boys" applauded the "hard-boiled palaver of Shad Ledue, the Corpo bully." The Suitcase show would perform until the following July, 133 performances in all. More Americans would see the play than had bought Lewis's novel: by the time it closed in February 1937, more than 379,000 playgoers had attended 584 performances, nearly a quarter of them on Broadway. After it closed in the original cities, companies took it on the road. Playgoers in Flint, Kalamazoo, Mount Holyoke, Camden, Bayonne, and other cities and towns all had a chance to see it too, and the show played for an extraordinary 260 weeks. It even took in $80,000 during the first four months, averaging thirty cents a ticket. And it continued to be revived; Lewis himself, as Jessup, starred in a production in Cohassat, Massachusetts, in 1938.

Critical reception was mixed. The reviewer for *Variety*, who saw the Broadway production, spoke for many when concluding: "Baldly stated it comes to this: if viewed as a show selling at 50¢ top and for the purpose of keeping unemployed actors from going hungry, it's very good; if viewed as the newest play of a Nobel prize winning writer, it's very bad. . . . Trouble is largely that the show doesn't head anywhere. Neither did the book it was taken from but there it wasn't so important." But even the harsher reviews—such as Brooks Atkinson's in *The New York Times*, who saw the same production and thought it "slipshod," acknowledged that "thousands of Americans who do not know what a fascist dictatorship would mean now have an opportunity to find out, thanks to Mr. Lewis's energetic public spirit and the Federal Theatre's wide facilities." Another influential reviewer, Burns Mantle of the *New York Daily News*, while conceding that the "New York production was not very good," recognized that this mattered a lot less than the fact that this "was a demonstration of the uses to which a people's theater might reasonably be put," and that the multiple and eagerly received opening across the country "indicated rather revealingly . . . what could happen here if the social body should ever become theater minded in a serious way."

The success of *It Can't Happen Here* would be measured in other ways. *Variety*, which surveyed the many productions across the country, noted that many of those who went to see it "quite obviously had never before been in a legit house." Its reporter in Birmingham, Alabama, wrote that most of those who saw it there were "obviously not accustomed to attending legit shows" and that some "appeared to be construction workers." Its correspondent in Seattle had a similar reaction: a "large percentage of non theatregoers" helped "pack the 2,300 seat . . . theatre," including "many Negroes in the audience, along with project workers, giving a proletarian aspect to the assemblage." Working-class playgoers who a half century earlier had frequented the theater were returning. The Federal Theatre surveyed audiences at many of the venues across the country after the show, and learned

that 80 percent preferred to see plays that dealt with "current issues."
It didn't much matter to them (as it did to the big-city reviewers) that
the actors weren't stars or that the rushed script was uneven and over-
long. A gratified Flanagan understood that "the venture was significant not so much in itself as in an augury for the future." In staging
it, she concluded, echoing Jessup, the "first government-sponsored
theatre in the United States was doing what it could to keep alive 'the
free, inquiring critical spirit' which is the center and core of a democracy."

Tamiris *(left)* and her dancers performing
How Long, Brethren?, New York, 1937.

CHAPTER FIVE

How Long, Brethren?:
Radical Dance

hen testifying before the House Un-American Activities
Committee in August 1938, Hazel Huffman, Martin
Dies's star witness, did her best to turn Hallie Flanagan's own words against her. To that end, she quoted from Flanagan's
closing remarks to the creative leadership of the Federal Theatre, who
had gathered in the summer of 1937 in Poughkeepsie, where Flanagan spoke of how vital protest was to their mission. Huffman then
pivoted to naming offending productions that embodied what she
deemed radical and un-American protest, including the antifascist
play *Professor Mamlock* (the tragedy of a Jewish doctor driven to suicide by Nazi persecution) and *How Long, Brethren?*, a dance project
that included "several Negro songs of protest." Flanagan had been so
impressed with *How Long, Brethren?* (its White dancers accompanied
by a Black chorus) that she had brought the racially diverse ensemble
to the Poughkeepsie gathering to perform. Huffman assumed that
the committee members would not object to her examples about

either the plight of foreign Jews or of Blacks challenging the status quo, since both groups were already linked in their minds to Communism. Flanagan saw the same pair of examples in a different light. She would write in *Arena* that *Professor Mamlock* was about "racial intolerance" and "the democratic principle of racial equality," and linked antisemitism to the persecution of American Blacks explored in *How Long, Brethren?*, quoting from a review in *The Washington Post*: "Until we check the vicious and illegal use of force against racial, religious, and political minorities, we shall face the same disaster that faced Professor Mamlock, who did not smell until it was too late the brimstone of hatred in the air of his once free country."

These "Negro songs of protest" were a new genre, or alternatively an old one that African Americans had not cared to share, and which threatened to unsettle what to Whites was the more acceptable and humble tradition of Black spirituals. Until their circulation in the early 1930s, the familiar form of Black song had been spirituals, songs of the enslaved, typically on biblical themes, that were more about perseverance and hope for the next world than a challenge to those in power in this one. White audiences (aside from slave overseers) first encountered African American spirituals in the 1860s, after abolitionists and missionaries traveled to the South and transcribed and published versions of these lyrics. The earliest of these was likely "Go Down Moses," which ran in the pages of the *New York Tribune* in 1861. Six years later a major anthology, *Slave Songs of the United States*, was published; W. E. B. Du Bois described it as "the first time the North met the Southern slave face to face and heart to heart." A score of other collections followed by the time that E. A. McIlhenny's *Befo' de War Spirituals: Words and Melodies* appeared in 1931, and spirituals were further popularized when touring Black choirs (initially Fisk

University's singers, then other groups from Black colleges) performed them, mostly in Northern churches and colleges. What had begun as an oral tradition of the enslaved had, by the early twentieth century, become commodified. Elaborately concertized performances largely effaced the horrors experienced by the brutalized slaves who first sang these songs.

Spirituals attracted considerable discussion: Were they derived from White hymns or rather a product of the African American experience of enslavement? Did their meaning change when removed from their original conditions of performance, especially if that had been co-erced? Frederick Douglass, who was haunted by the memory of these songs, wrote in *My Bondage and My Freedom* (1855) of singing them while enslaved, recalling that a "silent slave is not liked by masters or overseers. '*Make a noise,*' '*make a noise,*' and '*bear a hand,*'" Douglass added, were "the words usually addressed to the slave when there is silence among them." How did the process of their transmission— recorded, published, and set to music by Whites with various finan-cial, political, scholarly, and religious agendas—alter or partly erase their often coded meaning? And was there really a stark division be-tween spirituals and songs of protest, insofar as these thousands of songs, many lost, covered such a remarkable range, from Christian sufferance to contemplating violence in pursuit of freedom?

The label "protest songs" was the creation of leftists who first pro-moted them in the early 1930s, and, as Hazel Huffman had discov-ered, the earliest ones appeared—and would subsequently be used in the Federal Theatre's dance performance *How Long, Brethren?*—in the November 1930 issue of the leftist *New Masses.* These songs had been recorded and transcribed by Lawrence Gellert, who would publish others he had collected in subsequent issues, also under the heading

"Negro Songs of Protest," the title chosen by Mike Gold, the magazine's editor and a devoted Communist. *Time* magazine described Gellert as "an ardent Left Winger" and "lean, scraggly-haired New Yorker," who, with "an old-fashioned phonograph strapped on his back, a sawed-off megaphone and a bundle of blank aluminum records . . . has been touring the South . . . collecting Negro songs that few white men have ever heard." Born László Grünbaum, Gellert was seven years old when his parents brought him and his siblings to New York City, part of a great wave of Eastern European Jewish immigrants. The family first changed the name to Grunbaum, then settled on Gellert. His eldest brother, Hugo, was an accomplished illustrator, publishing in *The New Yorker* and the *New Masses*, where he was a contributing editor (which helps explain how the songs, for which Hugo provided illustrations, found their way into its pages). In the early 1920s, seeking seclusion and rest following what he later described as a "nervous breakdown," Lawrence Gellert left New York City for the comparatively liberal Southern enclave of Tryon, North Carolina. Gellert apparently knew little about Black history or music when he moved there. But soon after his arrival he began collecting and recording songs from local African Americans, songs that belied the local White assumption that Blacks were content with their subjected lot. A decade or so later, using better, if still primitive, recording devices, he had amassed hundreds of them in his travels through the South.

His publication of samplings of these in the pages of the *New Masses* were accompanied by brief descriptions of where and from whom he had first heard them. So, for example, an "old Negro in Greensboro," South Carolina—Gellert never named his sources— performed "When Marse He Gi' Me Freedom," in a tune he found "lugubrious, dirgelike, replete with pathos, grief and despair." Another "haunting" song, "Diamond Joe Wants Sack o' Flour," was sung to him to by a "young Negro chopper in a lumber camp near Anderson," South Carolina. He learned a third, "Stan' Boys Stan'," from a veteran of the Great War who was now "a tenant farmer in North Carolina." Gellert was struck by its "militant chord" that was "rather unusual for that section of the country," and it was sung to him in a "martial, guttural and snarlish" tune.

In 1936, Gellert published twenty-four of these in a slim volume titled *Negro Songs of Protest*, where they were set to music. The songs, he writes, offered a glimpse behind the "mask of the docile, amicable, treadmilling clown" that "the Negro must appear in if he is to survive," and "embody the living voice of an otherwise inarticulate resentment against injustice—a part of the unrest that is stirring the South." As he later told an interviewer, they went "way beyond the spirituals. . . . And you might really call them revolutionary songs." Their assertiveness came as a shock to some; the reviewer for the dependably progressive *New Republic* expressed discomfort with songs whose "explicit bitterness is not typical of Negro songs as we know them." Langston Hughes drafted an introduction to the collection (though it didn't get published with it) underscoring their importance to those impatient with passive, get-along responses to ongoing racial injustice in America: "These songs collected by Lawrence Gellert from plantations, chain gangs, lumber camps, and jails are of inestimable value, if they do nothing more than show that not all Negroes are shouting spirituals, cheering endowed football teams, dancing to the blues, or mouthing inter-racial oratory. Some of them are tired of being poor, and picturesque, and hungry. Terribly and bitterly tired." Hughes himself was providing a poetic equivalent to these grim songs in lyrics like "Open Letter to the South" and "Good Morning Revolution," whose speaker "ain't never had enough to eat," and calls Revolution "the very best friend / I ever had." Hughes wrote that radical poem while visiting the Soviet Union, and daringly sent it to *The Saturday Evening Post*, better known for its Norman Rockwellesque vision of America. The *Post* immediately rejected it, but the *New Masses* didn't, running the poem in its September 1932 issue. Two decades later, Hughes would pay the price for this when he was hauled before the Senate's Permanent Subcommittee on Investigations.

The appearance of these songs and poems of protest coincided with another emerging art form, modern dance, and would briefly and memorably intertwine with it. Nowadays, with thousands of modern dance programs at high schools, colleges, and community centers across the land, and with established companies performing regularly, it's hard to imagine a time, back in the 1920s and 1930s, when modern dance barely existed in America. At that time, when classical ballet still ruled, a handful of exceptional American modern dancers, especially women, following in the trailblazing path of Isadora Duncan, began to attract notice. To a significant degree their dances at this time were politically progressive. Their ranks, according to standard histories of modern dance, included Martha Graham, Ruth St. Denis, Doris Humphrey, Charles Weidman, and Katherine Dunham, all of whom struggled to reach a larger public. Talent was one thing, financing another: staging a one-off dance concert, for which they would have to book a venue and provide their own costumes and musical accompaniment, was prohibitively expensive, and aside from teaching classes the only decent-paying work that was available to these dancers—mostly in nightclubs and the occasional Broadway show—was at cross-purposes with their creative ambitions. And these were obstacles faced by the rising stars in the field. For their acolytes, a surprising number of them daughters of poor Eastern European Jewish immigrants, employment in modern dance was precarious at best.

One of the most celebrated modern dancers of that time, whose name has since dropped out of the pantheon of the founders of American modern dance, was Helen Becker, better known by the name she chose for herself, Tamiris (after a fearless mythological warrior queen). Tamiris's family, like Gellert's, were Eastern European Jews who settled in New York City at the turn of the century, though her family was much poorer. She recalled in a draft of an abandoned autobiography how her father worked sixteen-hour days in sweatshops. Two of her six siblings died, as did her mother. She grew up in a tenement, lice-ridden and hungry, running with a gang, and recalled these years as an "animal like—almost jungle existence." Her father saved to send her to dance classes at the Henry Street Settlement House, where she was taught "interpretive dancing." She went to public schools and in the summers worked long hours in a factory. At fifteen she was accepted at the Metropolitan Opera Ballet School, where she was trained afresh and danced for four years. After seeing Isadora Duncan perform at the Brooklyn Academy of Music she was determined to choreograph her own "American" dances. But that meant quitting the Metropolitan Opera and earning enough money—from a South American tour with the Bracale Opera, nightclubs where she would perform ethnic and exotic roles, and on occasion in musical theater— to stage her own solo concerts, the first of which took place in October 1927.

In her second, three months later, she introduced what would become an integral part of her repertory for the next decade, a pair of

"Negro spirituals": "Nobody Knows de Trouble I See" and "Joshua Fit de Battle ob Jericho." She writes in her unfinished memoir how in "these dances, I wanted to express the spirit of the Negro People—in the first, his sense of oppression—in the second, his fight—and struggle and remembrance when 'the walls came tumbling down.'" Tamiris had begun working on a third spiritual at this time, "Go Down Moses," of which she wrote (with no expectation that her presumptuous words in an abandoned memoir would ever be read by others), "I will make many Negro dances—I understand the Negro people so well!—their yearnings." Her flyer and program to this concert were accompanied by a manifesto declaring that "art is international, but the artist is a product of a nationality" whose "principal duty" is "to express the spirit of his race."

In 1932 Tamiris added a Black dance, "Gris-Gris Ceremonial," to her repertory and the following summer performed a revised version of it before a large outdoor audience at Lewisohn Stadium, this time with the Bahama Negro Dancers, in what for those times was a rare interracial performance. The following week, John Martin, the influential dance critic of *The New York Times*, praised her performance and noted that Tamiris "often has expressed her connection of kinship with Negro dance," before comparing her style with that of Isadora Duncan, with whom "she has a certain fellowship, in spite of differences which are racial and environmental as well as personal in their origin." That last sentence delicately underscores the extent to which Tamiris was viewed in the dance world as racially other; less polite members of the New York press called her "the Harlem savage." Other modern Jewish dancers shared Tamiris's interest in the African American struggle for equality. In 1934 Lillian Shapero, an early member of Martha Graham's company, in a program that included the New York City debut of Hallie Flanagan's *Can You Hear Their Voices?*, danced to "Negro work songs and spirituals" sung by members of the Black cast of *Stevedore*, and created a dance to accompany Langston Hughes's "Good Morning Revolution." Helen Bletcher, who, like Tamiris, had started dancing at the Henry Street Settlement House (and along with Shapero would dance for Martha Graham), similarly turned to Black spirituals and poems.

Venue figured as well in forging connections between Blacks and Jews through dance. The Young Men's Hebrew Association, located at Ninety-second Street and Lexington Avenue (now known as the 92NY), was at the forefront of promoting Black as well as modern dance, under the leadership of its educational director, William Kolodney. He created a subscription series of Sunday-evening dance recitals for his overwhelmingly Jewish membership, which included a pathbreaking "Negro Dance Evening" on March 7, 1937, a historical sweep led off by Asadata Dafora and Abdel Assen, who had been so crucial to the success of *Macbeth*. The program closed with Black dancers (two women and four men) performing to lyrics taken from Gellert's *Negro Songs of Protest*, increasingly a go-to source for politically minded dancers: Edna Guy choreographed "How Long, Brethren?"; Clarence Yates (who had helped choreograph *Macbeth* and was now serving as director of the WPA Negro Dance Unit) choreographed "Cause I'm a Nigger"; and Alison Burroughs did so for the final piece, "Scottsboro." When Kolodney tried to schedule an evening of Jewish dance, he had to cancel it, from lack of interest; his progressive subscribers were more interested in modern dance that was cutting-edge and political. As Naomi M. Jackson puts it in her history of dance at the 92NY, "In some ways, radical dance *was* a form of Jewish dance."

Tamiris was one of the first dancers to appear in Kolodney's series, dancing "Four Negro Spirituals" in a program that also included her radical *Cycle of Unrest* (with the dances "Protest," "Camaraderie," "The Individual and the Mass," and "Conflict"). In the years that followed, she would go on to perform nine "Negro spirituals" in all, which came to be seen, in the words of the contemporary dance critic Margaret Lloyd, as "the musts of her programs. Every new one was hailed with hurrahs. This was the thing she could really do, this was what she did best." Like other young assimilated Jewish dancers in the 1930s who shared her immigrant background and leftist politics, Tamiris identified strongly with the struggles of African Americans, and because many spirituals touched on the Jews' own journey from bondage to freedom, celebrated in songs about Joshua and Moses, it wasn't difficult for them to find common ground in the plight and art of Black America. Her other dance programs, including *Walt Whitman Suite* (1934), *Toward the Light* (1934), and *Harvest* (1935), were increasingly committed to exposing social and racial injustice. Moving from the universalism of the spirituals to more controversial racial issues, Tamiris turned to the violence experienced by African Americans at the hands of Whites in her November 1936 concert, *Momentum*, daringly featuring "Nightriders," on the lynching of Blacks (a dance she chose to reprise on January 2, 1938, at an all-star "Evening of Modern Dance" that also featured Martha Graham, Ruth St. Denis, Charles Weidman, and Doris Humphrey). For Tamiris, the "validity of the modern dance" was increasingly "rooted in its ability to express modern problems" and "to make modern audiences want to do something about them."

In the months following the creation of the Federal Theatre, both Gellert and Tamiris joined its ranks. Gellert, who was friendly with

Rose McClendon, was initially assigned to the Negro Unit, where he provided music for some of its earliest shows, *Walk Together, Chillun* and *Conjur Man Dies*, as well as *Swamp Mud*, which was canceled after Orson Welles poached its best actors, including Jack Carter, for his *Macbeth*—and, Gellert recalled, "we couldn't do a damn thing about it." He eventually transferred out of the Negro Unit, bouncing around to the Play Bureau and the Living Newspaper Unit and providing sound for a show in Atlanta, before eventually transferring to the Federal Writers' Project.

Two years earlier Tamiris had finally formed her own dance company. But unlike the other leading choreographers who affiliated with the Federal Theatre, she disbanded hers in order to contribute full time to the fledgling national project, one that was closely aligned with her political beliefs, her aspiration to bring American modern dance to a national audience, and her experience collaborating with actors. It was also a means to pursue her tireless goal of seeking economic security for fellow dancers (through the Dance Repertory Theatre, Concert Dancers' League, and most of all the Dance Association, all of which she helped found). As chair of the Dance Association, Tamiris met with Harry Hopkins and Hallie Flanagan and lobbied hard for the creation of an autonomous dance unit within the Federal Theatre. Permission was granted and in January 1936 the Federal Dance Theatre was created, with a modest budget of $155,000 and a quota of 185 dancers. For Flanagan, it was "impossible to think of the modern theatre without thinking of the dance," and she believed that the integration of dance into the unit would move contemporary theater forward, for directors needed "to learn the hard lessons of the dancer: how to emphasize and distort line, how to assault by color, how to design in space."

117

Securing this limited funding turned out to be the easy part, for the founding of the Dance Theatre quickly brought to the surface long-standing rifts within the dance community. There were many forms of dance after all, including ballet, ballroom, tap, and folk dance. But the scrappy modern dancers, who had long struggled to make ends meet and were experienced at organizing for better working conditions (lacking the union representation of actors, musicians, and stagehands or the longer-term security provided by ballet companies), quickly edged out their rivals. A backlash followed, with a coalition that included the Dance Masters of America, the English Folk Dancing Society of America, and the Dancing Teachers Business Association of New York accusing the modern dancers now running the Dance Project of "unparalleled unprofessionalism and shameful political agitation."

Internally, there was little agreement about the direction or leadership of the program. Byzantine rules about qualifying for relief, repeat auditioning, and specialized credentials (two years' work professionally plus three years of costly training with a known teacher or at established and largely segregated schools of modern dance or ballet, effectively excluding dancers of color) created obstacles. Neither of those whom Flanagan put in charge, first Don Oscar Becque and then Lincoln Kirstein, lasted very long in the face of organized resistance on the part of dancers Flanagan called a "volcanic group." Becque's fantasy of creating "a common denominator of movement technique" ran into a buzz saw of opposition from the other choreographers, who had their own ideas. After that, the Dance Theatre limped along under the direction of an executive committee made up of its leading choreographers, working under a rotation system that allowed only a few of them at a time to cast and rehearse shows. It didn't help that the Dance Theatre was established not long before deep, across-the-board cuts were mandated for the entire WPA. This meant that less than half the promised quota of 185 dancers was ever filled, and the persistent threat of even deeper cuts meant that dancers spent much of their time at sit-ins and street protests, sometimes leading to their arrest, and far less time in rehearsal studios or in actual productions.

The Dance Theatre's ambitious goal—staging eight productions in its first six months—was never met, with John Martin, ten months after its creation, complaining in *The New York Times* that "the project has been in a continuous uproar ever since its formation, and the possibility of its ever achieving a Broadway opening had begun to fade into the nebulous realms of fable." Most of its earliest productions were recycled from the repertories of its leading choreographers, including Gluck Sandor and Felicia Sorel updating the 1933 *The Prodigal Son* as *The Eternal Prodigal*, Charles Weidman reviving his 1933 *Candide*, and Tamiris her 1934 *Walt Whitman Suite* as *Salut au Monde*. The Dance Theatre lasted only twenty-two months before more deep cuts resulted in its reabsorption into the Federal Theatre in October 1937. Dancers continued to contribute, both in New York City and nationally, to the Federal Theatre, but under different auspices: Harlem's Negro Theater Unit performed a dance concert, *Bassa Moona*, and Myra Kinch's *An American Exodus* enjoyed a long run in Los Angeles under the Federal Music Project, while Katherine Dunham, dance director of the Chicago Negro Theater Unit, choreographed several pieces, including *Run Li'l Chil'lun* and *The Emperor Jones*. Tamiris herself would contribute to (and perform in) a play, *Trojan Incident*, and, shortly before the demise of the entire Federal Theatre, choreographed *Adelante*, a long dance program on the Spanish Civil War. The Dance Theatre never had the time, resources, or strong leadership to mature into something more consequential and only managed to stage a handful of original productions, including Becque's short-lived *Young Tramps* (whose three-night run, according to *The Daily Worker*, "failed miserably"). Another original work, and its greatest success, was Tamiris's *How Long, Brethren?*, a long-running Broadway hit that offered a glimpse of a different future for modern American dance had the Federal Dance Theatre survived.

Gellert's *Negro Songs of Protest* held an even greater appeal for Tamiris than the Black spirituals to which she had been dancing for nearly a decade. Their boldness better suited her temperament and political views, and Gellert's selection allowed her to construct a rough storyline through rearranging the order of seven of the songs, from the reenactment of body- and soul-killing labor in "Pickin' Off de Cotton" to the fierce call for resistance of its title piece, "How Long, Brethren?" Gellert had described these songs as "work reels," explaining that their "tempo and swing depended on the type of work performed and the required motion of the instrument used," offering rich material for a choreographer. "Pickin' Off de Cotton," according to Pauline Bubrick Tish, who performed in it, was typical, "composed of fast running steps, stopping and starting and collapsing from exhaustion," providing "a graphic depiction of the cotton pickers slaving away in the fields of the deep South." And in the final dance, "How Long, Brethren?," Tish recalled, the "ensemble acted as the voice of social conscience. They entered in groups of four, their bodies curved, their hands semi-fisted, their eyes focused on Tamiris, the leader who spurred them on until their final exit downstage" toward a red dawn. The songs themselves were sung by the Wen Talbert Negro Choir, both men and women—their names omitted from the earliest printed program—with the published score's repeated "Nigger" changed to "Darkie" throughout.

Tamiris oversaw eighteen dancers on the production, roughly a quarter of those employed by the Federal Dance Theatre, most of whom had already worked with her on *Salut au Monde* and three of whom had been members of her now disbanded company. All were White, and many, probably most, were Jewish. The WPA Federal Theatre Orchestra, conducted by Jacques Gottlieb, provided music, to a score influenced by contemporary jazz and arranged by Genevieve Pitot, who worked from a transcription for piano. This had been provided by Elie Siegmeister, who acknowledged that these "were 'concert hall-styled' and adapted for 'more urban tastes,'" and was praised in the *Baltimore Afro-American* for having "succeeded better than most" in trying "to suggest a racial feeling in his accompaniments." Henry Guilfond, reviewing the performance in the *Dance Observer*, noted that "rarely have audiences responded so wholeheartedly and rarely have dancers deserved such ovations," adding that this was "not night-club jazz, her syncopation no floor show. She has captured the rhythms as they have come up from hard folk experience." John Martin praised Tamiris's choreography in *The New York Times* for offering "a supplement to the score, underlying its mood and intensity and adding a stage counterpoint, without trying to overtop or even to parallel it with action."

The experience of hearing and seeing this performed back in 1937 is impossible to recapture, the handful of contemporary recollections or modern attempts to reconstruct and revive it notwithstanding. Watching a video of the 1990s version performed by the Cleo Parker Robinson Dance Ensemble, advised by several dancers from the original production, conveys a sense of Tamiris's distinctive choreography, but also underscores how much is irrevocably lost. Audiences at the time, most of whom had never seen a dance concert—and this one attracted standing-room-only crowds—brought a different political urgency and set of cultural values to it than modern viewers. All we know with confidence is that the show, staged initially at the Nora Bayes Theatre (where it followed Weidman's *Candide* on the program), in an unprecedented run that stretched from May 6 to July 4, "was interrupted many times by applause and shouts so loud the dancers could not hear the orchestra or the chorus in the pit."

You could sit in the balcony at the Nora Bayes Theatre for a quarter, what you would pay to see a movie. By the time that *How Long, Brethren?* had transferred to Maxine Elliott's Theatre (and, after that, the Forty-ninth Street Theatre), *Candide* had been dropped, resulting in a more coherent show, one that now focused exclusively on the African American experience. The program now opened with Bob Moman leading the Federal Theatre Negro Chorus in five spirituals. That was followed by Tamiris, appearing solo, dancing to four more spirituals. The production then climaxed with the defiant "How Long, Brethren?" Between May 1937 and January 1938 there were forty-three performances in all, attended by nearly twenty-five thousand people, numbers unprecedented in modern dance, a different sort of audience, one that "kept interrupting the dance out of sheer good will." It was praised within the dance community as well: that June *Dance Magazine* gave its "annual award of excellence in a formal presentation," calling Tamiris's choreography the "most brilliant for the year."

Early on in the run at the Nora Bayes Theatre, the production's progressive politics spilled over onto Broadway. According to the *New York Herald Tribune*, on May 19, after the show ended, five hundred of the capacity crowd of seven hundred joined the dancers, chorus, and musicians to protest impending cuts to the Federal Theatre. After the police arrived to break up the protest, the picketers decided to march, and the police were forced to close off traffic. When in June, musicians employed in the Federal Music Project faced cuts, audiences and performers once again protested. This, too, was part of the experience of a show that so explicitly advocated resistance.

For Hallie Flanagan and the Federal Theatre, *How Long, Brethren?* was a triumph. When the American Dance Association held its first annual convention in May 1937, Flanagan sent a message to the group that was read aloud, urging them to "broaden the dance so that it becomes a strong expression of the life of today," and urging that "any tendency to the 'esoteric' should be suppressed." *How Long, Brethren?* epitomized for her what modern American dance could and should be: "In its conception, execution, and implications," *How Long, Brethren?* "becomes not only a powerful social document, but an epitome of that freedom from racial prejudice which must exist at the core of any theatre for American people."

What did it mean for Black or White contemporaries to watch White dancers enact the suffering of Blacks? African American writers provide little insight in this regard, especially when compared with the heated debate stirred up by Blacks performing a work by a White author with *Macbeth* in Harlem. The limited commentary in Black newspapers only came at the end of the run, when a final revival, planned for early 1938 (and canceled for reasons unknown), was expected at the Lafayette Theatre. A pair of these came close to expressing reservations. The *Baltimore Afro-American* juxtaposed an image from Tamiris's production with one of the "orthodox singing" of Black performers from *Porgy and Bess*, then asked readers, "How do you like your spirituals?" The other, with more edge to it, appeared in the scare quotes in the headline accompanying a photograph of Tamiris's group in *The Pittsburgh Courier*, "Examples of 'Negro Art' Which Won Dance Magazine's Award," the irony—if it is that—repeated in the more elaborate description that followed: "The dance above is supposed to protest conditions among Negro industrial workers in the South."

Whites who commented on the production were mostly silent about its racial dynamics. The Federal Theatre asked audiences to fill out response forms, and one who replied, a writer by profession, race unknown, wondered: "Why not Negro dancers?" But otherwise, it seems that Whites who saw it largely shared the view of Margaret Lloyd, the dance critic of *The Christian Science Monitor*, who in a long profile of Tamiris concluded that these "modern songs of protest from the present-day deep South . . . focus attention on Negroes, not only as Negroes, but as a symbol of all the oppressed peoples of earth. It may be racial oppression, or religious, or political, but thus focused on one aspect of contemporary life," Tamiris's program "becomes in its singularity a poignant reminder of a universal problem." In making this claim, Lloyd echoed Tamiris's own words, shared in a radio interview in the course of the run, in which she said, "Many people have asked me why I am so interested—since I am a white person—in using this particular material." The answer she offered: "Although the focus of *How Long, Brethren?* is centered in the South, it becomes for me the means for projecting the life of all oppressed people."

Lloyd's first and more visceral reaction to *How Long, Brethren?* a month earlier had registered greater unease in watching White dancers trying to render Black experience: "You wonder a little, while admiring the tremendous vitality of the dancer, at what first seems an artistic miscegenation. How can a modern white girl feel the rhythms and tempo, the temperamental pulse, of these old-time slave songs?" Yet her initial misgivings, Lloyd goes on to write, were ultimately allayed: "Tamiris moves gloriously, compellingly, and prejudice is soon worn down when '*How Long, Brethren*' gets under way, and before the '*Let's Go to De Buryin*'" episode is over, you are ready to stand up and yell from sheer contagion of exuberance." But whose prejudice is worn down? And is "worn down" the same as "worn away"? In the end, for Lloyd, the issue isn't fully resolved: "Whether or not Tamiris dances as a Negro would dance or composes as a Negro would compose, she certainly catches the native idiosyncrasy in '*Let's Go to De Buryin*'." It is a stirring production." The question of "artistic miscegenation" is left unanswered, and Lloyd doesn't seem eager to delve deeper into it.

Looking back a decade later, Tamiris would write:

> In the early days, in the Twenties, there were many days when I doubted that modern dance would ever reach a large audience. But the years of the Great Depression and the experience of working as a choreographer for the Federal Theatre Project settled that doubt. When Charles Weidman's *Candide* and my *How Long, Brethren?* were presented to cheering audiences that had never seen a dance recital, I knew that the modern dance was not an esoteric phase of dance to be enjoyed only by the *cognoscenti*, but one that could reach large audiences.

By the time she wrote those words, it had all come crashing down. The Federal Dance Theatre, along with the Federal Theatre, was no more. Tamiris, identified so closely with an organization that Dies's committee had tarred as un-American, was effectively blacklisted. She tried taking up part of her old name, now going by Helen Tamiris, but presenting herself as less foreign didn't help much. After the Federal Theatre "was destroyed," Tamiris admitted, "the shock and sense of rejection made the job of starting all over again to build a group and a school seem almost impossible." She tried to nonetheless, converting a downtown basement into a cramped studio, where she and her dancers performed, but admitted that the "productions were of necessity not on the same level as the works in the Broadway Theatre during the Project days." The FBI had opened a file on her after a confidential informant alleged that in 1936 Tamiris was an active Communist. Her file also made note of the sit-in strike that accompanied *How Long, Brethren?* as well as her participation in a group that had called on Congress to abolish the House Un-American Activities Committee. The American Legion deemed her one of those "whose past activities make them untouchable or inappropriate for Legion sponsorship," and in 1950 her name was included among the 151 allegedly subversive artists in *Red Channels*, the bible of Hollywood blacklisters. No invitations were forthcoming to teach at Bennington, Juilliard, or other prestigious schools where leading choreographers found employment and recognition. When the FBI had finished its extensive surveillance of Tamiris in 1955, it had found no incriminating evidence that she had ever been a threat, and an agent "recommended that she be deleted from the Security Index." By then her concert career had been over for a decade. Tamiris would find work and a supportive home in the commercial theater between 1943 and 1957, choreographing eighteen musicals, most of them on Broadway, including *Annie Get Your Gun* (1945) and *Show Boat* (1946). She died, in 1966, at age sixty-one. Eight years later, at a gala celebrating the hundredth anniversary of the 92NY, five of her "Negro Spirituals" (performed by her nephew Bruce Becker and his "Five by Two" dance company) followed Alvin Ailey's spiritual "Fix Me, Jesus, Fix Me," a choice that suggests that her dances were not yet viewed as unseemly acts of cultural appropriation. It was one of the last times they would be performed and Tamiris singled out as "one of the pioneers of modern American dance."

It was no small irony that after having had her career as a leftist concert dancer ended by the right, Tamiris's legacy would be subsequently attacked from the academic left for engaging in what the leading dance scholar Susan Manning in her 1998 essay "Black Voices, White Bodies: The Performance of Race and Gender in *How Long Brethren*" called "metaphorical blackface" and "metaphorical minstrelsy." While Tamiris and her dancers didn't actually "blacken up" as, say, a Jewish Al Jolson did in the 1927 film *The Jazz Singer*, Manning suggests that what they did, by expressing Black experience though not Black themselves, amounted to versions of blackface in "alternate guises."

Manning also criticizes Tamiris for not including Black dancers in the production. Tamiris had been training her cohort of dancers for over a year, some of them for several years, and while there was a sole exception (Add Bates, a Black man who was part of Weidman's company and danced in *Candide*), the Federal Theatre, under Flanagan's leadership, had drawn a line at extensively integrated companies. While the restrictions and bureaucracy in the Dance Theatre would have made securing any of the twenty-two modern dancers employed by the Negro Unit at the Lafayette Theatre difficult, had Tamiris insisted on recruiting some of them for *How Long, Brethren?*, it's hard to imagine anyone standing in her way. They were available, and for the past two years had not been employed in *any* concert dance program. According to a sharply critical report submitted to the WPA by the Negro Arts Committee Federal Arts Council, the dancers at the Lafayette Theatre had asked "that they be used in general dance productions, along with white dancers," but were told that only "those with light complexions might possibly be used." And while they had rehearsed a performance based on Maurice Maeterlinck's allegorical play *The Blue Bird*, the show was "withdrawn" after they resisted efforts on the part of its White director, Jack Resnick, to impose what they felt was a conventional White approach to the material that had nothing to do with their experience. As one of those dancers, Beryl Banfield, put it many years later, they "did not want to be a white interpretation of anything," adding that they "were also very fiery," so the challenges Tamiris would likely have faced replacing some of her White dancers with Black ones from the Lafayette Unit would likely have been formidable—had she even considered doing so.

The ambivalence one of the dancers involved felt about the racial dynamics of the production is captured in the recollection of Anne Lief Barlin, who, like Tamiris, was a Jewish immigrant from a poor family on the Lower East Side. Decades after she performed in *How Long, Brethren?*, she was asked if it had been a controversial production and admitted in a halting reply to "mixed feelings about it": "There were very few Negroes. (Pause) I don't think anybody—no, I don't think, it caused enough of a stir to be controversial. . . . It was both, something borrowed—it seemed it didn't have the integrity of creating it yourself." Yet at the same time, she added, dancing to Black songs of protest was "a recognition of another group's contribution," one that "politically, intellectually we accepted."

In the end, *How Long, Brethren?* managed to do what meaningful art often does: disturb and unsettle. It certainly angered members of the House Un-American Activities Committee, unhappy at the prospect of federal funding of packed performances where audiences heard songs of protest sung by a Black chorus while watching White dancers enact the horrors of slavery in America. It forced critics like Lloyd to confront their own prejudices and consider whether White dancers were capable of embodying Black experience, even as it would lead more recent dance historians to dismiss the performance as minstrelsy. Even if Tamiris and her dancers may have believed at the time that theirs were abstract bodies that could assume other identities, that conviction was not necessarily shared by those who watched them dance. Complicating these issues were historical factors impossible to disentangle from them, such as the extent to which Jewish dancers were themselves seen by many as racially other, that should give pause to anyone rushing to pass judgment.

Gellert's fate after the Federal Theatre closed is no less dispiriting. His career imploded at much the same time as Tamiris's, and the FBI opened a file on him too. Interest in Gellert's work soon faded. His second collection of songs of protest, *Me and My Captain* (1939), sold poorly and he failed to find a publisher after that. It didn't help that he was difficult to work with. As a recent biographer put it, by the early 1960s Gellert would be "defamed as a fraud in influential circles": his "archive was tainted if not outright phony, went the charge, an example of white leftwing propaganda and interference rather than Black vernacular creativity and resistance." An earlier biographer, Bruce Conforth, who had once celebrated Gellert as a "pioneering collector-radical," had turned against Gellert after three decades of exploring his work, publishing a book in 2013—*African American Folksong and American Cultural Politics: The Lawrence Gellert Story*—in which he argued that some of the "Songs of Protest" were assisted, prompted, and even coached by Gellert, and were therefore inauthentic, leading Conforth to conclude that "it seems clear that 'Negro Songs of Protest' (as a special body of material collected by Gellert) never really existed within the folk music tradition, but were, rather, the creation of the left wing and U.S. Communist Party in order to use as propaganda, with Lawrence as either their unwitting or identity-hunting dupe." If this were true, the "metaphorical minstrelsy" Manning describes was itself based on an inauthentic leftist plot—and Tamiris (and her cheering audiences) dupes of an unwitting dupe.

Gellert's reputation and the legitimacy of those "Songs of Protest" have been badly tarnished. It remains to be seen if more recent scholarship will restore Gellert's reputation and the once valued place of those "Songs of Protest" in American culture. For seventeen years, a young scholar, Steven Garabedian, painstakingly reexamined every shred of evidence, including the hundreds of damaged but still partly audible items in the Gellert recordings archive, housed at Indiana University. In 2020 he published the results of his research in *A Sound History: Lawrence Gellert, Black Musical Protest, and White Denial*, having found "no compelling evidence that Gellert fabricated songs." The recorded protest songs were genuine. Gellert may have been a contrarian, but, Garabedian concludes, he was also "an honest collector with sincere political convictions regarding racial and economic justice."

After the collapse of the short-lived Federal Dance Project, Black modern dancers continued to perform spirituals and songs and poems of protest; aside from Tamiris's nephew when paying tribute to her, White ones no longer would. Modern dance stopped reaching large popular audiences, let alone Broadway, and traditional ballet, better

funded and less politically suspect, elbowed its way back into prominence. The leading modern dancer to thrive after the 1930s was Martha Graham, whose progressive period, exemplified by her antifascist
Chronicle (1936), was now behind her, though the FBI had opened a
file on her as well, no doubt because of "her pro-communist, if pro-
democratic, performances in support of medical assistance during the
Spanish Civil War." Graham and Flanagan had spoken about working on a project for the Federal Theatre, but nothing came of it, and
Graham never joined its ranks. By 1947, Victoria Phillips writes in
Martha Graham's Cold War, Graham had become "directly involved in
early Cold War experiments with dance as pro-American propaganda," and eight years later Graham toured the globe, funded by the
State Department, insisting that she was "not a propagandist" and
that her dances were "not political."

Opening scene, tenement fire, *One Third
of a Nation*, Adelphi Theatre, New York, 1938.

CHAPTER SIX

One Third of a Nation:
Riling Congress

On February 23, 1937, Hallie Flanagan left opening night of *Power* at Broadway's Ritz Theatre relieved by what she had seen. The sold-out show had been well received (and would run there for another 141 performances), and, unlike the previous Living Newspaper, *Injunction Granted*, *Power* had not steered into treacherous political waters. Joseph Losey, who had directed *Injunction Granted*, was exceptionally gifted, but his radical politics attracted what for Flanagan was the wrong sort of attention (and would later get him blacklisted). Arthur Arent, who oversaw the writing of *Injunction Granted*, described it, accurately, as "a militantly pro-labor account of the working man's fight for liberation through unionization." Losey had worked in Harlem's Negro Unit, where he clashed with both John Houseman and Orson Welles, before Arent and Morris Watson brought him over to the Living Newspaper Unit. The first play he directed there, *Triple-A Plowed Under*, staged five weeks after *Ethiopia* was censored, had attacked the free-market economy as well as the courts, and ended with a call for a "farmer-worker alliance." Losey wrote to a friend that Flanagan had tried to stop it before it opened, but that he, Arent, and Watson threatened to quit if she did. The Hearst papers pounced, calling it "the most outrageous misuse of taxpayers' money that the Roosevelt administration has yet been guilty of."

In the aftermath of deep cuts to the WPA arts programs two months earlier, including the Federal Theatre, which had to eliminate roughly a fifth of its personnel, and further cuts imminent in July, what might have been tolerated politically in the early and heady days of the project had become, for Flanagan, too risky. She told Losey and Watson to "clean up the script" of *Injunction Granted* and "make it more objective." They ignored her. Flanagan rarely lost her temper, but did so now, writing sharply to both men: "I cannot have federal funds used as a party tool. That goes for the Communist party as well as the Democratic party." An explosive meeting followed in which she told them that they "were both through." A few weeks after the play opened she wrote to them again, complaining that "the avalanche of unfavorable publicity on it is all ammunition against the project" and "against me personally." *Injunction Granted* was closed in October 1936, in the midst of a strong run already seen by sixty-three thousand playgoers, and Losey left the Federal Theatre, later saying that "Flanagan found my political militancy increasingly inconvenient."

While it was true that Flanagan was opposed to seeing the Federal Theatre promote Communist Party objectives, the same couldn't be said of her growing interest in aligning it with Democratic Party ones. *Power*, which celebrated the creation of that New Deal success story, the Tennessee Valley Association, had so impressed Harry

Hopkins, who had joined Flanagan on opening night, that he went backstage and told the cast: "This is a great show. . . . I want this play and plays like it done from one end of the country to the other. . . . People will say it's propaganda. Well, I say what of it? It's propaganda to educate the consumer who's paying for power. . . . I say more plays like *Power* and more power to you." Langdon Post, a close adviser to President Roosevelt who had been appointed chairman of the New York City Housing Authority, was also there. Post was overseeing what *The New York Times* called "the largest low-rent slum clearance project in the country," and would soon publish *The Challenge of Housing*, in which he criticized the "huge fortunes" made from inadequately housing America's poor over the past 150 years. After seeing *Power* that evening, Flanagan writes, she, Hopkins, and Post went to supper, where they "started to plan a living newspaper on housing." Even a few months earlier, a play advocating slum clearing and government construction of low-income housing might have been too controversial, but what was once radical was now, from a New Deal perspective, acceptably progressive. A month before this, following his landslide reelection in November 1936, President Roosevelt had belatedly thrown his weight behind the issue, telling the nation in his second inaugural address on January 20, 1937, that he saw "one-third of a nation ill-housed, ill-clad, ill-nourished." "The menace exists," Roosevelt had acknowledged earlier that month in his State of the Union address, "not only in the slum areas of the very large cities, but in many smaller cities as well. It exists on tens of thousands of farms, in varying degrees, in every part of the country."

America during the Depression faced a housing crisis. Construction had all but stopped. Half of home mortgage debt was in default when Roosevelt took office, and a thousand homes foreclosed every week. In many poor urban neighborhoods the housing stock was increasingly dilapidated and overcrowded, slum dwellings that suffered from infestation and inadequate sanitation, lighting, and ventilation. Roosevelt's administration had taken a number of immediate steps to build and maintain homes, but it was clear that considerably more was needed to clear slums and spur construction on a larger scale, and for that, congressional approval of a significant sum was needed. Housing had long been a political battleground in the United States, especially since the large-scale immigration of the late nineteenth century, and the issues—ideological, economic, legal, and logistic— nightmarish to resolve. With piecemeal solutions proving inadequate, pressure groups began lining up as the issue landed at last in Congress's lap.

Congressional debate on addressing the nation's ill-housed had begun six months before the 1936 presidential election, before Roosevelt announced his support for the legislation. New York senator Robert Wagner, who had grown up in tenements, was in charge of the Senate bill, and deftly steered it through, only to watch it defeated in the House. When the legislation was reintroduced by Wagner after the election, the chorus of objections was by now familiar: fear of government competition with the private sector; fear of overregulation; fear of cost overruns; and fear that it benefited the urbanized North at the expense of the rural South. The bill, with the president's support, though significantly weakened by a series of amendments that slashed Wagner's billion-dollar request in half, made its way through the Senate, then the House, and on September 1, 1937, was finally signed into law. Historians still debate whether the passage of the watered-down Housing Act of 1937 was a crucial first step or a pyrrhic victory; at the time it was clear that the battle over the government's role in public housing was far from over.

✦

By 1937 the Living Newspaper was in danger of becoming formulaic and stale. If it was going to be less offensive politically, it could at least be more daring aesthetically. To that end, Flanagan secured funding from the Rockefeller Foundation to bring forty leading Federal Theatre directors and designers to the Vassar campus for six weeks of intense collaborative work in the summer of 1937. They sat through lectures, watched performances, and worked collectively from 9:00 a.m. to 10:30 p.m. every day. The group was heavily but not exclusively male, and, with the notable exceptions of Shirley Graham of the Chicago Negro Unit and Byron Webb of the Harlem Negro Unit, all White. Tasked with choosing a play on which to collaborate, they voted for Arent's unfinished and provisionally titled *Housing*, and Arent volunteered to add a closing scene. There were close to a hundred roles, and each participant (though many had no acting experience) signed up for several of them. Tamiris was put in charge of movement and Harold Bolton chosen as director, Clair Leonard as musical director, Howard Bay as designer, Mary Merrill as costume designer, and Abe Feder as lighting designer—a formidable creative team. The day after they arrived in Poughkeepsie, the participants took a long bus ride to Bennington, Vermont, to see *Electra* performed. On the way there they decided that the play needed a better title than *Housing*; Pierre de Rohan suggested one that they agreed on: *One Third of a Nation*.

The participants debated "realism, expressionism, impressionism, and the related schools of art and design," with Feder and Tamiris introducing the group to fresh approaches to lighting and movement. Howard Bay's set design, akin to a "surrealist painting," was for many the highlight of the production. *Variety*'s reviewer described how audiences saw, rather than a realistic tenement, a symbolic one: a "huge garbage can, a cracked toilet seat, a rusty water tap, an old-law fire escape . . . dangle from the flies and set the mood of the entire presentation." After the two-day run at Vassar, Flanagan gave each departing participant a volume of Harry Hopkins's speeches, then delivered a final pep talk linking the work of the Federal Theatre ever more closely to that of the New Deal: "By a stroke of fortune unprecedented in dramatic history, we have been given a chance to help change America at a time when twenty million unemployed Americans proved it needed changing. And the theatre, when it is any good, can change things. . . . And if, in making people laugh, which we certainly want to do, we can't also protest—as Harry Hopkins is protesting and as President Roosevelt is protesting—against some of the evils of this country of ours, then we do not deserve the chance put into our hands."

By the time *One Third of a Nation* opened at Broadway's Adelphi Theatre six months later, much of that formal experimentation had been abandoned, including its innovative set design. Instead, the curtain opened on a realistic four-story tenement with its front wall partly torn away, filled with abandoned objects that Bay had scavenged from the streets of New York City. As the show begins, the tenement appears to catch on fire. Arent's script took audiences from that deadly conflagration (and the toothless investigation that followed) back in time to the root causes of substandard housing in New

York, a period when individuals and institutions (including Trinity Church, which wasn't happy about its portrayal) became fabulously wealthy through real estate ventures, divvying up downtown, then renting out small pieces of it for hefty profits. By the early twentieth century, living conditions for many New Yorkers had become untenable. There is even a brief nod to Harlem, where rent exploitation— including poor Black laborers sharing a cot in eight-hour shifts—is even worse than the miserable tenement conditions faced by the Jewish, Irish, and Italian immigrants the play depicts: infestation, outbreaks of cholera, high infant mortality rates, and juvenile delinquency. While the Broadway production focused on New York City, it made a brief detour to Washington, D.C., in a manic scene never mentioned by reviewers, where Robert Wagner's efforts to pass housing legislation are frustrated by senators opposed to the New Deal. In addition, in the penultimate scene an actor playing Langdon Post makes a cameo appearance, as does one imitating New York City's mayor, Fiorello La Guardia (who calls the recent Housing Bill merely "a drop in the bucket"). Yet when push comes to shove, when the underlying issue of private property is finally raised, the play is evasive. Following reports of fresh housing tragedies and calls for collective action, the show ends, as it began, with a tenement fire.

One Third of a Nation was one of the Federal Theatre's great successes. In its first two weeks alone 10,000 playgoers saw it, and 40,000 more bought tickets. By March it had broken the record for a Federal Theatre show. A shortened version was performed on radio. Matinee hours were altered to give working-class theatergoers a chance to see it, and student shows were added; "huge hordes of hatless, drama-starved youngsters" from the outer boroughs joined the 217,000 or so playgoers who came to see it before the run ended in late October. Critics almost universally praised it. John Mason Brown's review in the *New York Post* concluded that it was "every good citizen's duty" to see it. Joseph Wood Krutch wrote in *The Nation* that "what we have here is the most successful effort to use the stage for the purpose of propaganda that I have seen in some fifteen years." Even Stirling Bowen in the conservative *Wall Street Journal*, while labeling it "dramatized propaganda," grudgingly acknowledged that the play has given the New Deal "an increasingly pointed weapon."

The Federal Theatre moved quickly to stage productions of it across the country, modeled on the success of *It Can't Happen Here*, though with a more gradual rollout, as it took time for regional productions to adapt the New York City story to local housing concerns. It opened in Cincinnati and Seattle in May, and soon after in New Orleans, Detroit, Portland, Philadelphia, and Hartford. The play was a hit pretty much everywhere it was staged. *The Seattle Times* reported, "Seldom has any play so caught the public fancy"; the *New Orleans Item* called it "a dramatic bombshell"; and *The Detroit News* described it as "thrilling beyond description." A second Southern production was in the works in Atlanta but fell afoul of local ordinances forbidding Blacks and Whites from appearing together onstage. The show was still running in San Francisco when the Federal Theatre was shut down in 1939.

Some of the changes made in regional productions were extensive. For the two-month Philadelphia run, seen by twenty-five thousand playgoers, the focus was changed from White to Black slum dwellers, and the survivor of the tragic tenement disaster in the opening scenes is a Black woman rather than a Jewish man. Philadelphia had far fewer actors available than New York, so drew on its Negro Unit, vaudevillians, a dance unit, and even a children's marionette unit to cover the dozens of roles the play required. Arthur Jarvis, Jr., wryly notes that an "unexpected bonus for Philadelphia was that some cast members lived in the very conditions condemned by the drama and could bring their personal experiences to each performance." Poor construction, rather than fire, was one of Philadelphia's main housing problems: a substandard bandbox building had fallen on July 25, 1935, and another collapsed on December 16, 1936, killing seven and injuring fifteen others. So instead of opening with a tenement catching on fire, the show there opened with a frightening collapse of a bandbox building (all the more unnerving because the old Walnut Street Theatre was itself in disrepair, and on opening night, crews determined that the stage wouldn't support the opening scene's collapse without risking suffering the same fate itself). A new ending was added in which Black actors bearing coffins across the stage sing a "Negro Spiritual," and are joined by "all the inhabitants of the bandbox houses who have appeared in the play," as close as the Federal Theatre ever came to staging an integrated protest. Pennsylvania's governor, George Earle, attended on opening night, and that production (and other revivals across the country) led to regional improvements in low-income housing.

As popular and as impactful as this extended nationwide run was, Flanagan had made a bad bet aligning the Federal Theatre with New Deal policies in the hope that this would protect her project from further cuts, or worse. Far from sheltering the Federal Theatre, it had left it dangerously exposed, as those opposed to the New Deal found the WPA plays a more inviting target than the still popular president, even as Flanagan's superiors were edging away from her controversial project. Ironically, Losey and Watson's more radical solutions would likely have provoked less outrage than a theater that pulled its hardest punches and was now seen as a mouthpiece for Roosevelt's agenda. *One Third of Nation* marked a turning point for the Federal Theatre, one that was recognized at the time by an astute young critic, Mary McCarthy, who wrote a long essay for *Partisan Review* describing the "aesthetic fatigue" that settled in as the Federal Theatre "passed from an experiment into an institution."

For McCarthy, the play's aesthetic limitations derived from its failure to live up to the political imperative toward which it inexorably drives:

> The housing problem is far knottier than the power problem. It is, in fact, impossible of solution under capitalism, even the liberal capitalism of the New Deal. The Government can expropriate the power plants without upsetting the system. . . . It cannot, however, take over housing, for to do that would be to expropriate the land. *One Third of a Nation*, as a WPA play, is therefore in no position to offer the one effectual remedy for the evil it pictures. It can demonstrate, with many playful and distracting flourishes, that the origin of the housing problem lay in the private ownership and exploitation of the land; it dare not suggest that the cure lies in public ownership and public planning.

So what looks like "the most showy of Living Newspaper productions" turns out to be "inwardly the least ambitious." And the reason for that, she argues, rests not in the limitations of the play so much as

in its alignment with "an Administration which has exhausted its political resources, is itself becoming superannuated": the Living Newspaper "has already chronicled the victories of the New Deal; it can
hardly go on to immortalize the omissions and failures." It was clear
to McCarthy that having tied itself to the mast of the New Deal, the
Living Newspaper, and by extension the Federal Theatre itself, was
slowly sinking: "The Federal Theatre, like all the New Deal ventures,
is a half-measure, a makeshift. It is a work relief project which aspires
to be a National Theatre, and its ambition, unfortunately, is incom-
patible with its economic base." McCarthy concludes that this "is a
disappointment, but not exactly a surprise." The May 1938 issue in
which her requiem ran appeared on newsstands the very month that
Congress authorized the Dies Committee.

✦

An unexpected performance of a scene from *One Third of a Nation*
would cost the Federal Theatre dearly. It took place on the floor of the
U.S. Senate on February 22, 1938, where Senator Josiah Bailey of
North Carolina derisively performed much of Act 2, scene 4. Having
quoted the *Congressional Record*, *One Third of a Nation* was now part of
it. The words Bailey recited would have been familiar to his colleagues, for Arent had assembled the dialogue out of heated exchanges in the Senate six months earlier in the course of the debate
over housing. Arent had actors impersonate a dozen senators in the
scene, including the progressive William Borah of Idaho and Robert
Wagner of New York, and, facing them, Charles Andrews of Florida,
Harry Byrd of Virginia, and Millard Tydings of Maryland. Vice

President Garner stood near his fellow Southerners. The clerk of the Senate drives the action, entering repeatedly to announce yet another reduction to Wagner's initial request in response to a series of amendments, as the senators are "heard debating in a vague sort of mumbo jumbo" and then shout over one another, "PASS THE BILL!" and "POINT OF ORDER," against a background projection of grim slum dwellings. The scene made opponents of the housing bill look awful.

Bailey had timed his performance deliberately. A day earlier Wagner had been forced to withdraw an even more divisive piece of legislation, an anti-lynching bill that Bailey and other Southern Democrats had been filibustering for a month. It was galling for Wagner, for he knew that the majority of the Senate, and of the nation (even, polling showed, Southerners), favored that legislation. But White supremacists in the Senate decided that it was best to hold the line on lynching before even more progressive laws ending Jim Crow would be introduced. Wagner had no choice: if he persisted, the massive relief bill awaiting the Senate's approval would not come up for a vote in time, and millions of impoverished Americans would suffer. Wagner did not endear himself to those filibustering the bill when he threatened to head down South and speak to voters there in person. Earlier on the day of Bailey's performance, Wagner's opponents had piled on, putting into the *Congressional Record* page after page of editorials attacking the anti-lynching bill, including several suggesting that Wagner had backed it "for the sole purpose of winning the Negro vote in New York City."

Bailey was as strenuously opposed to allocating relief funds to the WPA as he had been to enacting an anti-lynching law, about which, two months earlier, he had told the Senate: "The moment it goes through here . . . we will have the battle of Reconstruction all over again in America. That will destroy the South." His mocking performance of *One Third of a Nation* allowed him to defend the South, undercut Wagner and his New Deal causes, and attack the WPA, which, Bailey declared, was wasting money "building country clubs, golf courses, and ski courses and all that sort of thing, all over the country." When Joshua Lee of Oklahoma reminded him that the mission of the WPA was "to furnish employment . . . regardless of what those employed work on," Bailey saw his opening and pivoted to how the WPA's Federal Theatre was spending its money maligning the Senate: "We read in the newspapers a few weeks ago that the WPA had a theater in New York, and had put on a play in which my distinguished friend" Senator Wagner "was the hero, and in which my other friend" Senator Byrd "was the villain, who was hissed by the audience. . . . I am going to read to the Senate a part of that play so Senators will see how we are spending our money. . . . It is entitled *One Third of a Nation*."

Before performing the offending scene, Bailey brandished a copy of the play and ridiculed the long list of books that Arent had consulted in writing it. Bailey's dramatic reading, stage directions and all, was accompanied by a witty running commentary. "Most of the laughs came from the Senator's ad libbing," the press reported, as well as "from his gestures and vocal inflections." When Bailey came to a line in which a character asks whether Congress "still passes laws," he noted (again to "laughter") that this "was not written during the filibuster"—reminding his progressive adversaries of their recent and stinging defeat.

Bailey apparently heard nothing cringeworthy when quoting Senator Andrews, a conservative from Florida, who had asked Wagner,

"Where do the people in the slums come from?"—insinuating that the immigrants crammed into New York City's tenements were somehow less American and therefore undeserving of federal support. When Wagner demanded to know "What does the Senator mean by 'Where do they come from?'" Andrews doubled down on his anti-immigrant stance: "If we examine the birth records in New York, we will find that most of the people there in the slums were not born in New York, but the bright lights have attracted them from everywhere and that is one reason there are so many millions in New York without homes." Those words would not have sat well with playgoers in New York. Andrews had also opposed the anti-lynching bill, proposing that an anti-rape bill be substituted for it, maintaining that Black rapists, not White mobs, were the real problem.

After his performance Bailey turned to his colleagues and sarcastically invoked a version of the "How many ages hence" speech in *Julius Caesar*, in which Cassius tells his fellow senators how often their actions will be reenacted. Bailey then mockingly suggested that the "play to which I have referred will be reproduced longer than *Hamlet*, and people will be talking about the Senator from New York instead of the Prince of Denmark." Thanks to the Federal Theatre, "we shall rank in the memory of men with Oedipus Tyrannus or King Lear," and actors, he added, sarcastically, "will walk the stage a thousand, two thousand, three thousand years from now, representing us in our proper persons and our dignity." For Bailey, *One Third of a Nation* was a travesty: "Whoever thought of the Federal Government getting into anything like that?"

It was now late in the afternoon, and Bailey had timed his dramatic reading to have the last word that day. But real drama ensued when Sherman Minton of Indiana, a strong supporter of the New

Deal, asked if he might speak for "a moment or so." Minton explained that "I could not sit here and hear the able senator from North Carolina in his eloquent appeal, his impassioned appeal, without feeling a bit of shame, and entertaining a feeling of sorrow for people who are not as well off, perhaps, as we are. We sit here and we snivel and we sneer at poor devils who are down and out, who are trying to earn enough to buy bread and butter for themselves and their wives and kiddies by writing a play under the WPA and producing it with actors who are out of work and walking the streets, and perhaps begging for bread with which to feed themselves and their families." Bailey, offended by this, ignored the rule requiring formal permission to speak and cut Minton off: "I hope the Senator is not suggesting that I either sniveled or sneered"—something of a trap, since insulting a fellow senator was forbidden. Minton sidestepped this and continued: "I did not say the Senator did, but the snickering went on all over the Chamber as he read that little playlet and pointed the finger of scorn at those engaged on WPA theater and writing projects. God knows, they could not go out and use a shovel, and you would not give them one if you could. All they want is a chance to eat, and you snicker and you snivel at them." Minton, who grew up poor, was clearly furious.

Bailey, now formally seeking permission to respond, engaged in what he imagined was damage control, and joked: "I sometimes thought I would apologize for the lines being so stupid, but when we recall that they were trying to reproduce the proceedings of the Senate I do not think we can blame them for that." But Minton would have none of it: "Oh, the Senator was not making a critical review of the play. We know better than that. He was making a critical review of the projects of WPA which permitted any such thing. Perhaps it was not a very good play. I don't think the play is very 'hot' myself. But here was a poor man, who sweats, perhaps, over that little play and tried to do the best he could with the tools he had at hand in order to make a dollar or two for his wife and children. I am not going to snicker and sneer at him, because perhaps he did not create a Hamlet or a Launcelot Gobbo or some such character, or some play of great fame. . . . I want to see those who cannot go out and use a pick and shovel have the same chance as those who can, and I am very sorry that a United States Senator could derive any entertainment from holding up to scorn that kind of project under the WPA."

And then, delivering a final counterpunch to Bailey's anti-relief polemic, Minton reminded his fellow senators that the Federal Theatre currently employed "8,693 people." "We hear talk about encouraging business by freedom of enterprise, so that business can put people back to work. We had all of that for 12 years under the Harding and Coolidge and Hoover administrations. Freedom of enterprise closed the banks of this country. It resulted in 15,000,000 men walking the streets of the land begging for an opportunity to work." It was now almost 5:30 p.m., and the Senate recessed. The following day the Senate passed the $250 million WPA appropriations bill. Bailey was the only one who voted against it.

As a senator from a Democratic state where Roosevelt was still extremely popular (securing nearly three quarters of the vote in North Carolina in 1936), Bailey felt compelled to support the president's policies while running for reelection that year. But he had since become increasingly emboldened, and would coauthor an "Address to the People of the United States," immediately labeled as a "Conservative Manifesto," put together by a bipartisan group of senators hoping to check New Deal policies. When on December 16, 1937, *The New*

York Times published a leaked draft of the "Conservative Manifesto," its authors were ridiculed and there were calls of treason from New Deal loyalists. But rather than denying his role, Bailey owned up to it, and by the time he read aloud from *One Third of a Nation*, he knew that there was a groundswell of support for his views. Remarkably, close to two million copies of the "Manifesto" had circulated in the previous two months, not including what had been reprinted in newspapers, driven by financing and endorsements from the business community. Roosevelt would huddle in the White House with loyalists in the Senate, including Minton and Wagner, to strategize on how best to counter this development.

Bailey's histrionics had been prompted by newspaper reports that members of his emerging anti–New Deal coalition had been hissed by audiences after *One Third of a Nation* opened at the Adelphi Theatre in New York. Those singled out in the play—especially Andrews and Byrd—were furious, and thought that by flexing their senatorial muscles they could force the Federal Theatre to retreat. On February 10, Byrd wrote directly to Harry Hopkins, and, in a coordinated move, a furious Andrews did so too, forwarding a clipping of the February 7 front-page story in the *Herald Tribune*. Andrews wanted to know who was "responsible for this play" and "what action, if any, has been taken by your department to have these particular scenes eliminated from it?" He also demanded a list of the names, addresses, and federal salaries of every actor, writer, and producer involved.

The national press was divided over whether the Federal Theatre, paid for by taxpayers, had the right to depict senators, or whether attempts to stifle free expression amounted to censorship. *The Washington Post* and other newspapers ran unsourced stories intimating that an investigation "was hinted in official circles." This looks like a testing of the waters, to see whether the public would favor such a probe. The *Post*'s own position was clear: on February 8, it ran an editorial condemning the ridicule of the Southern senators, calling it "an astounding display of effrontery" and concluding that "a publicly financed theater is not free to indulge in criticism of public servants, even less to malign them unjustly and possibly weaken the political support upon which they depend as officeholders." The criticism was met with defiance on the part of Arthur Arent, who insisted that there had been "no attempt made, whatsoever, to satirize any of these gentlemen," and reminded reporters that all "of the material used in *One Third of a Nation* and the particular speeches of the three Senators were taken from the *Congressional Record*." A more diplomatic Hallie Flanagan quietly tried—and failed—to meet and placate Andrews, and wrote to him saying that she had seen the production three times and invited him to see the play as her guest.

The senators were not yet done with *One Third of a Nation*—"this play about the Senators," as one now called it—that had turned their own words against them. The men (and one woman) who served in the Senate at this time were members of an exclusive club, and bristled at being mocked or having actors mouth their words. On February 27, 1938, Aubrey Williams, Harry Hopkins's right-hand man, was called to testified before the Senate Appropriations Committee. Senator Richard R. Russell of Georgia wanted "a little information" about play selection in the Federal Theatre and said he thought it set a "very dangerous precedent" when senators were "exalted" or "minimize[d]" with public funds, and Senator John Townsend of Delaware pointedly asked whether a play funded by taxpayers ought to be "carefully censored." Williams thought not. Townsend disagreed. Left unspoken: If the Federal Theatre could make U.S. senators look bad debating housing, what might it do with a play about lynching? The senators then moved on to other business, but their residual anger, and the implications of this last line of questioning, were unmistakable.

Senator Andrews had a hard time letting the matter go and told the *Motion Picture Herald*, "I don't think Americans are responsible for this kind of presentation," adding that "some foreign element must be behind this." The link between the Federal Theatre and an implied Communist threat was backed up in a letter soon after published in the *New York Herald Tribune*, signed by "Two Members" of the Federal Theatre, who preferred to keep their identities secret: "As professional WPA players, we have long observed that this 'foreign element,' of which Senator Andrews speaks has been working to distort the best interests of the Administration and to shape the purpose of the Federal theater to its own ends." In the end, the only satisfaction Andrews got was the addition of a single and ambiguous line to the published version of the scene, which read: "Despite his position during the debate, Senator Andrews voted for and supported the bill in its final form."

Ticket sales for the play soared in the aftermath of the controversy. A few at the time predicted that the confrontation over *One Third of a Nation* in the Senate might lead to a congressional investigation. One of those was Ernest L. Meyer, who wrote that what most "irks" the Southern senators "is that the Living Newspaper had the bad taste and impiety to reanimate dead words which had been decently buried in the catacombs of the *Congressional Record*. The technique holds terror for lawmakers." Meyer had spoken with Congressman Maury Maverick of Texas about the recent housing legislation, and Maverick recounted a conversation with a Southern congressman who insisted there were no slums in his district. When Maverick replied, "I've been in your district and I've seen acres of miserable shacks, whole miles of them," his colleague assured him that "those aren't slums. . . . That's where the Negroes live."

◆

The story would have one last twist. In June 1938, the Federal Theatre sold the film rights to *One Third of a Nation* for the modest sum of $5,000. Eight months later the movie opened across the country. Paramount, the film's distributor, hoping to cash in on the play's ongoing popularity, ran a four-page ad in the *Motion Picture Herald* linking the film to the "play presented by Federal Theatre," which had "won laurels of critics, attracting record crowds and reams of publicity." The ad promised more of the gritty realism of the stage original: a "huge tenement fire . . . tenants fighting for lives while flames scorch heavens. Actually filmed on streets of New York!"

It appeared to be an independent project, relying on a Hollywood distributor, filmed locally in Astoria, Queens. Those few in the know must have been smiling when newspapers reported that Harold Orlob, who had been providing music for Broadway shows for over thirty years, had purchased the rights. Orlob had never produced a film before and never would again. He was a front for more powerful investors, including Floyd B. Odlum, one of the ten richest men in America, who preferred to remain out of sight. Odlum had made a killing during the Depression, snapping up foundering businesses, including "hotels, department stores, transport and utility companies, a property portfolio and various entertainment interests" as well as a large stake (and soon a controlling interest) in Hollywood's RKO studio. No doubt it was thought wiser to claim that a Broadway veteran was behind the show than to acknowledge that a plutocrat with a sizable property portfolio was bankrolling a film based on a play exposing the damage done by callous landowners. Sylvia Sidney, who starred in the film as the slum-dwelling heroine, later recalled that "not only was Floyd Odlum's money invested in *One Third of a Nation*," but also that Odlum's yacht was used for the scene in which she has a shipboard date on the East River.

A Hollywood regular with no obvious political leanings, Oliver Garrett was brought in to write the filmscript. At this point he had written over twenty screenplays, including *Moby Dick* and *A Farewell to Arms*, and would work next on *Gone With the Wind*. Yet his first go at it failed to please the film's financial backers. Orlob told the *New York Herald Tribune* that "When we got the first draft of the script it was amazing to note how the writer had got so lost in his subject that he seemed to be a good candidate for the radicals. The story had plenty of fire, but too much for the Hays office. We would have had difficulty because of the propaganda involved and the language used, so it was sent back for softening." The "fire" Orlob speaks of is political, not the conflagrations that bookend the play. Extinguishing that fire and "softening" the message were polite ways of saying that Garrett was told to gut the story's progressive vision.

Dudley Murphy was hired to direct the film on a tight budget of $200,000. Murphy had directed Paul Robeson in *The Emperor Jones*, and had earlier in his career been a leading avant-garde filmmaker. More recently, he had worked on *Confessions of a Co-Ed* and *The Sports Parade*. Aside from a few pickup shots, Murphy gave up early on in his hopes to film on location and had art director Walter Keller build a realistic-looking tenement in the Queens studio, though he did hire local boys from Astoria to play in street scenes. Murphy's handling of the watered-down script was seen as too radical by the film's backers. Richard Kozarski writes in *Hollywood on the Hudson* that the *New York World-Telegram* reported that "trouble arose as soon as a rough cut was screened for the backers, 'a group of prominent bankers.'" The film began with a newsreel clip of Roosevelt reciting the "one third of a nation" section of his second inaugural address. "Before the next sequence was flashed, an indignant cry went up from a backer in the dark room. 'This is New Deal propaganda!' he yelled. 'Strike that scene out!'"

The film managed to transform a play about the horrors of tenement life, the indifference of landowners, the failure of free enterprise, the misery experienced by poor Black renters, the prejudice of senators, and the desperate need for federal intervention into a film with an all-White cast that ricochets between realistic scenes of slum life and a romantic comedy in which the rich absentee owner of tenements, Peter Cortlant (played by Leif Erikson), falls for the beautiful Mary Rodgers (Sylvia Sidney), who lives in one of his firetrap buildings. They meet at the beginning of the film when her young brother Joey (played by the future director Sidney Lumet) is injured in a fire, and Peter pays for his medical care. Joey is left crippled, and his relentless hatred of the infested tenement in which he lives is the best thing about the film (Joey talks to the building and the building mockingly talks back). Peter, "a kindly capitalist," would like to do the right thing while winning the heart of the woman he has fallen for, but he is dissuaded by his sister and business adviser. It is only at the very end of the film, after a second blaze, this one deliberately set by a suicidal Joey, that Peter swears that he'll tear down all his tenements—"I mean it this time." The film closes with footage of construction crews demolishing a tenement, with Peter looking on as Mary joins him. The music swells. We glimpse the future housing unit, with trees and a playground, as an image of dead Joey appears, smiling, projected onto the new building.

The argument of Arent's far-from-radical play had been that only government intervention on a large scale could fix the nation's housing crisis. The movie rejects that view, ending with a wealthy landlord voluntarily tearing down one of his slum dwellings and replacing it with an attractive building. There is no suggestion that other landlords will follow suit; it is a fantasy, a conversion experience for one, not many. As Joseph F. Coughlin wryly noted in the *Motion Picture Herald*, "According to the story's solution, it would seem that the best way to meet the slum problem is to have a bevy of young women from the Ghetto meet up with an equal number of plutocratic playboys, who are as socially minded and as generous as 'Cortlant.'" If the film has a moral, it's the one conveyed early on by the Irish cop who reprimands young Joey: "It's time you learned to respect private property." It was a box office disaster, closing after a week, and if an argument were needed for an unmuzzled and uncensored Federal Theatre, the film had made it.

Abram Hill, c. 1940.

CHAPTER SEVEN

Liberty Deferred:
Confronting Racism

From its earliest months, the Federal Theatre, in line with its progressive agenda, had tried to stage a Living Newspaper about racism in America. And, from early on, it repeatedly undermined its own efforts, so effectively that by the time it closed four years later not a single one of these plays was ever performed.

After Elmer Rice stepped down in protest over the censorship of *Ethiopia* in January 1936, he published a "Statement of Resignation" in *New Theatre* making clear that what had really panicked Roosevelt's administration was not foreign affairs but rather its discovery that even more explosive productions were in the works, including a Living Newspaper, *The South*, "on the situation in the Southern States, touching on such vital subjects as lynching, discrimination against Negroes and the plight of the sharecroppers (in other words, hitting the Democratic Party where it lives)." *The South* exposed entrenched racism in the Deep South, including the "legalized lynching" of the Scottsboro Boys' sentencing. Other scenes depicted an attack on a union gathering, the Georgia governor's defense of chain gangs, an account of the unequal sums spent on educating Blacks and Whites, police brutality against socialists in Florida, the anti-lynching bill debated (and filibustered) in the Senate, and the campaign to release the Black activist and labor organizer Angelo Herndon, convicted in Georgia of "insurrection" and slated for hard labor. A scrolling tele-type above the stage would list victims of Southern lynchings: "R. J. TYRONE SHOT TO DEATH BY LYNCH MOB. . . . RUBIN STA-CEY HANGED BY LYNCHERS. . . . LEWIS HARRIS HANGED BY MOB." Shortly after Rice's resignation letter was published, Harry Hopkins's assistant, Jacob Baker, wrote to the staunchly conservative Florida senator Park Trammell, reassuring him and his colleagues "that the WPA had no plans for a theatrical production of sharecroppers." After Rice quit, *The South* was shelved.

Over a year would pass before the Federal Theatre once again gave the go-ahead to a Living Newspaper about racial discrimination. Its initial title, *The Hartford Negro*, was changed to *Bars and Stripes*, and then again to *Stars and Bars* (alluding both to the design of the Con-federate flag and to the barring of Black advancement). A White playwright, Ward Courtney, wrote it in collaboration with the Negro Unit of the Federal Theatre in Hartford, Connecticut (identifying in the script the contributions of specific members of that unit), and it was cleared for development in April 1937. Emmet Lavery, who joined the Federal Theatre in September 1937 and was appointed director of its Play Bureau, signed off on it, saying, "It should be a good show."

Stars and Bars featured two of the Living Newspaper's by-now-familiar characters: the usually endearing "Little Man," who serves as an Everyman figure, as well as the unseen "Loudspeaker," who in earlier productions had been a neutral editorial voice. But surprisingly, the Little Man in *Stars and Bars* is an unsympathetic bigot, a Connecticut Yankee who embodies Northern prejudice against Blacks. The play opens in 1830, with a slave ship packed with manacled Africans whipped by White men. After witnessing this cruelty, the Connecticut Yankee responds: "They got worse in Africa than they got here. We gave them a chance to share in our Civilization!" The Loudspeaker also turns out to be biased and is intent on downplaying racism; to that end he reads aloud from a sanitized "history book" about "milestones in the history of the Negro in America." An unnamed "Negro," fed up with this, enters and interrupts the Loudspeaker, accusing him and his fellow Northerners of hypocrisy: "Most Northerners think and talk sympathetically while they discriminate and exploit," for in "the North Negroes are regarded as not quite human." The Loudspeaker at first tries to ignore him, then orders the unnamed "Negro" to "leave the stage," before calling him a Communist and, in desperation, demanding that stagehands stop illuminating him. But it is the Loudspeaker who departs (replaced by someone "more vital, younger") after confirming in a final speech his deeply patronizing attitude: "Why you impudent African. . . . Tonight I'm going to show these good people all the heroic qualities of your race. How they have progressed in the Arts, Music, Theatre, Education! I shall make them weep with tears of sympathy for the Negro's guileless soul. I shall teach Hartford to love and cherish her 8,000 Negroes like little children."

After the prejudiced Loudspeaker is replaced, *Stars and Bars* goes on to detail the unacknowledged history of racial discrimination in Hartford, from redlining and slums to unequal health care, shorter life expectancy, and higher unemployment. In its most harrowing scene Death enters, accompanied by Syphilis, Tuberculosis, Pneumonia, and Infant Mortality, who shoot dice for their victims and drag off Black children from their parents. The play then moves from the allegorical to the topical, quoting the discriminatory statements of local political and religious figures, before ending with both Black and White protesters marching off together to confront Hartford's current mayor, Thomas Spellacy.

Stars and Bars did not open, as planned, in November 1937. A few months later, in February 1938, Converse Tyler, from the National Service Bureau's Playreading Department, was asked to look over the script, and while acknowledging that it followed the guidelines for a Living Newspaper "pretty well," he thought its focus on Hartford too narrow. Tyler suggested revisions and recommended it "with reservations." Yet the Federal Theatre never staged the play. There may have been nervousness about its attacks on named and quoted local political and religious leaders. Or it may be that the extensive mixing of races in the cast demanded by the script proved a stumbling block. Or the storyline may have been too discomforting for Northern liberals who may have shared the Connecticut Yankee's view that Blacks in America had it "pretty good," and who, while happy to condemn discrimination in the South, didn't want to be thought of as racists themselves. Neither *The South* nor *Stars and Bars* is mentioned by Hallie Flanagan in her account of the Federal Theatre in *Arena*—a silence that extended to the third and most trenchant Living Newspaper about America's racist history, *Liberty Deferred*.

Around the time that *Stars and Bars* was expected to open in Hartford, a pair of young Black playwrights employed by the Federal Theatre, Abram Hill and John Silvera, submitted a now lost treatment or initial draft of *Liberty Deferred*. Hill, at twenty-seven, was five years older than Silvera. Born in Atlanta in 1910, Hill moved with his family to New York, where he attended the City College of New York before transferring to Lincoln University in Pennsylvania, a historically Black public university, where he studied theater and wrote and produced *Hell's Half Acre*, a play about Southern lynching. He also worked as a drama director at a Civilian Conservation Corps unit on Long Island. He submitted *Hell's Half Acre* for a playwriting competition, which led to his acceptance to study theater for two years at the New School for Social Research, where, he recalled, Arthur Miller and Tennessee Williams were classmates. Hill joined the Federal Theatre's newly formed Playreading and Playwriting Department, where he worked mostly on scripts dealing with Black subject matter and continued to write plays. He was a committed playwright from early on.

Not so Silvera. He grew up in what he later described as "very comfortable circumstances" in New Jersey. His father knew Marcus Garvey, and Paul Robeson had lived two doors down when he was a student. Like Hill, Silvera attended Lincoln University, where he was a track star. He too joined the Federal Theatre shortly after it was formed, for the chance "to do something interesting and still, of course, earn a living," though not, he recalled, "because of an overpowering interest in the theater itself." Silvera was assigned to public relations at the Harlem Unit and served as a resourceful advance man for the national tour of *Macbeth*, arranging for housing on the road for over a hundred Black performers—not an easy task in Jim Crow America (and Silvera himself, more than once, encountered bigotry on segregated trains). Silvera, who was also responsible for outreach to Black colleges and theaters, was committed to creating a more autonomous "Negro Department" within the National Service Bureau. After *Macbeth* closed, he was reassigned and asked to evaluate playscripts intended for the Negro Unit. One of those was Hill's *Hell's Half Acre*. While Silvera thought it was an "excellent play," he didn't recommend it for production: "Such gruesome realities," he wrote in his report, "as the old cracker Granny who has pickled as souvenirs the left ear of every Negro lynched for the past twenty years, and the fighting over parts of the victim's body, have no place in Federal Theatre offerings. There is a much more wholesome job to be done." The rejection didn't seem to damage his subsequent relationship with Hill. He later told an interviewer that his "interest in writing plays became sharper and then I was joined with Abe Hill, who was a well-known playwright, in trying to write a Living Newspaper. . . . We developed one called *Liberty Deferred*," a collaboration that, according to Hill, had begun around April 1937. Hill recalled that they initially named it *"One-Tenth of a Nation,"* a Living Newspaper documenting how Blacks "were depressed and deprived of full participation in American life," before changing the title to *Liberty Deferred*.

Little is known about which of the two playwrights contributed what, though it seems that Hill was the lead writer while Silvera was responsible for the most inspired scene in the play, set in "the fabled land where all lynch victims go," Lynchotopia. It's a dystopian fantasy in which once a year Blacks who have been brutally lynched meet up to see whose gruesome treatment was the worst. It's a mordant scene, one that spoke to Silvera's conviction that the unrelenting realism of plays like Hill's *Hell's Half Acre* didn't work as well as "ridicule and humor": "People get tired of the serious preaching about some of the things that are wrong, civil wrongs. And if you can laugh them out of existence, maybe you'd do a more effective job."

Lynchotopia, which begins on New Year's Day 1937, opens in an imaginary afterworld where the Keeper of Records, "an official-looking Negro" who wears a rope around his neck ("the insignia of Lynchotopia"), announces the number of lynch victims from the previous year. The thirteen new members bring the running total since 1882 to 5,107. Soon enough, the first victim of the new year arrives, Wesley Johnson of Alabama, his "clothes torn to shreds as though he had been through a severe mauling." Others soon follow: Roosevelt Townes and "Boot Jack" McDaniels of Mississippi, then Richard Hawkins and Ernest Ponder of Florida, each wearing a noose. When the Keeper of Records hears that Townes and McDaniels were tortured with blowtorches before being shot and burned, he's impressed by how lynch mobs were "going modern." At year's end there is a review for the eight victims of 1937, and "the one that has been through the most brutal lynching gets the prize," though he has to better the stories of victims from previous years. Each brutalized victim is convinced that he's the sure winner, but none can outdo Claude Neal, lynched in 1934. Neal enters and takes us through his horrific lynching, at which a large crowd gathered excitedly to hang and then burn him (their brutality reenacted behind a screen).

The scene then shifts, once news arrives in Lynchotopia that the Southern bloc in the Senate is filibustering an anti-lynching bill. Neal and the other lynch victims march off to the Capitol, to the tune of Walt Disney's recent hit, Snow White's "Hi Ho." It's off to Washington they go, to hear one racist senator after the next denounce the anti-lynching bill, with Senator Pat Harrison of Mississippi warning that if the legislation passes, a bill that allows "miscegenation of the races" and another that would strip from states the right to decide who can vote were sure to follow. The scene—arguably the most brilliant and devastating written for the Federal Theatre—culminates with the lynch victims filing out of the Senate as news arrives of a motion to put aside anti-lynching legislation.

Other scenes that share the same mix of facts, wit, and sardonic humor fill the play, including a scathing one on the suppression of voting rights. The stage directions for this scene call for a spotlight to rise on a large map of the United States, with small doors in each of the states that deny Blacks the right to vote. A carnival barker named Joe Lilly White then enters, cracking a whip, and asks, "Where can Negroes vote?" One after another the doors to the states of Florida, Georgia, Alabama, Mississippi, Louisiana, Arkansas, and Oklahoma swing open, as White men stick their heads out and shout "Not here," before slamming their doors shut.

When Joe Lilly White declares, "That's the way we handle Negroes who want the ballots," he is interrupted by a "Voice" from the audience, who wants to know how he defines "Negro." An extended exchange follows, with Joe Lilly White offering several unsatisfactory answers: "They're all black," "They have wooly hair," and then "Anyone having a mixture of African blood," before falling back on "Well anyone can tell a Negro when they see one." When the Voice mockingly responds that "only a Nazi could tell a pure race bred," Joe Lilly White calls on the Southern states for help. Florida volunteers, "Anybody with one-eighth African blood," Arkansas offers, "Anybody having a distinct admixture of African blood," and Texas says, "If one's parents were slaves—he is a Negro." The exchange is then complicated by the arrival of a crowd of "mulattos, quadroons, octoroons, whites, Indians, Mexicans and Chinese." Confusion follows, and Joe Lilly White orders them all to "scram," only to be confronted by a Black man named Nixon who demands to vote and is steered by him to Texas. Texas calls Nixon "one of them Gawd damn smart darkies," then tells him to "Get the hell out of here." But Nixon won't budge.

Audiences at the time would have known who Nixon was: a physician with a degree from Harvard Medical School who had long battled to secure voting rights for Blacks in Texas. In 1927 the Supreme Court had ruled in his favor (in *Nixon v. Herndon*), striking down a Texas statute that prevented Blacks from voting in Democratic primaries. But the Texas legislature got around this by then declaring that political parties could determine their own voting rules, and when Nixon tried to vote in the 1928 Democratic primary in Texas, he was once again denied the right to do so. He sued again, and this case, too, made its way to the Supreme Court. The outcome of its 5–4 ruling in 1932 (in *Nixon v. Condon*) is reenacted in *Liberty Deferred*, where a Supreme Court justice enters and tells Nixon that the "Democratic Primary in Texas is a voluntary organization . . . and like a private club. You are not a member of that club. You are henceforth denied the right to vote." Nixon then "rushes from state to state" asking if he can vote there—only to have doors slammed shut on him, as Joe Lilly White snaps his whip, cries out "DEMOCRACY," and the wild scene ends.

If such unconventional scenes—and *Liberty Deferred* is rich in them—were intended to shock White playgoers, its opening one was meant to unsettle them. *Liberty Deferred* begins with a well-dressed young White couple having a drink at a bar. Jimmy North is from New York and wants to show the city to his date, Mary Lou Dixon, a small-town Southerner. He suggests that they head uptown to Harlem to hear some music "and see how our darkies live." Mary Lou is less excited about this idea than he is, and shares why in an aside: "I know Jimmy means well and all that—but—mixin' with niggers—I suppose they're alright, some of them, but—in their place—and I can't forget my place, either." But she agrees to go, and the location shifts to a nightclub in Harlem, where Jimmy explains to Mary Lou how well he knows "these people": "gin, swing, trucking and sin. That's all they ask . . . just a happy-go-lucky-devil-may-care bunch of God's chillun." While clichéd Black music plays, a series of stereotypic Blacks enter in an "elaborate, satirical manner," offering a "caricature of the Negro as most Whites insist upon seeing him," including a subservient Red Cap "bowing and scraping" for a tip; a "Hollywood version of the plantation worker" cheerfully picking cotton; "vulgarly dressed" young Black men shooting craps; a "Steppin' Fetchit" performing a vaudeville routine; and an old Uncle Tom reenacting "the thousand-versioned classic about what the old darky said to the Judge." The sequence, the stage direction explains, captures "the Negro as he is too often shown on the screen, stage, and over the air; in fact, as he is seen by Jimmy and Mary Lou, who represent White Supremacy."

As the music dies down, a young Black couple, Ted and Linda, appear, dancing slowly, and when the Black entertainers see them, they stop and stare, "almost accusingly, as if each had dropped his clownish mask in self-disgust." The caricatures exit, leaving just the two young couples, one White, one Black, onstage. Ted and Linda have been observing the different sorts of racist responses of Jimmy and Mary Lou, and Linda asks Ted, "Can't they see anything else?" Ted tells her no, Whites only see what they are shown at the movies or hear on the radio. Ted and Linda are bitter; Ted has been laid off at work, his job given to a less experienced White man, while Linda, who has trained as a nurse, has tried to find employment but can't get off "the waiting list." The scene continues in a kind of duet, with Jimmy going on about how Blacks like to dance, and Ted saying sardonically, "They love to watch us dance. Dancin' on the levee. Dancin' on the end of a rope."

This opening scene marks a groundbreaking moment in American theater, as Blacks call out the racism of privileged and prejudiced Whites, both Northern and Southern, while implicating theater, film, and radio in perpetuating damaging stereotypes. This sets up what follows: a first Act depicting the long history of the oppression of Blacks from the origins of Anglo-American slavery in 1619, dramatizing how and why Blacks were first sold as slaves in colonial America, up through post-Reconstruction and the discrimination faced by returning Black veterans who had fought in World War I. The material was deeply researched and documented; Hill later provided a four-page bibliography, typical of Living Newspapers, attesting to the accuracy of every factual claim and quotation, and drawing on such historical sources as W. E. B. Du Bois's recent *Black Reconstruction in America* (1935). The second Act focuses on the 1930s (equally well documented, though relying here more heavily on newspaper accounts), including the Lynchotopia and voting rights scenes. It culminates in a scene depicting the National Negro Congress of 1936 and the determined efforts of Blacks and Whites—even Jimmy, after hesitating, joins in—to defeat Jim Crow, who makes a cameo appearance, and fight together against discrimination. It ends with the singing of the hymn often referred to as the Black National Anthem, "Lift Every Voice and Sing," which the audience is invited to join. The National Negro Congress, in which civil rights, labor, and religious organizations opposed to racial discrimination allied with the Communist Party, was Martin Dies's worst nightmare, one that he believed exploited "racial hatred" and whose ultimate goal, he would write in his 1940 book, *The Trojan Horse in America*, was "to eventually bring about an overthrow of the capitalistic system, using Communist terminology and the establishment of the dictatorship of the proletariat." Yet after all that precedes *Liberty Deferred*'s powerful conclusion, it's hard to tell whether its optimistic ending is heartfelt or merely an ironic take on the uplifting social realism of earlier Living Newspapers.

◆

On November 8, 1937, Emmet Lavery—to whom the early script or treatment for *Liberty Deferred* had been submitted—wrote to Silvera inviting him to get in touch "regarding our discussion of the Living Newspaper for the Negro theatre," adding that Philip Barber, who chaired the Production Board, also wanted to speak with him. With Barber (who had replaced Elmer Rice) involved, the young playwrights may well have believed that *Liberty Deferred* was being fast-tracked and its production imminent. Lavery, now in his midthirties, had joined the Federal Theatre a couple of months earlier, after stumbling upon and then attending the previous summer's workshop in his hometown, Poughkeepsie, while on vacation. He had been in Hollywood before that, working as a screenwriter, after the success of his play about Jesuits, *The First Legion*, which had a Broadway run in 1934. Shortly before he joined the Federal Theatre, Lavery founded the National Catholic Theatre Conference, to "promote theatre in harmony with Catholic principles." Deputy director of the Federal Theatre John McGee reached out to him while Lavery was back East and persuaded him to join Flanagan's project. Flanagan must have also been behind the invitation, for she knew Lavery quite well and had set in motion his career as playwright and screenwriter. Lavery recalled that he and Flanagan "had a wonderful working relationship. Our tastes were not identical but we knew each other's state of mind after seven or eight years of being neighbors in Poughkeepsie and audit[ing] her classes for seven years." In an unusual arrangement, Lavery, as a young lawyer, had been permitted to study theater under Flanagan (the president of Vassar made an exception for him, and charged no tuition, as only women could take classes there).

Any hopes that *Liberty Deferred* would soon be staged were dashed when on December 21, 1937, Lavery wrote a long letter to Silvera (he ignored Hill in his correspondence). It began promisingly enough—"I like very much the material you have gathered for *Liberty Deferred*"— then pivoted to a call for a radical overhaul: "What it now needs is (1) the addition of story techniques which will convert it into the Living Newspaper set-up; and (2) occasional consideration of the advancement which has been made by the Negro people, even in the face of all the deferred liberties (this could be nicely pointed throughout by the inference that the Negro has been given prominence in the arts, in the sciences—in fact just about everything—except liberty." Much like the first Loudspeaker of *Stars and Bars*, Lavery wanted to foreground all the good things that had happened to Blacks in America. In Kate Dossett's wonderful formulation, Lavery was bent on making *Liberty Deferred* "a liberal critique of racism rather than a critique of liberal racism."

He made no mention of Lynchotopia or the voter suppression scene, or the play's remarkable opening or stirring conclusion. Lavery wanted these replaced by the sort of stereotypes Hill and Silvera were desperate to demolish, an old Uncle Tom figure, "minstrelsy," and a pair of "black face" characters. "Let us begin and end the story," Lavery wrote, "with a school room scene in which a Negro professor is lecturing to his young students on the Bill of Rights." By eliminating Jimmy and Mary Lou and having these Black students challenge their professor, Blacks would be at odds with one another, rather than with Whites. "All through the play," Lavery continues, "the professor is a pathetic figure" who "tries to convince the announcer that things are getting better." And to "give this production value in song and humour," Lavery then recommended "that the professor, in the course of his journey, produces triumphantly at stage right and left, two figures—the eternal con-men of minstrelsy—Pagliacci in black face." Lavery also let Silvera know that he was assigning a young White writer, Ira Knaster, to oversee revisions "in a play doctoring capacity."

Four months later, on March 5, 1938, the *Baltimore Afro-American* reported that "*Liberty Deferred,* written by Johnny Silvera and Abram Hill of Lincoln, will be produced shortly in one of the Broadway WPA houses." But that announcement was premature. The following month Lavery informed Silvera and Knaster that "there is a great deal of work which must be done at once before it can be typed out and sent out to the field." Lavery was annoyed that most of his advice had been ignored. In their latest draft Hill and Silvera had failed to highlight how good things were for Black artists even if their civil rights were denied: "You will remember," Lavery wrote, that "we discussed in detail how important it is to show the Negro's achievements in the arts at the same time that he is meeting reverses in the field of civil liberties." Lavery also wanted their Living Newspaper to be less episodic ("There is no character who is common to the whole story . . . no thread or continuity which links up the major sequence"). Hill and Silvera thought they had addressed this by bringing back the young Black couple, Ted and Linda, in a reunion scene in which Ted is now working as a Pullman porter, but Lavery continued to insist that the framing device that he had previously suggested—"opening and closing on a Negro school-room"—worked better. He assured them that "I am not trying to weaken your story—I am trying very hard to strengthen it."

Liberty Deferred inched closer to production. On May 8 *The New York Times* reported that the play was in its "final draft stage." And in an undated memo, likely from this time, Lavery wrote that the play, now in a "Final Draft," was to be directed by Halsted Welles, who had previously directed a much admired Federal Theatre production of T. S. Eliot's *Murder in the Cathedral*. In early July, Silvera handed in three typed final copies, and Lavery wrote back immediately saying that he had read the "completed script" and would "urge its production in several units of the Federal Theatre." On July 11, 1938, Lavery confirmed in his weekly roundup that the play was "now ready" and that it would "be sent to Mrs. Flanagan as soon as some additional revisions have been made." The daring play, it seemed, would be staged nationally: on July 13 the *Amsterdam News* reported that *Liberty Deferred* was "soon to be released for production in Federal Theatres throughout the country as well as a probable production in New York this Fall." At month's end, Silvera and Hill submitted a freshly revised and (they hoped) final draft, in which they had made changes to the end of the first Act, sharpened characterization in the second Act, and gave their final scene a "more realistic interpretation," but otherwise, apparently, had retained most of their original design. In September, Lavery informed Flanagan that Halsted Welles didn't think the play "good enough in its present form to warrant production by the Experimental Unit" (most likely the "Test Theatre" Welles had set up in New Haven), then told Knaster that the Chicago Unit didn't want to stage it either, and that he "had heard nothing more from the Eastern Region, which at one time seemed interested," and would let him "know as soon as I hear anything definite from New York. At the moment there doesn't seem to be any interest there." The project was effectively stalled.

If Lavery's concern about the ongoing Dies Committee hearings was a factor in his efforts to defer or scuttle *Liberty Deferred*, there's no record of his mentioning it, either to Silvera and Hill or to his superiors. He did complain to his colleague Ben Russak that "one of the fundamental weaknesses of *Liberty Deferred*" was that Whites like he and Russak couldn't identify with its Black leads: "One can only have sympathy with a people if the protagonist of that people means something to us." He asked higher-ups—Flanagan, Barber, George Kondulf (who ran the New York City Unit), Brehon Somervell (who headed the WPA in New York), and Howard Miller (deputy director of the Federal Theatre)—to weigh in, not one of whom urged that *Liberty Deferred* go forward. Lavery belatedly commissioned a reader report in the summer of 1938, and its author, "M. S." (perhaps Morris Surofsky), faulted the script for its "over-indulgence in sheer fact . . . that would serve to bludgeon an audience rather than convince it" and for failing to emphasize that "white skins and black skins conceal the same thoughts, desires, ambitions, and hopes." All this was complicated by the backroom drama at the National Service Bureau, where Silvera's proposal to establish a "Negro Department" was co-opted when Lavery assigned Russak to oversee it, rather than Silvera himself, exacerbating the very discrimination Silvera was trying to overcome. Tensions no doubt intensified when a letter that Silvera had sent on May 17, 1938, to Alfred E. Smith, a top WPA administrator in Washington, D.C.—in which he wrote of "several instances of gross discrimination on the Federal Theatre Project which I think you are in a position to help us adjust"—was leaked.

It may have been coincidental, but around this time Lavery became enamored of the work of another Black dramatist, one whose play showed, as Lavery put it, how slavery "really started." Called *Panyared*, it was by Hughes Allison, whose *The Trial of Dr. Beck*, a courtroom drama about eugenics, had been staged by the Federal Theatre on Broadway in August 1937. *Panyared*—which, in Lavery's words, meant "the shanghaiing of African natives"—was to be the first of a three-play trilogy, beginning in Africa in 1800, which turned on a Black man selling his brother into slavery. Lavery admired how "Allison looks at the Negro in a new light," insofar as "the slave trade could never have flourished as it did had not African princes, like their Biblical brethren before them, sold their brothers into bondage." Lavery believed that Allison had shown "the Negro's initial contribution to his own travail," without "shifting one iota of the burden which properly belongs to American traders and planters for their share in the exploitation of the Negro." *Panyared* ends on a positive note, at Reconstruction, when the hero's grandson becomes "one of the first Negro public officers in the South." Lavery pressed the play on a skeptical Flanagan, even sharing with her an enthusiastic reader report he had commissioned Abram Hill to write, but she was dismissive of *Panyared*, not only because "a play dealing so violently with miscegenation is not possible for us" but also because of its stilted language, which she found "impossible to swallow" (a criticism Lavery took issue with, "because the play makes a point of the fact that the American Negroes speak a patter much inferior to the original language of the African Blacks").

In September 1938, after several months of hearing nothing about a potential production, a frustrated Hill wrote to Flanagan directly, reminding her that "We have made efforts to carry out the suggestions made by Mr. Lavery, Mr. McGee, and yourself to the fullest degree," and requesting that at this point a director and group of actors be assigned to see how stageworthy the script was. Two months later, Hill wrote again to Flanagan. He told her that the New Theatre League (a leftist federation of little theaters and amateur groups with strong Communist backing) had praised the manuscript and recommended it to its affiliated theaters, though he still believed that the Federal Theatre was the right home for it. His letter was ill-timed, as Flanagan had just appeared before the Dies Committee. Hill now pushed for a production in Harlem rather than in a Broadway theater, and enclosed a clipping of a review of the script that had run in the *Amsterdam News* on December 10, 1938, by its star critic, Dan Burley, one of the most influential Black journalists of the day. It seems that he and Silvera, frustrated by the delays, decided to reach out to influential members of the Black community for support.

It's clear from his column that in the draft Burley read, Hill and Silvera had ignored Lavery's advice to overhaul the frame (*"Liberty Deferred,"* Burley writes, presents "its history through the eyes of two white youngsters and two colored"). Burley grasped immediately what was groundbreaking about the play: "The philosophy of the American White man and what gives him his viewpoint has never been so graphically discussed for theatre purposes as in this script." He also saw how controversial this would be: "Many reading *Liberty Deferred* will contend that the piece is vicious propaganda aimed at perpetuating racial discord. Others will be equally as sure that it will place the Negro's position in America before America as it has never been done before." Either way, the play spoke powerfully to the reality long experienced by Blacks in America: "It is virulent in places, and expresses, no doubt, the reaction of the educated Negro to the pogroms black people endure in order to live in the United States."

Having identified what was at stake in the play, Burley turns to the reluctance of Whites in the theater world to confront this and stage the play:

> Of course, the theme of the play is the accepted model of the black and white problem. That never seems to change: The white man has his foot on his colored brother's neck: the latter squawks in piteous tone, digs deeper ditches, picks more cotton, shoots more craps, and hollers to the high heavens for the Lord to give Gabriel the order to toot the horn. While I have no quarrel here with this familiar method of presenting the Negro, whether in play, story, or song, I do concern myself deeply with the fact that the white market has persistently decided against this viewpoint as commercially impossible.

After three years of unfulfilled promises, some in the Black community had had enough. In early 1939 Black activists even considered turning to the Dies Committee to air their grievances, a plan quickly squashed by Walter White, executive secretary of the NAACP, as well as its legal counsel, Thurgood Marshall (who recognized that the Dies Committee was not keen on providing "any relief for Negroes" and that it was wiser to "fight within the WPA set-up"). At roughly the same time, a newly formed organization, calling itself the Negro Arts Committee Federal Arts Council, sent a long brief on "The Negro and Federal Project No. 1 (WPA Arts Projects) for New York

City," sharply criticizing everything from labor relations and discriminatory employment to the absence of Blacks in supervisory roles at the WPA, in violation of "the principles and ideals of the New Deal Administration." "If a true democratic culture is to prevail in America," the brief urged, "a greater proportion of Negro people should be employed as artists and artist-teachers in all the arts on the Federal Arts Projects, for the benefit of both the Negro and White people in this country." Its findings were endorsed by a wide array of Black organizations, including the NAACP, the Brotherhood of Sleeping Car Porters, the Southern Negro Youth Congress, the National Negro Congress, and the New York Urban League, as well as by such prominent Black public figures as the labor rights activist A. Philip Randolph and the philosopher and critic Alain Locke.

The brief singled out the failings of the Federal Theatre. Black playwrights have "begun to look upon the Federal Theatre with apprehension," since they have "met with very little success" there. Most of its plays about "Negro life" have been written by Whites, and the Federal Theatre "cannot receive credit for having launched one Negro playwright upon a career as a dramatist." Burley's piece on *Liberty Deferred* seems to have struck a nerve in the Black community; quoting from his account, the brief saw reflected in the treatment of *Liberty Deferred* "the fate of *numerous* Negro plays by Negro playwrights." The brief went on to note that John Silvera and Abram Hill had "spent two years in preparing the documented script under the direct supervision of Emmet Lavery," and that Lavery had told "a regional meeting of the directors in New York City in the fall of 1938" that "*Liberty Deferred* was a play 'the National Service Bureau was indeed proud to recommend.'" Yet six months had already passed since "publicity was officially released concerning *Liberty Deferred*," and its authors were still waiting for word that the Federal Theatre would stage it.

Stung by this personal attack, Lavery replied, denying that his treatment of Hill and Silvera was representative, promoting Allison's *Panyared*, and explaining that just because he had authorized press releases to be sent out announcing the play's production, that didn't obligate the Federal Theatre to stage *Liberty Deferred*:

> It is true that, in order to encourage the authors, I allowed some publicity to be released regarding the preparation of the script, but you will see this in no way committed the project to a production. And certainly this play does not, as your brief maintains, illustrate "the fate of numerous worthy Negro playwrights." As soon as this particular script was finished I advised the authors that it did not come up to my expectations but that I would not keep them from submitting it to the New York project. Surely therefore, the disinclination of the New York project to produce a script far from completion is no indication of the discrimination against Negro plays. This office in particular has always had a rigorous concern for the development of Negro drama, has in fact given Mr. Hill and Mr. Silvera every opportunity, and is at the present moment keeping close contact with Hughes Allison on the development of a Negro trilogy.

Lavery tellingly calls *Liberty Deferred* both "finished" and "far from completion"; it would remain in that state of limbo until the Federal Theatre closed three months later.

It's hard to know what to make of the outlier draft of the play now housed in the New York Public Library ("By John D. Silvera and Abram Hill," and in handwriting added, "Thru Ira Knaster"), which likely dates from the final months of the Federal Theatre. Reading it is a dispiriting experience. Perhaps desperate to see their play staged, the authors (if the draft is indeed their work, rather than Knaster's) largely capitulated to almost all Lavery's demands for revision. The opening of the two-page synopsis that precedes the script is representative:

> *The complacent old school teacher Professor Hat-in-Hand is thoroughly upset when one of his star pupils, Douglas, refuses to pledge allegiance to the flag. Douglas does not feel that "with Liberty and Justice to all" applies to the Negro. The professor attempts to correct this viewpoint and talks to them about Negro slavery. His idea, at least that which he teaches his students, is the old stereotype Uncle Remus version. A scene of dancing and singing Negroes dramatizes in entertaining fashion the type of plantation life that Professor wishes to tell about. Out of the dancing group comes Sam, a young Negro who interrupts the professor and explains to him and to the children the real story of American slavery; tracing its development from London England in 1600 through the Civil War.*

The searing exposure of White liberal self-satisfaction is transformed into a story of Blacks arguing with each other about their past. While many original scenes are retained, they are often carelessly reworked into this new frame (with bits and pieces of earlier versions not fully edited out). Rather than exposing offensive racial stereotypes, this draft reproduces them, laying it on thick, sanitizing the original's controversial message and channeling Lavery's advice:

Dancing, singing and music is so placed throughout the play as to provide light entertainment following heavy spots. The achievements of Negroes as well as the defeat of their ambitions are so designed as to give offence to no sector or locale. Ample opportunity is provided for a Negro chorus.

Sam has replaced the embittered Ted and Linda, and his journey takes him to Lynchotopia—yet even that experience has not dampened his optimism about this country. There turns out to be little difference between the professor's Pollyannish views and Sam's, who, at play's end, removes a noose from around his neck and declares: "Not Black Americans but just Americans." America's problem, we learn, turns out not to be systemic racism but merely a failure to enforce existing laws. Urging patience rather than collective action, Sam closes the play with the words: "There'll be no more of this if that Constitution is enforced. We've got to enforce it. Then we'll have real liberty[;] until then our Liberty is deferred." Had Hill and Silvera—if the draft is their work—attempted a parody of their original, they couldn't have done much better than this.

After the Federal Theatre closed, Lavery accompanied Flanagan to Poughkeepsie, assisting her at the Bureau of Theatre Research established for her at Vassar, where she wrote *Arena*. He set to work on his own book, a "postscript" to hers, "The Flexible Stage," which he prepared for publication in 1940—down to directions for captions and appendices—but which was never published. In the chapter on "Negro Drama," Lavery writes: "I think it is not overstating the case to say that Federal Theatre completed the emancipation of the Negro, gave him his full and true stature for the first time in theatre, and in giving him that stature in the theatre gave it to him in life as well."

Allison's "nobly planned" though never staged *Panyared* comes in for special praise: "Here, for the first time in the history of the American stage, a Negro playwright has gone to the roots of the situation which introduced the Negro to American life in the role of a slave." Hill and Silvera's *Liberty Deferred*, which had been listed in an earlier chapter on "New Plays and New Playwrights" among plays in the works when the National Service Bureau closed its doors, is never mentioned in Lavery's chapter on "Negro Drama."

Thirty-six years later, in January 1976, John O'Connor and Mae Mallory Krulak interviewed Lavery as part of the oral history project "Voices of the WPA" at George Mason University and asked him about *Liberty Deferred.* Lavery replied that "I only have a vague recollection of that, and I recognize it as a title in the National Service Bureau, but offhand now I couldn't tell you what it was about." When reminded of his extensive correspondence on it and the Negro Arts Committee brief, his memory was refreshed. Though his interviewers had not accused him of discrimination, it was clearly on Lavery's mind in his response:

> Well, you know, oftentimes in a project like that, the ultimate decision to produce or not to produce isn't necessarily a matter of discrimination, but I can see how playwrights, who were properly hopeful, would find it hard to believe that if everything had been going well, then suddenly it wasn't going well. But I think in the theatre particularly—well, in films also—there are so many questions of taste and style involved that the ultimate acceptance or rejection of a script may have nothing to do with the personality of the author, or even the worth of the enterprise. So many peripheral factors.

After the Federal Theatre closed, Abram Hill cofounded the American Negro Theatre in Harlem, whose mission was to "break down the barriers of Black participation in the theater." John Silvera, who left playwriting, enlisted in the Army Air Corps, serving as an intelligence officer and public relations officer for the Tuskegee Airmen, published *The Negro in World War II*, and later served as human rights commissioner for New York. Emmet Lavery returned to Hollywood to write screenplays, serve as vice president of the Motion Picture Academy of Arts and Sciences, and then president of the Screen Writers Guild. *Liberty Deferred* has never been staged.

The newly formed House Un-American Activities Committee, June 1938. From
left to right: Congressmen Joe Starnes, John Dempsey, J. Parnell Thomas,
Martin Dies, Arthur Healey, Harold Mosier, and Noah Mason.

CHAPTER EIGHT

The Creation of the Dies Committee

When Martin Dies first ran for Congress in 1930 he proudly told voters that he was "a native of East Texas" and "heir to her sacred traditions and priceless memories." He would later claim that he was born in 1901 and had graduated from the University of Texas at Austin. None of this was exactly true. He wanted to be known as the youngest member of Congress, so sliced off a year; he was born in 1900. And though he lived for most of his life in East Texas, Martin Dies was born in Colorado City, in West Texas, closer to New Mexico than to Louisiana, where his father had briefly moved the family in what seems to have been a successful attempt to overcome a drinking problem. He did attend the University of Texas, but only for a month, after enrolling in January 1920. Among those "sacred traditions and priceless memories" of White voters (for only Whites voted in Texas primaries) were a reverence for the Confederacy and an insistence on White supremacy. So when Dies gave a stump speech, he made sure to remind those gathered to hear him that his grandfather had fought in the Civil War, and that had "these heroes in gray" come home "and exclaimed 'All is lost' the South today would be ruled and governed by ignorant niggers instead of intellectual whites."

Martin Dies deeply admired his father, who had represented the same congressional seat—the fourteen counties of Texas's Second District—from 1909 to 1919. Martin Dies, Sr., never sponsored any major legislation while in Congress but was respected as a talented orator. He opposed immigration and was against American intervention abroad as well as the right of women to vote. He was above all a nativist: anti-foreigner, anti-Catholic, and anti-radical political thought, for whom all non–"Anglo-Saxon" peoples were "beaten races." He was on record saying that the "Pacific . . . is a barrier against the hordes of the Orient" and that "White supremacy is as secure and unshakable as the eternal hills." His son would inherit both his name and these values.

Martin Dies, Sr., moved his family around a lot, and the young Martin Dies experienced even more dislocation after his father divorced his mother, Olive M. Cline, in 1909, leaving her for a woman who worked in his office. The divorce seems to have been amicable and Cline was granted custody of their son and two teenage daughters. There are conflicting accounts of where Dies attended elementary school; he was variously educated after that in his mother's hometown of Greenville, Texas, then at a boarding school in Cluster Springs, Virginia, from 1914 to 1917, a nonmilitary academy of seventy or so boys, where Dies served as president of the Dramatic Club. He would likely have stayed there through graduation had the school not closed. He returned to Texas and spent his senior year at Beaumont High School in 1917–18, where he was on the debating team and acted in a school play. He graduated in May 1918, and both he and his father spoke at the ceremony.

Dies's education after high school continued to be itinerant. Following in his father's footsteps, he pursued a law degree, and to that end attended several schools: Wesley College (a Methodist junior college in Greenville), then briefly the University of Texas at Austin, followed by Hickman College, and finally the National University in Washington, D.C., where he received a bachelor of law degree in June 1920. Dies also claimed that while attending law school he went to "a school of Dramatical Art and Public Speaking," underscoring how important oratory was to him. At the age of nineteen his formal schooling was over, and in 1920, soon after he passed the Texas bar, Dies married Myrtle McAdams of Greenville, with whom he would have three children. He had a more stable domestic life than his father, and the marriage lasted until his death fifty-two years later. The young couple moved around East Texas, first to Marshall, then to Orange, where for the next decade of his life Dies practiced law in a small firm established at this time by his father, and dabbled in real estate. Not much else is known about how he spent his twenties. If he aspired to a national political career early on, he might have worked his way up the ladder, as his father had done before him, running for and holding local offices. But he chose not to do so. His father contemplated campaigning for his old seat again in 1922, but died fairly suddenly that year, at age fifty-three.

On February 1, 1930, at the age of twenty-nine, having briefly considered running for Congress two years earlier, Martin Dies announced that he would challenge John C. Box, the incumbent who had succeeded his father. In the interim the Depression had hit and the stock market had crashed. Rural America—and Texas's Second

Congressional District was mostly rural—was hit hard, and Dies's campaign speeches spoke to these voters' anxieties. It is surprising how much he sounded like the Communists he would be vilifying before the decade was out, as he slammed "capitalistic tyranny" and "high pressure financiers," and warned voters that the "centralization of wealth and power in the hands of monopolies and the control by these monopolies of the priceless resources of this country is rapidly destroying the equality of opportunity in this land." The excesses of capitalism and the resulting income inequality were to blame for the sad state of things: "These great trusts and monopolies are rapidly transforming America from a land of free and independent citizenship into a land composed of the ultra rich and the ultra poor." Whether Dies said all this because he believed it or because it was politically expedient to do so is impossible to know. As one contemporary critic observed, early on in his political career "Martin Dies seems to have expressed almost every point of view at least once." He couldn't easily run to the right of Box, the son of a Confederate veteran best known in Congress for writing the so-called Box Bill in 1926 that sought to impose severe quotas on Mexican immigration.

The population of Texas's Second Congressional District had swelled since Dies's father first held office, more than doubling from 203,373 in 1900 to 430,881 in 1930. Of these, roughly 125,000 were African Americans. Only a tiny percentage were foreign-born. Most of those who lived there were Whites of Scotch-Irish or English descent, or a mixture of both, farming cotton or rice, cutting timber, or working in the oil refineries. Two laws had been passed in Texas since Dies's father had first entered Congress that had a profound effect on elections. The first was a state poll tax, instituted in 1902, which sharply restricted the political participation of the poor. It wasn't much—only

$1.75—but the tax was enough to discourage two-thirds of adult Whites in the state; when a poor family in Texas (where the median income was around $800 a year) had to decide whether to pay for groceries or for the right to vote, food usually won.

The second, which almost completely suppressed Black political representation, was enacted by the Texas state legislature in 1923 and declared that "in no event shall a negro be eligible to participate in a Democratic party election held in the State of Texas." When this law was challenged and the Supreme Court ruled that it violated the Fourteenth Amendment, the Texas legislature got around that ruling, ensuring that only White votes counted by delegating authority to political parties to make their own primary rules and exclude Blacks (a law not overturned by the Supreme Court until 1944). Because Democrats vastly outnumbered Republican voters, Texas was effectively a one-party state; winners of the Democratic primary went on to win elections. So while African Americans constituted over a quarter of the inhabitants of Texas's Second District in 1930, they could be safely ignored.

Which meant that while running for office Martin Dies could appeal directly to fellow White supremacists. On the campaign trail on March 29, 1930, in Center, Texas, he made clear his staunch opposition to racial equality, attacking Oscar Stanton De Priest, a Republican from Chicago, the child of former slaves and the first African American to be elected to Congress in the twentieth century. De Priest, Dies told the crowd, had "insulted the honor of the South marching two buck negros [sic] down the aisles of Congress the other day and introduced them as 'gentlemen of his race.'" "Had I been in Congress," Dies added, "the voice of the Second District would have been heard in clarion note protesting against the gross insult to the memory of a torn and bleeding South." De Priest had also riled Southern Democrats when he hadn't prevented his wife from attending a tea at the White House to which Mrs. Hoover had invited the wives of congressmen. When delivering this stump speech a few months later at Port Arthur, Dies went off script about this offense, assuring the crowd, "Had I been a member of Congress when Oscar De Priest made a speech assailing the southern white man, I would have taken a swing at that nigger's jaw. That burr-headed wife of De Priest may be good enough for Mrs. Herbert Hoover, but I'll tell you here and now that she's not good enough for you and your wife nor me and mine."

The only newspaper that reported on Dies's racist remarks was the African American *Chicago Defender*, which noted that Dies had "said more of this nature" and concluded that Dies "has joined the Blease clan." Senator Coleman Blease of South Carolina was a staunch defender of lynching ("Whenever the Constitution comes between me and the virtue of the white women of the South, I say to hell with the Constitution"), who, after the tea scandal at the White House, insisted that it was called the *White* House for a reason and proposed prohibiting interracial marriage by constitutional amendment. *The Chicago Defender* supposed that Dies "feels that he must appeal to the lynch spirit if he wants to get to Congress from Texas," and unless "there looms up a candidate more vicious, more ribald and more vulgar than Dies, he has the election in his pocket. Of such is the electorate of Texas made."

Lynching was not a thing of the past in Texas. During Dies's senior year of high school in Beaumont, where roughly a third of the population of thirty thousand or so was Black, a pair of Black men were lynched: Charles Jennings, a forty-year-old married woodcutter, on

September 3, 1917 ("The body of the negro hung on the square for a number of hours following the hanging, and it was finally cut down, after hundreds had passed by and viewed it"); and on May 25, 1918, the week Dies graduated from high school, Whites in Beaumont lynched another Black man, Kirby Goolsie, for an "alleged attack on a white girl."

The political assessment of *The Chicago Defender* was correct: Dies went on to defeat Box in the Democratic primary by 7,326 votes: 34,101 to 26,781. Dies ran unopposed in the general election, which meant that fewer than 8 percent of those living in the Second District—all of them White and of sufficient means—voted to send Dies to Congress. After his victory, the *Austin Statesman* declared: "Now the brilliant son of a brilliant father has pushed his face into the picture gallery of national celebrities. No land like this."

President Herbert Hoover's Republican Party suffered huge losses in that 1930 midterm election. Before this, they had controlled the Senate (54–39) and the House (268–164). But in 1930 that advantage in the Senate was nearly erased, and Dies and other Democrats narrowed that edge in the House to 217–216, then took the majority (after a few special elections) by the time the Seventy-second Congress was seated. Sworn in on March 4, 1931—the same month that Hallie Flanagan was writing *Can You Hear Their Voices?*—Martin Dies would have to wait until the following December before Congress convened. In the interim he hired a staff and asked them to ensure that his office was nowhere near De Priest's.

Even before his first day seated in Congress, Dies engaged in a bit of grandstanding. In late September 1931, he and Representative Fletcher Swank of Oklahoma made national news when they visited the White House and demanded that President Hoover call for an "extra session of Congress to deal with the unemployment problem."

They challenged him to enact what amounted to New Deal legislation (with a plea to halt immigration added to an otherwise progressive list): "a large undertaking of public works, involving road, Federal building, waterways and flood control," along with "a year's moratorium on mortgage foreclosures on homesteads, the prohibition of immigration for five years, and legislation to end 'speculation' on the stock exchanges and stricter regulation of the banking system."

The demand that America's doors be temporarily closed to all immigrants was undoubtedly Dies's idea, repeated in his first act in the House, on December 8, 1931, when he introduced a bill urging Congress to "suspend for a period of five years general immigration into the United States." The bill went nowhere, as immigration had already been severely restricted in 1924, but Dies warmed to the issue and pressed it hard, using it to draw national attention to his emerging America First agenda, which was nationalist, anti-immigration, and increasingly anti-Communist. After his first major speech in Congress, on December 17, 1931 (in which he argued that there "is no justification for immigration to the United States"), failed to enlist the support of his colleagues, he turned to radio, public lectures, and newspapers to make his case, initially in a piece called "Nationalism Spells Safety" that ran in the *National Republic*, a right-wing magazine of "Fundamental Americanism." "It is safe to say," he wrote, "that we invited the evils of the Old World's social and economic disorder by offering our fertile lands and priceless resources . . . as a refuge for the jobless and dispossessed of Europe," and he called for the deportation of three million illegal immigrants, whose numbers, he claimed, without evidence, included "hundreds of gangsters, murder[er]s and thieves unfit to live in this country."

Dies followed that up with an essay on "The Immigration Crisis," this time in the mainstream *Saturday Evening Post*, where he recounted how he had seen "100,000 Communists parade in New York on May 1," adding: "I did not see an American in the crowd. They openly insulted and derided everything we hold sacred. If I had my way I would deport every one of them and cancel citizenship of those aliens who have been naturalized." On June 6, 1932, he again tried and failed to persuade Congress to "expel alien communists," on the grounds that they promoted labor unions as well as "discontent among the negroes." Dies's anti-immigration campaign soon sputtered, and while he had begun to make a name for himself, it was, for many, as a bigot: the *New York Herald Tribune* reported that "Martin Dies, whose alien-baiting campaign hasn't been doing so well recently, managed to get himself in the newspapers by raising the cry of 'racial and religious bigotry,'" and called what Dies proposed "hare brained" and a "stock maneuver of the bigoted, of whom the 100-percent native variety represented by Mr. Dies may be numbered among the less lovely specimens."

Dies badly needed a winning issue that would keep him in the public eye. He didn't have to worry about reelection, running unopposed in both the primary and general election (and comfortably fought off challengers after that). Yet it wasn't easy standing out. When Roosevelt took office in March 1933, and the Democrats controlled the White House, the Senate, and the House, Dies, like most other members of his party, enthusiastically supported the wildly popular president's New Deal, and dutifully voted the party line. Dies wrote at the time to his aide Robert Stripling, "I am voting the President's program one hundred per cent regardless of the political consequences to myself," even if that meant he couldn't easily distinguish himself, and meant as well disappointing wealthy supporters back home who chafed at regulations placed on big business. Dies was impatient to attain a higher office, but he had not yet gained enough political visibility to do so. In late 1935 he contemplated challenging Senator Morris Sheppard for his seat, but changed his mind, given the likelihood that he would be defeated by the much-admired incumbent.

One of the most astute observers of the Washington political scene at this time, the novelist and journalist Marquis Childs, sketched a vivid portrait of the young congressman. Childs was fascinated by Martin Dies and considered him "a case history in ambition, by Shakespeare out of *True Story Magazine*." His description is worth quoting from at length:

> When Martin Dies first came to Washington from Orange, Texas, he had the most complete and utter scorn for the whole institution of Congress. A protective rind of cynicism was what he showed to the world. I doubt whether I have ever encountered a more cynical man than this lank Texan with the sallow grey face. He was a leading member of the Demagogies Club, made up of younger members like himself who had pledged themselves to vote for any appropriation bill that came on the floor of the House, no matter what it was for. . . . You would see Dies standing at the back of the House, surrounded by two or three fellow members of his club, a good natured grin on his face. When a roll call came, he would stalk onto the floor and roar out his yea in a lusty voice, usually drawing tolerant laughter.
>
> Seeing him in that phase you would have said that here was another easygoing Texan who had patented for himself a

political formula guaranteeing his return to Washington ad infinitum. What happened to him is anyone's guess. It may have been merely Washington, the frustration of obscurity and neglect, some gnawing force beneath the outer surface of cynicism. Whatever it was it fed on itself.

His ambitions checked, Dies tried out a succession of sensational issues, none of which gained any traction. Looking back in 1940 at Dies's early political trajectory, another contemporary, Frederick R. Barkley, neatly summarized how Dies "changed his tactics" after his anti-immigration campaign failed "to get more than a line or two on the press wires":

> In three years he proposed to probe into seven different subjects. First he sought authority to investigate charges made by the late Senator Schall—a violent critic of the New Deal—that the Administration was restricting freedom of the press and of radio. Next he volunteered . . . to discover whether or not it was true that resigning government officials were accepting lucrative private jobs. Nothing came of these proposals and in 1937 he struck out at sit-down strikers, next against the German-American Bund's camp operators, and finally against an alleged sugar lobby. Still, the House remained uninterested, as it did again when Mr. Dies wanted to probe Secretary Ickes' charge that "Sixty families" control the United States.

To this long list Barkley might have added the Silver Purchase Act of 1934, Dies's only major piece of legislation (one that forced the government to buy up silver, though it did little to help the economy). The seeming arbitrariness of these causes suggests a sense of frustration, if not desperation.

Viewed one way, Dies was a loser, failing time and again to find an issue that would lead to the attention and power that he craved. Viewed more generously, he was learning from every setback, developing a playbook, one based less on policy differences than on fomenting a culture war. It turned out that, to this end, there was little reputational damage done in floating one trial balloon after another. He also learned that identifying immigrants as dangerous Communists proved more effective than maligning those who had come to America to make a better life for themselves. It was also a winning way to attack unions (which were supported by Communists) and racial equality (another Communist goal). After *The Saturday Evening Post* turned down more pieces by him (a racist-titled one on "Sambo Gets a New Deal," another on inflation, a third attacking Secretary of the Interior Harold Ickes, and a fourth, "The Immigration Showdown," on his hobbyhorse), Dies came to understand that it was a lot easier getting attention by having others speak and write about *him*. To this end, he was quicker than almost every other politician of the day to recognize the value of both traditional and emerging mass media— newspapers, direct mail, radio, and newsreels—and was thrilled when a newsreel was made of one of his speeches against immigration. He also planted stories in his local paper, *The Belmont Enterprise*, to head off potential rivals.

Dies also knew that most major newspapers, especially those in the Hearst chain, had swung against the New Deal and its progressive policies, and with his own swerve to the right, and his embrace of nationalism and opposition to foreigners and Communists, he was sure to have their support. And he was learning that he could charm reporters, who didn't investigate his claims very thoroughly and rarely followed up. With his oratorical gifts, he could also impress audiences on radio and newsreels with "a voice," Joseph Alsop and Robert Kinter wrote in a nationally syndicated column, "that would call the ghosts of hogs back from the lower regions, a manner so heavily, pompously hearty that you feel he could slap you on the back at a distance of 50 feet." Much has been made of how President Roosevelt used his thirty-one "fireside chats" to reach a national audience over the airwaves. But Dies found a no less successful path to millions of Americans, especially disaffected White and rural ones, and his savvy use of the airwaves would prove one of the most consequential parts of his playbook.

In the decade that followed his successful run for Congress in 1930, the percentage of American households that owned radios had more than doubled, from 40.3 to 82.8 percent, and by 1938 Americans were listening to radio, on the average, five hours a day, a cheap form of entertainment and news during these Depression years. Conservatives and evangelicals had been among the earliest groups to seize upon radio's reach in the 1920s, with their independent broadcasters offering a popular mix of old-time religion, music, and politics. But by the early 1930s these independent stations were in decline, due to the licensing policies of the Federal Radio Commission, and these voices remained largely excluded from the increasingly dominant national radio networks. There were exceptions. The rabidly antisemitic Father Charles Coughlin, "the radio priest" who stoked the disaffected on the right, had a weekly Sunday program on CBS in 1930, but the network canceled it when Coughlin refused to allow its officials to review his incendiary speeches. Anticipating those banned from social media sites in our own day, Coughlin turned to non-network airwaves (including WJR in Detroit and WOR in New York) and was soon reaching as many as forty million listeners every week. But by 1938 he had lost his license and was largely forced off the air. His base would have to turn to others to give voice to their grievances.

Dies, like many others, aspired to be that voice, but what set him apart was that he also grasped that, given his status as a member of Congress, he could safely appeal to the dominant mainstream radio networks—ABC, CBS, and NBC. He cultivated all three in order to secure a platform as a suitable, and soon regular, conservative speaker, one deft at framing his speeches in language that juxtaposed ungodly Communism with an American democracy grounded in "the Christian principle that the fundamental rights of man come from God and God alone." In a recent and detailed analysis of Dies's move into radio—"Populist Conservatism on the Air: The Dies Committee and Network Radio"—Joy Elizabeth Hayes unpacks how Dies developed "strategies for attacking liberal policies that became central to the conservative media playbook" so influential today, and he did so largely by forging "a politics of identity that pitted rural patriots against urban subversives."

A major break came Dies's way when in January 1935 he was appointed to the House Rules Committee. It took luck, timing, opportunism, and patronage to secure one of the twelve spots on the most powerful committee in the House. As Frederick R. Barkley explains it, the "big Texas delegation in the House had been held entitled by custom to one membership on the Rules Committee, but it had lost its representation through death in the previous session. Mr. Dies looked over the Texas list; found all the other members unavailable because they either held or were in line for important party chair-manships; campaigned for the Rules Committee job despite his lack of seniority and got it." But it would not have happened without the backing of his fellow Texan, Vice President John Nance Garner, and coincided with Garner's (and soon Dies's) break from Roosevelt's progressive agenda and alignment with the Southern Democrat–Republican coalition determined to thwart the New Deal agenda and protect White supremacy by defeating anti-lynching legislation.

A number of factors contributed to this realignment. One was Roosevelt's unsuccessful and, for many, disturbing efforts in the aftermath of his landslide reelection of 1936 to pack the Supreme Court to prevent it from thwarting his legislative agenda. Another was the so-called Roosevelt Recession that began in the summer of 1937, when a reduction in public spending led to a sharp economic downturn and a steep rise in unemployment. The New Deal was now beset by headwinds—ideological, cultural, and economic—and Americans were increasingly unwilling to support it, or the president, with the same enthusiasm they had shown just a few years earlier. The conservative Rules Committee was at the heart of this newly forged coalition's opposition. Garner still held considerable sway in Congress, and one of the ways he was able to undermine Roosevelt's policies (while still serving as his vice president) was to get allies in Congress to do his bidding behind the scenes. Martin Dies was all in on this, and clearly this was part of the deal that landed so inexperienced a congressman on the Rules Committee. Dies saw which way the political winds were blowing. Once pro-labor, he turned sharply against unions, especially sit-down strikers and those he now labeled "outside agitators." Once an opponent of rampant capitalism, he was now the staunch defender of property and the money behind it.

By the end of his second term in office, an impatient Dies had learned that amassing power in Congress was a painfully slow business. It typically involved a lot of horse-trading and compromise, as well as putting in the years and slowly climbing to the chairmanship of an important standing committee. The only way to get immediate attention was to chair the investigation of a controversial issue of national interest. And the only way to do that was through a "special committee," one that offered a shortcut to vast media attention, as well as the power to subpoena and interrogate witnesses. Congress had long been averse to establishing special committees, except under extraordinary circumstances, recognizing how easily they could be used to serve personal or partisan ends and put at risk the civil liberties of those harassed by overzealous investigators. Nonetheless, knowing that whoever submitted the resolution to form a special committee would likely be named its chair, Dies set to work.

After failing to win support for a special committee that he had proposed to investigate autoworkers engaging in sit-down strikes (over which Roosevelt and Garner, who wanted to suppress the strikers, had split), Dies tried—and failed—to persuade the House to investigate Hollywood. He kept trying though, and in July 1937 failed again, when the House rejected his proposal to establish a special committee to investigate "Un-American propaganda." Undeterred, six months later he proposed that monopolies and the manipulation of big business be investigated. That effort failed as well. But by now, Dies's playbook was nearly in place. He had discovered weak spots in the legislative process that would enable him to act without much oversight or constraint. His privileged position on the Rules Committee, which had to approve resolutions, meant that a fresh proposal to establish a special committee would likely clear its first hurdle. If the chance came his way, he was ready to make the most of it.

♦

Two things typically drove the creation of special committees in the House of Representatives: the pressure of the times and the relentless lobbying of a colleague. Without both, members of Congress were wary of establishing a committee they knew would have few restraints. The first House special committee to investigate subversive activities was the short-lived Fish Committee of July to December 1930, named after its chair, Hamilton Fish III, of New York. The Depression had begun, with massive unemployment and the threat of social unrest, and it was a good time to seek out enemies to blame. Fish, a Republican scion from an illustrious family of public servants, was isolationist, antisemitic (he handed out copies of *The Protocols of the Elders of Zion* in his congressional office), and an unrelenting foe of Communism, which he called "the most important, the most vital, the most far-reaching, and the most dangerous issue in the world." Fish's proposed investigation passed by a lopsided vote of 210–18. Like most subsequent special committees, its targets reflected the bias of its chair, who declared from the outset that it "is not the purpose of this resolution to interfere with any group except the Communists." At the end of the hearings Fish told the press that he would urge the Justice Department to investigate Communist activities in the United States and expressed his concern that "the Communists sought to stir up discontent among Negroes." He also advocated deporting alien Communists, whose departure would make jobs available "for honest, loyal Americans who are unemployed." The Fish Committee interviewed 225 witnesses in fourteen cities, returned $5,000 of its $25,000 authorization, and made thirteen recommendations, none of which had much to do with its actual findings, and none of which led to legislative action. The Fish Committee wrapped up its proceedings shortly before Martin Dies arrived in the House, and Dies later admitted he had never even heard of it.

Just a few years later, the House found itself under growing pressure to authorize a fresh special committee to look into the rise of Nazism, fascism, and Communism in America. This time the tireless advocate was Samuel Dickstein, who represented New York City's Lower East Side. Dickstein was especially alarmed by the growing strength of Hitler's supporters in America. The son of a rabbi, Dickstein was born in Russia and was two years old when his family immigrated to America in 1887. In 1922 he was elected to Congress, defeating a Socialist incumbent, then reelected eleven times. In 1931 Dickstein was appointed chair of the Committee on Immigration and Naturalization, where his sympathies for those fleeing persecution alienated others on the committee (especially Martin Dies) who were fixated on ending immigration, and where he established a subcommittee for nine months that investigated Nazi inroads in America, paving the way for his call to establish a more extensive special investigation. In pursuit of this, Dickstein sought allies wherever he could find them, joining Hamilton Fish in 1930 in denouncing religious persecution in Russia, and a year later bringing one of Dies's anti-Communist bills to the House floor.

In March 1934, Dickstein's resolution to establish a "Special Committee on Un-American Activities Authorized to Investigate Nazi

Propaganda and Certain Other Propaganda Activities" was passed by the House, 168–31. Its title emphasized Dickstein's concern with Hitler's rise, while enshrining the dangerously undefined label of "un-American." Because his colleagues were uncomfortable appointing a foreign-born Jew to head the committee, Dickstein was relegated to vice chair; the more trusted, Christian, and native-born John William McCormack, of Massachusetts, a foe of both Communists and Nazis, was appointed chair. While there were no rules governing the procedures to be followed by a special committee, McCormack ensured that every witness was first heard out in an executive session, and insisted as well that evidence be admitted much as it was in court procedures, which meant that witnesses were allowed counsel. When the measured McCormack conducted hearings, they ran smoothly; when the histrionic Dickstein took over, they were often sensational, as he sparred with witnesses, who baited him in turn. The McCormack-Dickstein Committee ran for less than a year, and cost just under $30,000. Its final report, in February 1935, reflected McCormack's temperament and concerns more than Dickstein's: neither fascism nor Communism, it concluded, had yet made serious inroads in America. The committee's sensible recommendation that foreign agents who distributed propaganda in America face compulsory registration became law.

Members of the House who had witnessed Fish and Dickstein in action had seen enough of what could happen when a special committee investigated what it deemed subversive. Lindsay C. Warren, a Democrat from North Carolina, spoke for many when he said that "investigations of this nature, and the membership of the House knows it, are generally for the self-glorification and advertisement of those who conduct them, and who have an itch and flair for publicity." But

Dickstein wasn't done, and in January 1937 began urging his colleagues to open a fresh investigation. His resolution went nowhere and the backlash was fierce, as Congress was weary and wary of witch hunts led by publicity seekers, Dickstein in particular. Maury Maverick, a Texas liberal, was blunt: "Kill this resolution. Cut it down." Even Hamilton Fish was opposed to a bill "that sets up an un-American *Cheka*, more or less." Jewish newspapers, fearful of an antisemitic backlash, joined in, lambasting Dickstein. In April 1937 the House overwhelmingly rejected Dickstein's resolution by a vote of 184–38. And that seemed to close the door on such an investigative committee for a good long while.

Yet Dickstein persisted. After he again began calling for a new investigation in late 1937, Harold Knutson of Minnesota said on the House floor that "the gentleman from New York has an obsession, and it seems to be growing on him." His colleagues attacked him for naming individuals in the *Congressional Record* as suspected Nazis, based only on hearsay. Dickstein wrote to Roosevelt to secure his backing, which was not forthcoming. In October 1937 he reached out to Martin Dies: "Conditions have gone from bad to worse. The resolution dealing with these activities will again be before the [Rules] Committee when Congress convenes. Is it your intention to help me out?" Dies had plans of his own, which he did not share with Dickstein, though he was happy letting the congressman from New York canvas for support and stir up media interest in a new committee. The tempo of Dickstein's campaign picked up: four months later, on February 23, 1938, he was once more haranguing his congressional colleagues. He did so again the following day and yet again a week later, hoping to reassure them, as he put it, that "I am not asking for any personal power and do not care whether I am chairman of any committee that might be created; as a matter of fact, I do not care to be on the committee; I do not care who is chairman; but it is the duty of Congress to ferret out the enemies within." Dickstein's attacks on Hitler were getting attention in the press, and members of Congress weren't happy about seeming unconcerned, especially after Hitler annexed Austria on March 12, 1938. But yet again, on April 12, the House shot down another Dickstein resolution to investigate "un-American propaganda."

But then, a month later, newspapers across the country reported that the House Rules Committee was putting forward its own resolution on un-American activities, proposed by its youngest member, Martin Dies, "after hearing Samuel Dickstein . . . assert that there would be 'riots and bloodshed' unless Congress acted." Both the timing and the explanation were surprising. On May 11, 1938, the *New York Herald Tribune* noted that while Dies's resolution made "no mention of Nazi, Fascist, or Communist organizations," the "committeemen made it plain that it was aimed in their direction." Perhaps Dickstein was blindsided by the action of the Rules Committee. But more likely he learned that it had been in the works, and believed, as the press reported, that his relentless pressure, culminating in this latest threat of imminent violence provoked by Nazi rallies, had forced the most powerful committee in the House to act. In either case, there is little doubt that he was confident that he had earned the right to be named as one of the committee's members, if not cochair.

Dickstein was genuinely concerned about growing domestic support for Hitler. But his recent and frantic appeals, along with this latest threat of "riots and bloodshed," can better be explained by information that only came to light after the collapse of the Soviet Union and the records of the NKVD (the forerunner of the KGB) became available. Researchers discovered that Dickstein had contacted Soviet agents in mid-1937 and soon after engaged in negotiations to spy for them. His handlers were not keen on paying him much unless Dickstein, code-named "Crook," could provide valuable intelligence and influence American policy. Dickstein was demanding a lot: $2,500 a month. When the Soviets made a counteroffer of $500 a month, Dickstein told them that when he had sold secrets to the British and the Poles they had paid up "without any questions." An NKVD memo reported: "'Crook' is completely justifying his code name. This is an unscrupulous type, greedy for money, consented to work because of money, a very cunning swindler. . . . Therefore it is difficult to guarantee the fulfillment of the planned program even in the part which he proposed to us himself." Dickstein had likely proposed a great deal—and a sure way to gain access to information the Soviets wanted, and influence public policy, was having subpoena powers while serving on an unchecked special committee.

In the spring of 1938, as Congress inched closer to once again establishing a special House committee to investigate un-American activities, the Soviets had come to terms with Dickstein and began paying him $1,250 a month—considerably more than his congressional salary. It's no small irony that a committee that would soon devote itself to hunting down Communists was a byproduct of Soviet efforts to infiltrate the U.S. government. It was Dies, not Dickstein, who was chosen to chair the committee, from which Dickstein was excluded. The disappointed Soviets cut Dickstein off in early 1940, having paid him a total of $12,000 for little of value in return.

The strange history of how the committee that Dickstein had campaigned for came into being, and how Dies was put in charge, goes back a year or so before its authorization on May 26, 1938. John

Garner, the Texas politician nicknamed "Cactus Jack," is best remembered nowadays for having said that the office of vice president is "not worth a bucket of warm piss." Garner surrendered considerable power when he agreed to run as Roosevelt's vice presidential candidate in 1932. By that time, after twenty-eight years as a congressman, he had risen to become Speaker of the House and a leading candidate for the presidency. After three ballots at the Democratic National Convention, Roosevelt was still short of the votes needed for the nomination and his support seemed to be peaking. Fearing the possibility of deadlock and a compromise candidate chosen instead—perhaps Al Smith, who was running ahead of Garner, in second place—Garner agreed to throw his support to Roosevelt; in exchange, Garner would be chosen as his running mate. It proved to be a winning ticket, though Garner himself had little interest in serving as vice president and only agreed to do so for the sake of the Democratic Party, to which he was fervently committed.

Cactus Jack may have posed as a populist, but he was a crafty politician, a master of the House rules, a consummate backroom dealer, a bank owner who charged usurious interest, as well as a pecan farm owner who paid his immigrant workers only "a penny a pound" for shelled nuts. A fiscal and political conservative, Garner had not signed on for all of the progressive New Deal policies that Roosevelt pursued in his first hundred days in office. Nonetheless, his skill in getting bills through Congress proved crucial. By 1936 their relationship had begun to sour, though Garner remained on the ticket for a second term. He much preferred a Democratic Party that represented a broad coalition rather than the more narrowly progressive one that Roosevelt was now trying to build. In their second term Garner set about putting the brakes on the president's agenda, especially what for him were its more radical goals, such as packing the Supreme Court (which Garner deftly sank in a Congress he knew how to manipulate far better than the president did). Roosevelt soon found Garner "pretty much against everything." By 1937 Garner had made clear to the president that he no longer supported relief measures. He was also concerned about what he believed was a growing Communist influence on the administration.

If the first two years of their second term were fraught, the next two turned adversarial, especially after Roosevelt tried to purge the Democratic Party of New Deal opponents, including those serving on the Rules Committee (Martin Dies was named in the press alongside those Roosevelt wanted to see voted out of office, though, as the press reported, Dies and a few others "are considered so firmly intrenched in their districts that it would be impossible to displace them at this time"). For a party man like Garner—who proudly declared, "I believe in partisanship"—the purge was unconscionable. So too was the role that left-leaning unions were now playing in elections. There was little love lost between Garner and the labor movement; CIO leader John L. Lewis described him as a "poker playing, whisky drinking, evil old man who would destroy labor." Roosevelt's attempted purge backfired, and in the midterm elections of November 1938 the Democratic Party lost seventy-two seats in the House and eight in the Senate. A month later, the president and vice president met in private, which they had regularly done until now, for the final time. Roosevelt's popularity was declining, though he cagily wouldn't declare whether he would seek a third term. Garner saw his own power growing and gave up the pretense of deference, interrupting the president at cabinet meetings and shouting at Secretary of Labor Frances Perkins.

Garner harbored hopes of being elected president in 1940 and quietly worked to weaken Roosevelt's chances for a third term in office. One way of doing so was getting Congress to defy the president. Garner may have left the House of Representatives, but he still held great sway there, especially with the Texans who ran some of the most influential committees. To the extent that the Texas congressional delegation was committed to the New Deal, it had only been to the first stage of it—recovery—not to the second—reform. Garner needed dependable surrogates in Congress, and he chose well in Martin Dies, whose father he had served with. It helped that Dies was unprincipled and ambitious, and ready to turn against Roosevelt and the New Deal.

Dies's loyalty test came in 1937, in the wake of the wave of sitdown strikes against auto factory owners in Michigan. Here's how Dies recalled their conversation a quarter century later, worth quoting at length for what it reveals about their relationship:

> At the height of the 1937 sit-down strikes, Vice-President Garner sent for me. He expressed in the strongest language his alarm and disgust at the Administration's inaction, obviously due to fear of antagonizing labor and Left-wing supporters. Garner said he had telephoned Roosevelt at Warm Springs, and that Roosevelt had finally agreed to support a Congressional resolution condemning sit-down strikes as unlawful and dangerous, and establishing a committee to investigate them. Garner said the President wanted me to introduce the resolution in the Rules Committee, where Speaker Bankhead and Sam Rayburn would call it for a vote immediately. Accordingly, I assured the Democratic members of the Rules Committee that the resolution had Administrative support,

and that the President would issue a statement in favor of it. Before the resolution came up for consideration, Garner telephoned me, so angry he could hardly talk. "Martin," he said, "I've got some bad news for you, and for the country. That two-faced, cowardly President had reneged on his promise to support your resolution. I have just finished telling him what I think of him." With Administration support withdrawn, the resolution had no chance. . . . Successful politicians swim with the tide, and the tide of Liberalism, led by Communism, favored sit-down strikes.

This version of what took place, however self-serving, offers a glimpse of what it meant for Garner to call Dies in and instruct him on what to do. If there is a grain of truth in the reported conversation with Roosevelt, had Garner won over the president, Dies might well have chaired a special committee to investigate striking workers rather than un-American theatrical activities. Dies's resolution to investigate the strikers was voted down on April 8, 1937, 236–150.

Dies's biographer, Dennis Kay McDaniel, writes that "Garner's chosen tool to hack away at the New Deal on the sit-down issue in early 1937 was Martin Dies," and that "it is certain" as well "that Garner told Dies to submit the resolution that established the House Special Committee on Un-American activities." Dies would confirm Garner's support in his memoir, where he writes, "Since I was classified as a supporter of the President," Garner, Speaker of the House William Bankhead, and House Majority Leader Sam Rayburn "asked me to introduce a resolution to establish a special committee on un-American activities." Dies's 1937 proposal to investigate "un-American activities" had long sat, dormant, in the Rules Committee. No longer.

Garner destroyed his papers after leaving office, and in any case was not the kind of politician to put his plans in writing, so there is no paper trail to corroborate this, or clarify when he decided that a vaguely worded resolution to investigate "un-American" propaganda, in the right hands, could be turned against the New Deal and hold the president in check, or even why he decided to play this hand when he did. But there is little doubt that he was behind the special committee, Dies his surrogate, and their objective to throttle the New Deal. Dickstein's clamoring for a committee would serve as a Trojan Horse. Garner, as savvy as any politician who ever served in the House, accurately predicted that "the Dies Committee is going to have more influence on the future of American politics than any other Committee of Congress."

Some at the time speculated about what had taken place behind the scenes. On November 2, 1938, after the investigative journalist Paul Y. Anderson—who would hound Dies in story after story in *The Nation* until his untimely suicide shortly before Flanagan's testimony—suggested on national radio that Garner was pulling the strings. Dies strenuously denied it, telling the *New York Herald Tribune*, "Mr. Garner has never talked with me about the committee," and that same day *The New York Times* quoted Dies's condemnation as "infamous lies" and "echoes of the White House" reports that Garner was the "master mind" behind his committee. A year later, on October 29, 1939, a sharply critical piece by Richard L. Stokes ran in the *St. Louis Post-Dispatch*, based on an interview with Dies, reflecting back upon the first sixteen months of his committee. Stokes recalls "the general astonishment" that greeted the news that so undistinguished a congressman as Dies had been asked to chair the special committee. He goes on to suggest that the committee had really been created to further Garner's agenda: "The idea had flashed upon the Democratic faction led by Vice President Garner that the committee could be used for tying up alien propaganda first with the Congress of Industrial Organizations and second with the Roosevelt administration itself, for the purpose of discrediting the New Deal and averting a third term."

Stokes's article was accompanied by a sidebar that lists Dies's claims for what his committee had already accomplished (though it's unclear how much of this list is really by Dies and how much by Stokes himself). After taking credit for having "proved that the German-American Bund and the Communist Party of the United States are agents of foreign governments," Dies turns to domestic political victories. The entries read like a Garner wish list, including having "paralyzed the influence of the left-wing faction of the Roosevelt administration, which is now declared to be conducting a quiet purge of radical elements"; defeating Governor Frank Murphy of Michigan (who had supported sit-down strikers); and destroying "the legislative power of the Workers Alliance of America." Sitting uncomfortably alongside these successes was another of Dies's "triumphs": that he had "led Congress to eliminate the Federal Theater Project of the WPA."

Though Dies's resolution had Garner's blessing, and the House leadership could be depended on to secure the votes to pass it, members of the House still had to debate and approve the resolution, only a month after they had soundly rejected Dickstein's similar measure. Efforts to tie up the administration—with midterm elections looming, and perhaps Roosevelt's planned purge of conservative Democrats—may have influenced the timing. The delay may also have reflected the challenges in locking in the support of an emerging anti–New Deal coalition of Republicans and mostly Southern Democrats required to pass it.

The debate was overseen by Alabama Democrat and Speaker of the House Bankhead, who, according to Dies, was one of those who had asked him to put forward the resolution. Until now Bankhead had dutifully promoted Roosevelt's agenda (despite his unhappiness with court packing and the "wage and hour" bill). He was unrivaled at managing debates in a way that allowed little time for discussion or amendment, and his gravity was such that he didn't have to pound a gavel to restore order; he merely had to stand up. His job was to juggle the competing demands of seeming impartiality and his majority party's interests. His implicit support for the Dies resolution would have sent an ominous signal to liberal New Dealers in the House. As one of them put it late in the debate, doesn't this bill "put the Democratic Party in a silly position when it looks like we are going to be investigating ourselves?"

The ensuing debate was anything but perfunctory. Texas Democrats were at odds with one another, while big-city Republicans from the North found themselves on the same side as Democrats from the rural South. Bankhead had at first restricted discussion to an hour, but when that was objected to, allowed a second hour of debate. The transcript of the ensuing exchanges might suggest that the resolution would fail, or at least that the vote would be close. But the outcome, given the strong support of the Rules Committee and House leadership, was assured in advance, and the resolution handily passed, though not before its opponents had a chance to say, for the record, how dangerous a threat to democracy the Dies Committee posed. The strategy of Dies and his supporters was to speak tirelessly of the dangers posed by Nazism, fascism, and Communism, in a resolution that never explicitly said it was going to investigate any of these.

The bill's vague language was immediately challenged. Lindsay Warren, from North Carolina, called it "most unusual." He had never seen anything like it. For one thing, there was no mention of a report. For another, there was no time limit set to the investigation: "This means that the lid is off. It would mean that you could come back here next January and ask for permission to file a report or to extend the inquiry over a period of years, if you cared to do so." Dies was forced to give ground on this, saying, "I believe the committee ought to conclude its hearings by that date" and he agreed to the recommendation that the committee would finish its business by January 3, 1939.

Gerald Boileau of Wisconsin also questioned the bill's language. Worryingly, the resolution included a clause that allowed it to address as well "all other questions in relation thereto that would aid Congress in any necessary remedial legislation." That wording, Boileau pointed out, would give Dies a blank check to investigate anything he pleased. Dewey Johnson of Minnesota, who represented the Farmer-Labor Party, agreed: "They could investigate Old Faithful geyser in Yellowstone National Park." Boileau shrewdly proposed an amendment that would have undermined the committee's unspoken mission, by limiting its investigations to those who "have as their objective the overthrow of the government of the United States by force or violence." It was not an unreasonable amendment, and even won the support of the influential centrist John McCormack. But given that the procedures were controlled that day by Bankhead and Dies, working in tandem, the suggested amendment would never be voted on.

Others criticized the slipperiness of what it meant to be "un-American." Luther Patrick, a Democrat from Alabama, put it directly: "It seems to me the most important thing involved in this matter is what is an un-American and what is an American activity? Who is to pass on that question?" Rather than address this highly charged issue, a strong supporter of the resolution, the flag-waving Republican from Tennessee J. Will Taylor, countered with a long and time-killing speech meant to stir up patriotic sentiment, denouncing a recent Communist rally at Madison Square Garden in New York and decrying how red paint had been splashed on Plymouth Rock in Massachusetts. "It is only a question of a short time," he added, "until a revolution will ensue and the soil of our great country will be soaked in blood." Taylor also deflected credit for the resolution from Dies to Dickstein, concluding, to cynical applause, that because of Dickstein's "gallant fight against the sabotage of our American institutions, he is entitled to your support today, and to show our appreciation of his valuable services, I trust this resolution will be adopted by a unanimous vote." This nod to Dickstein seems to have confused some of those in the room. Robert Stripling, a Dies aide who was working as "doorkeeper" in the House chamber that day, recalled that John E. Rankin, a Democrat from Mississippi who didn't much like Blacks, Asians, or Jews (*Time* magazine quotes him casually calling one a "little kike"), was initially predisposed to vote no, until assured that Dies, not Dickstein, would run the new committee.

Everyone in the room knew that the fiercest enemy of the resolution was Maury Maverick, the liberal congressman from Texas, who lived up to his namesake (the term "maverick" had been coined to describe his no less unconventional grandfather). "What this resolution is going to do," Maverick warned, "is give blanket powers to investigate, humiliate, meddle with anything and everything in people's affairs in America." The resolution's language, he noted, was "slipshod," especially the deliberate vagueness of "un-American": "Oh, you say, we are going to investigate un-American activities. Un-American! Un-American is simply something that somebody else does not agree to."

Maverick's attack was countered by a firebrand Republican from New Jersey, a committed anti–New Dealer named J. Parnell Thomas. A year earlier Thomas had been elected to fill the seat of Randolph Perkins, who had served uneventfully since 1921 then died unexpectedly, after surgery, in May 1936. Thomas began his remarks by saying that he was initially opposed to the committee but came around after seeing what was taking place in Nazi recruiting camps in his home state. Thomas would have done well to stop there. But he couldn't resist going on to say that Communists were a greater threat to America than Nazis, repeating claims he had made on the House floor back in March: "They are right in our own Government. They control certain WPA projects."

This accusation angered Boileau, who responded that "the danger of writing a resolution as broad as this certainly is apparent," after hearing what Thomas had to say. Boileau was applauded when he went on to predict that were Thomas chosen to serve on the committee, "you will have from him an effort to investigate the New Deal, as he claims it to be un-American." Their exchange made explicit what supporters of the bill had hoped to downplay: its ultimate objective was undermining the New Deal. When Dies asked him to yield, sensing the mood was shifting against the bill, Boileau refused, saying, "I am very sorry, I cannot," then offered what would be a prophetic warning: "If we pass this resolution, we will in effect be saying to American citizens, 'Be careful! Be careful with whom you associate, and be careful where you go, because a handful of Members of Congress . . . will hold you before the American people as enemies of our great democracy. They will call you unpatriotic, and it will take you the rest of your life to convince the American people that you are really patriotic."

John Coffee, Democrat of Washington State, also spoke for fellow progressives, calling the proposed investigative committee "a smelling expedition aimed at liberal organizations in the United States." Coffee wanted to know "who is going to define un-American?" And he sketched out a fairly accurate picture of what would ensue if the resolution passed: "Why establish a committee, the chairman and members of which can march into your State and into mine, sit around a table surrounded by newspaper reporters and motion-picture photographers, and receive endless publicity designed to mitigate or curtail all independent thinking?" Coffee also acknowledged what everyone there well knew: the ranks of loyal New Deal supporters in the House had thinned, as many Democrats were now turning against the president's agenda: "Some of the men who came here as liberals, elected by the common people on the representation that they were going to fight for the liberal cause, have now become tired and exhausted." Support for the bill was clearly a reflection of the growing reluctance to advance a progressive agenda.

Members of Congress had their eyes on the calendar as well as the clock. As the time allocated for debate neared its end, John Cochran, Democrat of Missouri, pointed out a problem confronting those who in a few months would be facing primaries and then voters in the midterm elections in November. Given the attention to the bill in the press, he said, "I do not want to be accused of refusing to vote for legislation to investigate un-American activities." He wasn't wrong in fearing that; less than two months later, Maverick, facing a primary challenger, was narrowly defeated and lost his seat in Congress. Some may well have wanted to oppose a president still wildly popular in their districts without voting against Roosevelt's legislative agenda. Who better to give Roosevelt a black eye than the young upstart from Texas who had threatened to punch Oscar De Priest in the jaw?

As time ran out, opponents of the bill scrambled, to no avail, to invoke parliamentary procedures to amend it. But once Martin Dies had spoken the magic words—"Mr. Speaker, I move the previous question on the amendment and the resolution to final passage"—the rules, Bankhead explained, would not allow for that. A vote was called, but so few members of Congress had bothered to listen to the debate that there wasn't a quorum. More members were ushered into the House Chamber and the vote finally taken. The bill, one of the most consequential in the history of civil liberties in the country, es-tablishing a House committee to investigate un-American activities (one that would not be dissolved until 1975), comfortably passed on May 26, 1938, with a vote of 191–41. Samuel Dickstein, who until this point had not said a word (and may have been told not to), asked Bankhead for three minutes to address his colleagues. "Not at this juncture," he was told. The House turned to its next item of business, the World Poultry Congress, to be held in Cleveland.

Hazel Huffman, testifying before the
House Un-American Activities Committee, 1938.

CHAPTER NINE

The Dies Committee
v. the Federal Theatre

W̶e have four thousand American Nazis goose-stepping in Andover, New Jersey, three weeks before the House voted to authorize the Dies Committee, to thank for the demise of the Federal Theatre. Or perhaps responsibility should be shared with the doctors who failed to save Randolph Perkins's life at Georgetown Hospital, where the moderate New Jersey congressman died of a kidney infection. Had Perkins survived, J. Parnell Thomas would not have been chosen in a special election to succeed him. And had those American admirers of Hitler not paraded in Thomas's backyard, the congressman might not have changed his mind and supported the creation of the special committee. If blame were truly to be apportioned, it would also include the WPA for first silencing and then failing to defend Hallie Flanagan; Communists within the Federal Theatre who thought it was fine to distribute their literature during working hours; the Federal Theatre itself for failing to lobby early or hard enough in its own defense; and a mainstream press more interested in selling papers than in investigating unsubstantiated claims. It would also have to include members of the House and Senate, and President Roosevelt, all of whom officially signed off on the program's demise. But it was Thomas, working independently, who first targeted and privately investigated the Federal Theatre. Without his efforts it would not have ended when it did.

Eager to join the Dies Committee, Thomas sought out Senate Minority Leader Bertrand Snell and asked that his name be put forward. Snell, an anti–New Dealer and former chair of the Rules Committee, took the measure of his ambitious colleague—whose attack on New Deal spending on propaganda had made the pages of *The New York Times* back in March—and did so. When in early June, William Bankhead named the seven-man committee, Thomas was included as one of its two Republican members. Thomas's initial investigation of the Federal Theatre depended, in turn, on two key players: one was a former New York City policeman and investigator, Stephen Birmingham; the other, a registered nurse from Ohio named Hazel Huffman, who had briefly worked for the WPA.

Like the proverbial dog chasing a bus that finally caught up with it, Martin Dies found himself at a loss how to proceed once put in charge of the special committee. His young aide, Robert Stripling, who volunteered to serve unpaid as secretary to the committee, recalled in an interview a half century later that "he and Dies stumbled into it, and did not at first know what they were doing." In the immediate aftermath of the vote, the House leadership seems to have had some misgivings about Dies. A concerned John McCormack sent Bankhead a letter about how he thought Dies should proceed. Bankhead forwarded it to Dies, who sent back a contrite note reassuring Bankhead, "I announced that our committee was not going to be a three-ring circus," and insisting that he was "not seeking publicity": "I have avoided the press and shall strive to conduct an investigation that will reflect credit upon you and the House of Representatives." Unpersuaded, the House leadership handcuffed the investigation; Dies, who had refused to give a dollar amount when challenged to do so during the debate, then asked for $100,000 to cover the cost of a team of investigators and staff. When the authorization was approved by the House Committee on Accounts, it was for only $25,000. Dies would have to make do with even less than the modest sum that the McCormack-Dickstein Committee had been given for an investigation of similar duration.

Dies initially imagined that he would employ a dozen or more skilled investigators who would fan out across the country. His limited budget would not allow for that, but the language of the resolution specified that he could also draw, at no additional expense, on the experienced personnel of the Department of Justice, the FBI, and even the WPA: "The head of each executive department is hereby requested to detail to said special committee such number of legal and expert assistants and investigators as said committee may from time to time deem necessary." When pressed by reporters three weeks after the vote about what progress his committee was making, he assured them that while it would take until August to gather everything that was needed, "agents of the committee, including the G-men and operatives of other Federal investigating units, will go into the field immediately," and "their reports will largely determine the course the investigation will take." He envisioned the hearings touring nationally, moving from city to city, beginning on the West Coast and ending back East.

Dies asked for a dozen additional investigators from the executive branch, but his requests were stonewalled, then rejected. Over the ensuing weeks he would appeal unsuccessfully to the president, and then to the press, and complained bitterly about it. He managed to place six investigators in the field, three of whom he soon had to dismiss, including Edward Sullivan, who was fired after the press reported that he had previously been engaged in labor espionage and involved in antisemitic organizations. Sullivan had been sent to California to look into unionization there, as well as Communist influence in Hollywood. John Metcalfe, who as a journalist had investigated the Bund for the Chicago *Daily Times*, would focus on Nazis in the Midwest. Chester Howe, who had worked on passport fraud for Immigration Services, was dispatched to Detroit to look into Communist support for sit-down strikers. Stephen Birmingham, the former policeman who had served as an investigator for the McCormack-Dickstein Committee (and before that in military intelligence during World War I), covered New York City.

The clock was running. At the beginning of July, with his report to Congress due in six months, Dies had little to tell the press. He was no longer sure that his committee would tour, telling the *Austin Statesman* that he hoped to begin hearings in Washington in early August and that the committee "would then decide whether to send a subcommittee or go as a body to the West Coast." Perhaps sensing that Dies had no real plan, J. Parnell Thomas went rogue. On July 26 he announced that he had been holding what he called his own "informal hearings" since early July at the Federal Court Building in New York City. Stealing the headlines from Dies, he revealed that the committee would be going after the Federal Theatre. The news came as a surprise to Hallie Flanagan, and may have to Martin Dies as well. Parnell said that he would call on Flanagan "to answer questions concerning alleged Communist activities of the project." Thomas went on to allege that "the Federal Theatre Project not only is serving as a branch of the communistic organization but also is one more link in the vast and unparalleled New Deal propaganda machine," that it "is infested with radicals from top to bottom," and that "practically every play presented under the auspices of the project [is] either centered on a plot sympathetic to the cause of communism or serves as a vehicle for the propagation of New Deal theories." He went into considerable detail, including the fabricated claim that Flanagan had written *Can You Hear Their Voices?* while in the Soviet Union. The *San Francisco Examiner* declared that Thomas was "on the war path." *The New York Times*, which gave extensive coverage to these accusations, noted that it had tried, and failed, to reach Flanagan. The next day, responding from her office in Washington, Flanagan, who had heard nothing of these secretive hearings, told the press that she would "be glad to answer any questions" and that some of what was reported was "obviously absurd." Thomas—and Dies—must have noted to their satisfaction, and perhaps surprise, that the official response was so tepid.

A few days later, Dies, eager to show that he was still in charge, reached out to the press, sharing with a friendly reporter at *The Hartford Courant* that he was "sitting on a briefcase supposed to contain sworn confessions by former officials of the German American Bund" showing "how the Hitler Bunders got their money from abroad and what they did domestically to promote the Nazi cause." He also intimated that he was in possession of a confession by "a former official of the Communist Party . . . relating how domestic Communist policies were guided from abroad," which "gives the ins and outs of subtle Communist penetration into patriotic liberal organizations." The

New York Herald Tribune reported on July 30 that while Dies had no intention of subpoenaing Nazi and Communist leaders, he claimed that he had enough evidence "without their testimony." Dies made clear that he was not "going to let cranks come on and make this a smear session. . . . This will be no three-ring circus."

A week before the hearings began on August 12, Dies finally landed his front-page headline in *The New York Times*—"Dies Opens War on Propagandists"—after serving a subpoena on George Sylvester Viereck, a Nazi propagandist, to testify before his committee on August 18. Dies had done so before Viereck could set sail for Germany, having learned of his plans to meet with Hitler "in his mountain retreat." After initially threatening to ignore the subpoena, Viereck canceled his trip and agreed to appear before the Dies Committee. Ten days later Dies reversed course and decided to let Viereck depart the country; they had arrived at a "gentlemen's agreement" allowing Viereck to appear before the committee on his return in October. He did return to America, but Dies never asked him to testify. Viereck, it later emerged, had been on the German government payroll since Hitler took power in 1933 and was precisely the kind of individual that Dies should have been investigating. Had Dies done so, he might have exposed a propagandist secretly in the employ of the German Foreign Office. Let off the hook, Viereck would soon enlist senators and congressmen, including Hamilton Fish, "to take propaganda from the Hitler government . . . and deliver it in Congress in floor speeches. Then he'd use their offices' franking privileges to get thousands, in some cases millions, of reprints of this Nazi propaganda" to mail out nationwide. It wasn't until 1942 that these activities were exposed by the Department of Justice; Viereck was convicted for violating the Foreign Agents Registration Act and imprisoned until 1947.

While declaring war on Nazi propagandists (and then ignoring them) was a good way to get headlines, as the first day of his committee hearings approached, Dies remained unsure whom to target. A day after that Viereck story ran, Dies received a letter from Hallie Flanagan, volunteering to testify on August 11, when she and her regional directors would all be in Washington. It's unclear at this point whether Dies planned to pursue the Federal Theatre very aggressively; he wrote back letting her know that she wouldn't be needed anytime soon, as the committee had a "heavy schedule of witnesses." The day before the hearings opened, Thomas kept the pressure on, telling the *Chicago Tribune* that "he would demand before the committee that the Federal Theatre Project be closed pending a house cleaning."

Flanagan and those higher up at the WPA weren't particularly concerned. They had already weathered similar attacks in April 1936, when Harry Hopkins appeared before the House Appropriations Committee and deflected accusations that the Federal Theatre had been staging propagandistic drama. Hopkins asked if they had seen any of the plays, especially the Living Newspaper *Triple-A Plowed Under*. They had not. He then patiently explained that "a play is subject to many opinions," and what really mattered was whether it is "good theater, is it artistic, is it well done," then followed that up by reading into the record high praise for the project's early productions from leading theater critics. That blunted their attack, and the members of the Appropriations Committee turned to other concerns. Later that month, Pennsylvania senator James Davis's attack on Flanagan and her early writing, as well as on her project's use of "American money to spread communistic propaganda in this country, through the theatre," similarly failed to gain traction. Flanagan and her superiors took away precisely the wrong message from this: the mud that was flung wouldn't stick. For their part, critics in Congress, based on this dry run, had learned not only which lines of attack on the Federal Theatre worked and which didn't, but also that it was best to deny opponents a chance to defend themselves.

What would soon turn into a three-ring circus opened at the Old Congressional Building in Washington on Friday, August 12, 1938. It began, however, with Dies offering a statesmanlike speech about how he planned to run things:

> The Chair wishes to reiterate what he has stated many times— namely, that this committee is determined to conduct its investigation upon a dignified plane and to adopt and maintain throughout the course of the hearings a judicial attitude. . . . We shall be fair and impartial at all times and treat every witness with fairness and courtesy. . . . This committee will not permit any "character assassination" or any "smearing" of innocent people. We wish to caution witnesses that reckless charges must not be made against any individual or organization. The Chair wishes to make it plain that this committee is not "after anyone." All that we are concerned with is the ascertainment of the truth, whatever it is. . . . Statements and charges unsupported by facts have no evidentiary value and only tend to confuse the issue. It is easy to "smear" someone's name or reputation by unsupported charges or an unjustified attack, but it is difficult to repair the damage that has been

done. . . . The utmost care, therefore, must be observed to distinguish clearly between what is obviously un-American and what is no more or less than an honest difference of opinion with respect to some economic, political, or social question.

Over the next four months every one of these promises would be spectacularly and repeatedly broken. Reputations would be smeared, impartiality abandoned, hearsay evidence accepted as fact, and those with honest differences of opinion branded un-American.

Dies burned through his best witnesses in the first few days. On day one his investigator John Metcalfe, who was also his main witness, declared that there were a half million Nazi sympathizers in America. But in the absence of any deeper digging into the Bund's activities, or Viereck's, the Dies Committee was pretty much done with Nazis. Metcalfe would sporadically return in the ensuing months, his visits best explained by what Robert Stripling later told Dies's biographer: whenever "there was a hearing on the Bund or the Silver Shirts," Dies would have breakfast at the Mayflower Hotel with the "bagman" for Jewish organizations. In exchange for a cash payoff, Stripling explained, "if they wanted six hours of hearings, they got six hours of hearings."

On day two of the hearings Dies pivoted to Communism. His main witness was John Frey of the American Federation of Labor (AFL), who alleged over the course of the next three days of testimony that the Civil Liberties Committee in the Senate, chaired by the progressive Senator Robert La Follette, Jr., had Communist connections and that his archenemy John Lewis's Congress of Industrial Organizations (CIO) had a Communist "tinge." Frey named, without proof, many names—both individuals and organizations. Dies could not have been happy with the limited media coverage of these opening sessions, especially because in these dog days of August there was little other domestic political news. Congress had adjourned, its members heading home from the sweltering capital to campaign for reelection (which he, running unopposed in the Democratic primary, didn't have to do), and Roosevelt summering in Warm Springs, Georgia. Dies had the Washington-based press to himself, but reporters covering the hearings were beginning to lose interest. Nearly a week in, neither *The Washington Post* nor *The New York Times* bothered running stories.

Hazel Huffman was sworn in on Friday, August 19. Her testimony marked a turning point in Martin Dies's fortunes, for it triggered enormous media attention—attention that grew exponentially in the weeks and months that followed. Birmingham, the investigator in New York who had been working closely with Thomas, wrote to Dies in advance to say that he had focused his investigations on the Federal Theatre and was planning to send eight witnesses to the hearings: "This many seem like a lot . . . but I have figured this being a Governmental agency, and the Committee is practically making charges against the different executives in the Project, that we should be fully covered." Huffman, who was key to his investigation, topped the list, along with a half dozen or so disgruntled Federal Theatre employees. A few of them were fiercely anti-Communist, others upset about the influence on the project of the Workers Alliance, a leftist labor union which, according to Henry Frank, who testified briefly, was passing out literature, such as the circular he had been handed a day or so earlier declaring that the "Dies Committee, which made a farcical whitewash of the inquiry into naziism, continues its red-baiting witch hunt, which has as its purpose to smash Roosevelt, labor, the New Deal, and the Workers Alliance." Birmingham was on the fence about including one last witness, Sally Saunders. He wrote to Dies that Thomas already had a copy of her statement, and that he should "see what you think about using it, and advise me as to bringing her down to Washington."

Dies asked Thomas to lead the questioning of Huffman, and he was interrupted almost immediately by Starnes. Having some inkling of what was in store, Starnes insisted that Huffman's testimony "be restricted to Communism" and to what is "un-American or subversive." But the well-prepared and supremely confident Huffman bulldozed her way past his objections, insisting that to "correct a disease we must first know what is causing it," and to that end felt justified in attacking Flanagan herself: "If there is any doubt left as to Mrs. Flanagan's active participation and interest in things communistic, let me try to remove that doubt." She proceeded to read incriminating passages cherry-picked from Flanagan's *Can You Hear Their Voices?*, taking turns with Thomas, who had his copy open to pre-marked pages as well. Starnes, still disturbed with where this was heading, interrupted their performance and asked whether it was Huffman's contention that Flanagan was a Communist. Huffman was unable to back up her accusation with hard evidence. Much hung in the balance. "I have never seen a [Communist Party] card bearing her name," she acknowledged, "but I can prove Mrs. Flanagan was an active participant in Communist activity, and that her Communist sympathies, tendencies, and methods of organization are being used in the Federal Theater Project." When a wavering Starnes then asked, "Have these theater projects been used to spread Communistic propaganda?" Huffman answered, "That is what I intend to prove conclusively," and without further interruption—she clearly didn't like being challenged—she took the committee through one play after another, twenty-six in all, to show that cumulatively and collectively they revealed how the Federal Theatre disseminated Communist propaganda. *How Long, Brethren?* had included "Negro songs of protest," some of which had first appeared in the Communist *New Masses*. *Revolt of the Beavers* had tried to inculcate Communist beliefs in young children. *The Case of Philip Lawrence* had referred to "Negro discrimination." *One Third of a Nation* had been about "social housing." *Medicine* promoted socialized health care. *Power* had been celebrated for causing private utility companies "headaches." *Professor Mamlock* had unmasked "ugly fascism," as had Sinclair Lewis's *It Can't Happen Here*, which was "anti-Fascist in the extreme." Progressive, integrationist, anti-corporation, liberal, anti-fascist—to Huffman it all amounted to the same thing: Communism.

Until now Dies had sat quietly, listening and watching as the chain-smoking Huffman, her elbows firmly planted on the table, took command of the room. She was physically unprepossessing—*The Boston Globe* described her as "matronly"—her simple dress belied by a brooch of a large spider, which seemed to be crawling across her body. Everything she had to say was unchallenged hearsay, with a bit of character assassination thrown in. But it was enthralling. Rather than restore his promised guidelines, Dies began to inject himself into the flow, underscoring and reshaping her testimony into material that reporters could use. When Huffman concluded that the plays were "Communist activity," Dies chimed in, "I do not see how they could be any more so." And when Huffman described a scene from Flanagan's *Can You Hear Their Voices?* in which a drunken congressman appears, Dies wondered aloud whether that offending scene "had anything to do" with Flanagan's "promotion" to head the Federal Theatre.

Whenever Huffman steered off course, complaining for example about mismanagement in the Federal Theatre, Dies gently nudged her back: "We do not want to go too far afield here. It is not our function to investigate . . . inefficiency, or alleged mismanagement on the part of the WPA. Do you want to tie that definitely with Communist activities?" She got the hint, and continued her attack. Soon after, Dies, playing to the press again, rephrased Huffman's lengthy responses into a more digestible sound bite: "It is almost unbelievable to me that they would use public funds of the taxpayers intended for relief, for the purpose of spreading Communism in the United States, or for the purposes on building up the Worker's Alliance?" The next day *The Boston Globe* quoted his leading question (which sounded more like a statement) word for word, as well as her emphatic reply: "Yes, sir."

Toward the end of Huffman's testimony, Dies finally asked a question that had been hanging in the air. "I do not think you have cleared up one point that is confusing," he said. "You were once employed by the Federal Theatre Project?" To which, to his obvious dismay, Huffman replied: "I was never on the Federal Theatre Project payroll. I was employed by the WPA." And she further clarified, "While working for the WPA I was put on the Mail Division at WPA doing analyzing, to analyze the mail. . . . In fact I worked as investigator, although I was classified as receptionist." When she insisted that she was really an investigator, not a clerical worker, he did his best to help her resolve this contradiction: "You were not designated as investigator, but, in fact, that is what you were?" She agreed. When he then asked whether she had worked "undercover," she said yes. It was a nice way of legitimating how someone hired to handle mail was spying on an organization she wasn't employed by. But nobody on the committee was disturbed by that—nor was the press, except for the reporter for the *New York Herald Tribune*, who questioned her independently and wrote on August 20 that "Mrs. Huffman's professional status was not inquired into by the committee, but it was determined privately that she was a registered nurse who had played one part, in the road company of *Grand Hotel*, with one night on Broadway." Nor did anyone ask Huffman whether she was illegally employed by the WPA, since only one member of a household could be on relief, and her husband, Seymour Revzin, who would testify after her, already worked for the Federal Theatre. Moreover, Huffman's boast that she represented a nine-hundred-strong organization that nobody had ever heard of, that she was "secretary on relief status of professional employees of the New York Federal Theatre Project"—a group that, as she admitted, had no membership list, dues, or records—was also accepted without question. Left unchallenged, Huffman had come across as the perfect witness: forceful, assured, deferential to the men who questioned her, encyclopedic in her recollections, and exceptionally well prepared.

According to Philip Barber, who had headed up the New York Unit, Hallie Flanagan had only herself to blame. Huffman had come "vaguely over from the WPA administrative headquarters" and asked to be put in charge of the mail room, "which was enough," Barber later recalled, "to make me suspicious." When he turned her down, Huffman went directly to Flanagan, saying "she only wished she could work for her, that she was sure she could handle the mail," and "she'd always be there, a person she could rely on." Despite the warnings of Barber and his assistant Walter Hart that "she was putting a rattlesnake in with her," Flanagan hired her, telling them (in Barber's words) that Huffman had said "the loveliest, sweetest things. She was so nice. I like her so much." Barber wasn't surprised when Huffman quit six weeks after she was hired by Flanagan: "It's not that she learned so much in that position. It's that having had that position, she could say anything, and they would assume that she had learned it." Huffman's congressional testimony could not have come as a surprise to Flanagan. Two years earlier she recounted in a letter to her husband how a member of her staff requested that Huffman be dismissed, which Flanagan initially refused to do. Flanagan was then shown "an affidavit" from Huffman, "made to the Hearst press (she is rumored to have received $1000 for it), that she had opened my mail for 3 months and found it 'incendiary, revolutionary, and seditious.'" Flanagan had concluded at the time that Huffman "was clearly a stool pigeon."

What motivated Huffman remains unclear. But she left the hearings proud of what she had accomplished. She soon began writing an essay, most of it consisting of correspondence and documents, with the odd title "Why Throw the Baby Out the Window." In it, Huffman writes: "There is little question in my mind that in the event the Federal Theatre Project closes down I shall be blamed! . . . Any credit given me for having been instrumental in bringing the investigation about I am willing to accept." When Dies read the headlines about Huffman's testimony, he found that they far exceeded expectations: *The Washington Post* led with "WPA Theater Run by Reds, Inquiry Told." *The Boston Globe*: "Nurse Says Reds Dominate Federal Theatre Project." *The Baltimore Sun*: "Says Radicals Dominate WPA Theater Unit." The *Los Angeles Times*: "Reds Sway in Theater Project Told." *The New York Sun*: "Secretary of N.Y. Actors' Relief Group Tells House 'Hallie Is Communist.'" *The Hartford Courant*: "Dies Is Told WPA Theater Red Infested." And the down-market *New York Journal-American* went with the more sensational "Reds Urged 'Mixed Date' Blonde Tells Dies Probers."

The "blonde" in that last headline was Sally Saunders. Dies had told Birmingham to bring her along too, and she testified early Saturday morning. Pleased with how things were going, Dies decided to steer into the treacherous waters of race, hoping to insinuate that the Federal Theatre's support of racial equality was fundamentally Communist. Saunders had her own agenda, so Dies went out of his way, before she was allowed to say a word, to make clear that his committee was not interested "in the racial question, except insofar as it forms a vital part of Communist teachings, practices, and doctrines," and disingenuously added, "We do not want to do anything that will stir up or increase any hatreds." To his exasperation, Saunders wanted to begin by addressing the Fifteenth Amendment (which had granted Black men the right to vote), and Dies had to remind her that this was neither the time nor place for that. Saunders, who acted with the Federal Theatre, then recounted how she had received a phone call at her lodgings from a Mr. Van Cleve. When she said she didn't know him, he explained that a day earlier, during a rehearsal break for a show they were both in, *Sing for Your Supper*, he had sketched her portrait. Saunders suddenly remembered that a "Negro" had done so. At first she thought that someone was playing a practical joke on her, then grew "very angry" that a Black man had dared to call and ask her out. Dies wanted to know whether she had reported Van Cleve to her supervisor after "he asked permission to make a date with you." Saunders said that she had, only to have Mr. Hecht, who was in charge, tell her that Van Cleve had "had just as much right to life, liberty, and pursuit of happiness as you have."

Saunders immediately requested a transfer from the show, which was granted. Unwilling to stop there, she then reported "the matter through a personal friend to Senator Pat Harrison," who represented her home state of Mississippi. The senator would understand what this was about: a Black man hitting on a White woman. Many had been lynched for less. After Saunders was finally coaxed into saying what Dies had brought her to the hearing to declare—that "social equality and race merging" was part of the policy of the Workers Alliance involved in the Federal Theatre—the committee was done with her, and Saunders was thanked for her testimony. Dies chose not to delve further into what Saunders had shared with Birmingham: "The unvarnished truth," she told him, is "that I could not work with negroes because of odor which seems part of their race. . . . On my last tour with *Post Road* my roommate, Betty Brown Widmer, or Manager, William Riley, could testify to the fact that if a negress did my laundry, it had to air a week before I could wear it." Saunders added that a "mutual friend of my father and Senator Pat Harrison wishes to give the story to the newspapers, and when he does a wave of revulsion will sweep the country."

The first week of the committee hearings set Martin Dies on a new and unfamiliar path, so extraordinary that social scientists would soon be scrambling to explain his growing influence on domestic politics, as pollsters tried to register his popularity and seismic impact. Looking back today, when so much of what Dies introduced has become normalized in American politics, it is hard to fathom how unprecedented it once was. Much of Dies's success that summer had to do with his deft handling of the media. He was determined to play to the press, and through it the nation, by dispensing with executive sessions and barring the general public from his hearings. The press alone would be his audience. Dies also recognized that he had to keep reporters and photographers entertained, and relieved the inevitable tedium of covering hearings with stunts like having his young son Tommy come up and light his cigar or wield his gavel, photographs of which started accompanying stories. There was, by now, a deep-seated bias in the press against the New Deal; Harold Ickes had estimated that 85 percent of American papers were against it, and Dies depended on this. Dies also guessed—as it turned out, correctly—that as long as he kept a fresh stream of accusations coming, this press wouldn't have time to investigate unsupported allegations, and that the handful of corrections or objections that were newsworthy would be buried in the back pages.

The courtroom reporters who almost universally gave Dies glowing coverage (further amplified by headline writers), nonetheless admitted, when polled, that the hearings were being conducted unfairly. In late October 1938, a pair of columnists for the *New York Daily News*, John O'Donnell and Doris Fleeson (at the public suggestion of President Roosevelt, who thought it would make a "swell story"), canvassed these journalists and reported that eleven of the eighteen writers covering the hearings on a daily basis (including four who worked for conservative big-city papers) thought that the hearings were unfair. Only two thought that the hearings were conducted in a fair way, another two as fair as other congressional hearings had been, and the other three were noncommittal. Dies didn't much care about the hostile accounts, read by comparatively few, that began to appear in *The New Republic*, *The Nation*, or *The Daily Worker*; for him, these leftist mouthpieces only confirmed his arguments about growing Communist influence. His committee was rewarded, it was soon tabulated, with "more than five hundred column-inches of space in *The New*

York Times alone during the months of August and September 1938, and many of the major national dailies gave the hearings comparable space.

The restraints that the McCormack investigation had carefully put in place to protect time-honored rights—allowing witnesses to have lawyers present, rejecting evidence that would not be accepted in a court of law, first interviewing witnesses privately—were abandoned from the start. Dies had a canny sense of where American democracy's guardrails were flimsiest, and chairing a special committee allowed him to shatter these protections, and violate rights, in ways that none had dared do before. When Dies saw that administration officials did not push back on obvious falsehoods and insinuations—they badly underestimated him, and their misguided strategy was to let things blow over—it gave him confidence to press even further. He also saw that his colleagues in the House remained silent when he trampled on every promise he had made to them about how the hearings would be conducted. It helped that he was a charmer and a great talker, adept at making himself the aggrieved party. He also knew better than to apologize when he was in the wrong. And unlike most politicians, Dies wasn't afraid of hurting his own ratings if he could damage the reputations of those he was vilifying.

He quickly got behind Thomas's assault on the Federal Theatre, in part because it was a sure way of meeting Vice President Garner's goals of frustrating Roosevelt's agenda, in part because he saw how easy it was to garner headlines by attacking progressive plays as "un-American." Martin Dies would harden into an ardent anti-Communist in the years to come, but in the summer of 1938 he wasn't one yet. He was, rather, an opportunistic, America-first, anti-immigrant, anti-labor, racist politician with few scruples, for whom power and popularity mattered more than ideology. The Federal Theatre embodied pretty much everything he despised: unions, liberals, foreigners, intellectuals, and promoters of racial equality. It wanted to change America, and he was stubbornly resistant to those changes, especially when it came to treating Blacks as equals. In combating the forces of change—driven by the New Deal and embodied in play after Federal Theatre play—the elastic term "Communist" proved to be the best of all catchphrases, one through which he could persecute anyone and anything he deemed "un-American." Assessing the public response to the testimony of Huffman and Saunders, he saw that scaring people (your children are being indoctrinated and Black men want to sleep with your daughters) was a lot more effective than the arduous and consensus-building business of legislating. What the conservative commentator Jeane J. Kirkpatrick later said about Senator Joseph McCarthy's war on Communism was even more true of Dies's battle with Flanagan: McCarthyism was not so much about Communism as it was a struggle for "jurisdiction over the symbolic environment. . . . What was at issue was who would serve as the arbiter of culture and whose narrative would prevail."

In the weeks following Huffman's testimony, Dies, still facing no significant pushback from the press or WPA officials, went on the offensive. He used a national radio address on the evening of August 29 to attack the Federal Theatre, whose plays, he said, were threatening American values and institutions: "I wish I had time to read some of the excerpts from these plays," he told listeners: "They attack the capitalistic system and ridicule the government of the United States. These plays, together with Communist literature and pamphlets which were distributed on the project and exhibited on the bulletin boards, corroborate the testimony of numerous witnesses to the effect that Communism is playing no small part in the activities of the Federal Theatre Project."

Employees of the Federal Theatre grew increasingly alarmed by the WPA's inexplicable silence. Emmet Lavery spoke for many when he wrote to Flanagan on September 2 that "day after day the hearsay testimony floods the newspapers of the country, so that slander and libel thrive on the simple fact of their constant repetition and our administration does nothing." "What," he asked her, "is the WPA going to do?" As it turned out, very little. J. Parnell Thomas took to the radio ten days later, declaring that the Federal Theatre was "a hotbed of un-American activities" and accusing Flanagan of harboring Communist sympathies. Finally, on September 17, Flanagan's immediate superior in the WPA, Ellen Woodward, wrote to Dies all but insisting that the national directors of the theater and writers projects be invited to testify. Flanagan and her staff began assembling a detailed two-hundred-page brief. Flanagan also requested that a public relations expert be assigned to draw on this evidence and feed the press factual corrections. This idea was rejected, as were her efforts to persuade higher-ups to let her bring a production of *Prologue to Glory*, a story of young Abe Lincoln sure to please politicians, to Washington. Dies waited until October 6 to let Flanagan know that she would be called to testify, though he didn't know when that might be. He had more important business in hand: using the committee hearings to tarnish the reputation of Roosevelt-backed politicians, especially Michigan governor Frank Murphy. Still, when he had the chance, Dies kept up the drumbeat of attacks on the WPA, telling the *New*

York Journal-American on October 19, 1938, that the theater and writers' projects were "doing more to spread Communist propaganda than the Communist Party itself."

Harold Ickes, who thought Dies "wants the stage all to himself," had prepared a scathing counterattack on the committee chair, a speech titled "Playing with Loaded Dies," which Roosevelt initially approved but then, right before it was to be given, forbade Ickes from delivering. Finally, two weeks before the midterm elections, with a massive defeat for progressive Democrats looming, the president publicly attacked the Dies Committee, declaring that it had "made no effort to get at the truth, either by calling for facts to support mere personal opinion or by allowing facts and personal opinion on the other side." He also slammed its "flagrantly unfair and un-American attempt to influence an election." But the rebuke came too late, and Dies knew it. He counterpunched, hard, the press reporting that in "open defiance of President Roosevelt, Chairman Dies . . . yesterday declared that the President was himself guilty of 'violating the fundamental principle of Americanism.'" The "lanky Texan . . . angrily and sarcastically reminded the President of the recent so-called 'purge' of conservative Democrats," and in response to Roosevelt's charge that his committee was "'flagrantly unfair,'" Dies said that "'the president had not read the hearings record' and was 'grossly misinformed.'"

Smelling blood, Thomas weighed in as well, dropping the pretense that the investigation was really about exposing un-American theater, saying that "the President is annoyed and angry because most of the evidence unearthed by the Dies Committee shows a definite tie-up between the New Deal and the Communist Party." The loyal New Dealers on the committee, Arthur Healey and Dempsey, were shocked and called for the increasingly politicized hearings to be halted until after the midterm elections. Dies refused. Dempsey threatened to resign, but didn't. After this Roosevelt told Ickes that he was confident that Dies would not be able to secure more funding to continue his committee and thwart them. Ickes disagreed, telling Roosevelt that the Texan's "chief object in life is to smear the Administration, incidental of course to getting publicity for himself. Some people now feel that no one can control Dies." He thought it "not unlikely that, as the result of [Dies's] efforts, a Communist scare will be fomented and kept fanned in this country, following which some man on horseback may arise to 'protect' us against the fancied danger."

An August 1938 Gallup poll had indicated that a majority of Americans wanted Roosevelt to pursue more conservative policies, and in the ensuing midterm elections the president's party suffered serious losses (seventy-two seats in the House, eight in the Senate, and nine governorships, including Frank Murphy's). Dies immediately began calling for the renewal of his committee, asking during an Armistice Day speech for $200,000 to $300,000 to continue his work, the following day upping that figure, with the *Chicago Tribune* reporting that Dies was now asking for a million dollars to look into "charges of corruption and graft" in relief spending. Dies began calling for the resignations of Roosevelt's most trusted administrators, Harold Ickes, Frances Perkins, and Harry Hopkins, whom he "held responsible for the WPA's infestation with communists and other radicals." Had the WPA flexed its muscles back in August and demanded that Hallie Flanagan immediately be allowed to refute Hazel Huffman's outrageous testimony, the outcome might well have been different. But in the ensuing months Dies had grown wildly popular. Fellow Texan Sam Rayburn (who had recently been returned to office with 97.9

percent of the vote) ruefully acknowledged that "Martin Dies could beat me right now in my own district."

When Hallie Flanagan testified on December 6, she more than held her own, *Variety* awarding her "the first round" in her "skirmish" with the Dies Committee. But that was no longer enough. Soon after she and Dies debated the place of theater in American democracy, Gallup released the results of its national poll. Americans wanted the Dies show renewed for another season: a significant majority—three quarters of Americans who had heard of the much publicized work of the Dies Committee—supported its ongoing investigations. Two months later, twenty thousand supporters of Hitler gathered under giant swastikas at an antisemitic and anti-Communist rally in Madison Square Garden in New York, where President Roosevelt was mocked as "Franklin Rosenfeld," the crowd "gave a great ovation to Father Charles E. Coughlin, of Detroit, Adolf Hitler, and Benito Mussolini," and "words of praise were voiced" as well for Martin Dies.

It received scant coverage, but the day after Flanagan testified, Hazel Huffman was once again invited to testify. The committee had wisely rejected the plan Huffman had concocted to appear by surprise at the previous day's hearing and personally accuse Flanagan again and again, forcing the head of the Federal Theatre to admit to or deny each accusation. Martin Dies didn't even bother showing up for Huffman's testimony that day. He went off to New York City to deliver a speech at the Biltmore Hotel, attended, apparently to Dies's surprise, by the American Nazi leader Fritz Kuhn. *The New York Times* reported that Dies had wanted to use the speech to attack "administration critics and journalists 'who secretly are in sympathy with Russia,'" but with a Nazi and his entourage in the room, he improvised, condemning "the treatment of Jews in Germany," but then called upon "the government to condemn the massacre of millions of Christians in Russia and Spain."

Representative Dempsey, who until now had been restrained and had said almost nothing in defense of Woodward and Flanagan, turned prosecutorial and deftly took Hazel Huffman's claims apart. He got her to admit that it was not a crime in America to be a member of the Communist Party, then turned to the allegedly un-American plays she had cited, especially *Power*, to underscore the difference between communistic and propagandistic. "What is there in *Power*," he asked, "that is Communistic? . . . Can you point to a single thing in *Power* that outstanding and splendid members in Congress have not made reference to in connection with Government ownership?" Huffman, caught off guard by this unexpected attack, said that she really couldn't remember the play, but Dempsey would have none of that, pointing out that it was one that she had "complained about very bitterly," and again demanded to know what was communistic about it. When Huffman responded that *Power* was anti-capital, anti-fascist, and antiwar, Dempsey replied: "Do you charge the men and women of America who thoroughly believe that war is a thing that should not occur under any condition—I have received thousands of letters from people who do not believe in war—and are we to consider them un-American because of that opinion?" Huffman replied that antiwar protesters were really "pro-Soviet," but Dempsey rejected that too, adding that he was unaware of "any revolutionary theater here in the United States." When Huffman insisted on her greater authority to speak about theater, Dempsey countered with a surprising revelation: "The theater is my hobby and I have been attending as many theaters as it is possible for me to do, and at one time I had control of the Brighton Beach Theater of New York. I know theatrical people and I know writers. And I am afraid that this committee is going rather far afield in permitting some of this testimony to go in; because certainly it is far beyond the scope authorized by Congress."

Huffman couldn't believe where this was heading and demanded to know whether Dempsey would like to say "for the record" how he would distinguish a propagandistic play from a Communist one. Dempsey brushed this off and rebuked Huffman, informing her once again that she was confusing propagandistic plays with communistic ones. Huffman wanted to continue their back-and-forth, offer more examples, but Dempsey was done with her, as was the committee, and the next witness was called. While their heated exchange failed to make the news, fixated as the media was on the attention-grabbing Martin Dies, it offered a glimpse into what might have been had Dempsey, back in August, found the courage to speak out when an unchallenged Huffman had so effectively traduced the Federal Theatre, or even the previous day, when Flanagan could have used the support of a theatergoing member of the committee.

Federal Theatre workers protest congressional efforts to close the project, 1939.

CHAPTER TEN

The End of the
Federal Theatre

L ike a picador deftly wielding a spiked lance, Dies had wounded the Federal Theatre, though it was not his job to kill it. That task would fall to others—with President Roosevelt himself forced to play a reluctant matador, delivering the death blow. Between Flanagan's testimony before the House Un-American Activities Committee in early December 1938 and the last day of June 1939, when the president signed a relief bill eliminating all government funding for the Federal Theatre (which alone of all WPA projects was singled out for elimination), half a year would pass. After that, shows were closed, scripts were put in storage, and thousands of actors, designers, and stagehands would lose their jobs.

Dies had until January 3, 1939, to submit a report. But he understood that his future depended less on what fellow members of Congress thought of it than on the groundswell of public support, and the Gallup poll of December 11 had confirmed that the country was now solidly behind him. So, almost daily, in the days and weeks that followed his clash with Flanagan, he made his case directly to the nation through the press and radio, daring "the President and his leaders to tell the American people exactly where they stand on the question of continuing my investigation." Roosevelt chafed at this, but lacked sufficient leverage, so failed—the press duly reported—to get congressional leaders to terminate Dies's committee.

Surprisingly, given the prominence of the Federal Theatre in the committee's hearings, the official report, which ran to 124 pages, had almost nothing to say about it, aside from a brief paragraph describing how some of its "employees and former employees" testified that unspecified Communist activities had been carried out there "for a long time," including Communist meetings "held on the project during work hours," leading the committee to conclude that "a rather large number" of the project's employees "are either members of the Communist Party" or "sympathetic" to it. That was it. No offending plays were mentioned or testimony quoted. Why provide ammunition for those attacking the biased accusations on which these conclusions were based?

Dies had not fooled his congressional peers, nor did he much care. His fiercest opponents dutifully rose and denounced his findings. Kent Keller of Illinois called Dies's hearings "the most infamously conducted . . . in the history of our country," a "one-man investigation . . . carried on apparently with one principal objective—that of getting publicity for the chairman." John Martin of Colorado went further: "This committee is having the effect of identifying in the public mind New Dealism, liberalism, and labor, with radicalism and Communism. . . . If it keeps on, it will dig more graves for Democrats than for Communists." Their objections were swept aside, and on

February 3, 1939, the Dies Committee was renewed, by a vote of 344–35.

By then, Dies's allies had already begun acting on the next step: slashing WPA funding. On January 13, Clifton A. Woodrum of Virginia, a leading member of the House Appropriations Committee, announced that the "WPA could do several things to reduce expenditures," while Republican John Taber of New York, calling for deep cuts to the program, urged his fellow representatives to read the Dies report and learn about the "un-American activity in which the WPA is engaged." On March 15 a subcommittee of the House Appropriations Committee began hearings on the $1.7 billion Relief Act, at which Woodrum steered the proceedings to Federal One, especially the Federal Theatre. Though the subcommittee uncovered nothing notable, on March 27 the Rules Committee of the House called for an investigation of the WPA by the Appropriations Committee, to report back to Congress "as soon as practicable." Investigators were quickly dispatched to New York, Chicago, and Los Angeles. They had less than three weeks to uncover abuses, and, like the Dies Committee investigators before them, focused their attention on the Federal Theatre.

Even a year earlier it would have been surprising to see Woodrum take such a prominent role in opposing the WPA and targeting the Federal Theatre. Back in 1922 he had narrowly won the Democratic primary over a more conservative opponent, entering the House in 1923 at age thirty-six, where he rose steadily in the ranks, joining the Appropriations Committee in 1929. He had been an avid supporter of Roosevelt from the outset, and rode his coattails in 1936, winning 60 percent of the vote. But the midterm election of 1938 was a wake-up call for Woodrum, who now found himself too liberal for his district; his Republican foe, who had come close to unseating him, was determined to do so in a rematch in 1940. Woodrum hoped to be appointed as a federal judge, or run for the Senate, but Roosevelt passed him over for a judicial appointment, and his path to the Senate was blocked by popular incumbents. Political survival meant turning against the New Deal and its increasingly unpopular relief program.

Woodrum was friends with the un-American Activities Committee member Joe Starnes and shared with Dies a desire to constrain the leftist Workers Alliance. He followed Dies's playbook closely, directing attention to the now vulnerable Federal Theatre, relying on some of the same biased witness testimony, using the smear of Communism, and turning to the press and radio to generate attention. Like Dies, he was disturbed by how the Federal Theatre promoted racial equality, and made much of an investigator's account of several shows in which there was racial mingling, including *Sing for Your Supper*, in which the "colored and white are mixed together" and even "dance together." Woodrum took care not to repeat Dies's mistake of allowing Hallie Flanagan to testify, and ignored her letter to him. A frustrated Flanagan, who saw how things were once again playing out in Congress, bypassed her superiors and shared her letter to Woodrum with the press, in which she categorically denied his accusations and, alluding to how Woodrum had picked up where Dies had left off, condemned "the 'false impression' given to the country by constant repetition of 'so distorted a picture of the project.'"

Woodrum tried his best to pry apart the two strands that held Flanagan's project together: relief and theatrical excellence. He first lambasted the Federal Theatre for employing "ham actors" on worthless and expensive shows, and then, using the all-Black *Swing Mikado* as a key example, attacked the project's success, for that show had made money and delivered that profit directly to the Treasury Department. For Woodrum, this went beyond the intended relief, undermining free enterprise by moving the government into "the field of amusement and entertainment, touring over the country, from place to place, and charging admissions at cut rates in open competition with the theatrical industry," which, he argued, was "going beyond what I think Congress intended." Woodrum also wondered aloud whether the cast of *Swing Mikado* was made up of "colored people that had been picked up and trained" or were truly "theatrical people."

Hoping to forestall even more severe cuts, the WPA announced on June 13, 1939, that the Federal Theatre would slash the number of those employed in its National Service Bureau from 268 to 25, while eliminating 1,500 workers from its New York roster. All the Federal One programs were now shrunk to a total of 5,500 workers, half the number employed two years earlier. That same day Colonel Francis Harrington, an army officer and engineer who in late December had replaced Harry Hopkins (who had been appointed commerce secretary), assured Woodrum's committee that he planned to overhaul "the Federal Theatre Project with a view to improved organization and efficiency." Two days later *The Baltimore Sun* called for the end of the Federal Theatre, noting that abuses had always dogged national theaters, and, echoing Woodrum, argued that the Federal Theatre was set up for relief, not so that "the American government would be the liberal patron and subsidizer of all the arts and of the dramatic arts especially." The Dies playbook, with its fixation on subversive infiltration, had leached so deeply into the culture that even Eleanor Roosevelt, in her published plea to save the Federal Theatre, conceded "that this project is considered dangerous because it may harbor some Communists, but I wonder if Communists occupied in producing plays are not safer than Communists starving to death."

Flanagan had no doubt attended a lot of dispiriting performances in her years as a playgoer, but that was nothing compared with what she endured on the evening of June 16, 1939, when she took a seat in the gallery of the House of Representatives and watched Congress debate the fate of her project. She was spotted by reporters, who described her as looking "red and grim." The young congressman Everett Dirksen of Illinois recognized how much savage comedy and newspaper coverage could be extracted from stringing together the titles of Federal Theatre plays and reading them aloud, punctuated by sarcastic commentary—*A New Kind of Love* ("I wonder what that can be"), *Up in Mabel's Room* ("There's an intriguing title for you"), *A Boudoir Diplomat* ("The State Department might well take note of this"), *Lend Me Your Husband* ("surely adapted to the tempo of modern age"), and *Love 'Em and Leave 'Em* ("a very happy title"). The "more titles he read," the press reported, "the louder and the more heartlessly the House howled." "'If you want this salacious tripe,' Dirksen shouted, 'then vote for it!'"

A few rose to defend the theater project—William Sirovich, Emanuel Celler, and Vito Marcantonio of New York; Adolph Sabath of Illinois; and Mary Norton of New Jersey, the first woman that Democrats had elected to the House, whose proposed amendment that the Federal Theatre be spared was greeted with laughter, then rejected. At that point Flanagan rose and left the gallery. The mood on the floor, the *New York Herald Tribune* reported, was "belligerent" and the "repudiation of the Federal Theatre" was "overwhelming." The vote on the relief bill, which specifically terminated funding for the Federal

Theatre, passed, 373–21. On Saturday, June 17, Woodrum, who was greeted with a three-minute ovation, stood before his peers, basking in his triumph, and piled on, declaring that the Federal Theatre "has produced nothing of merit so far as national productions are concerned." Holding up a copy of *Sing for Your Supper*, he added, "If there is a line in it or a passage that contributes to the cultural or educational benefit of America, I will eat the whole manuscript. . . . It is small, trashy kind of stuff. . . . So we are going out of the theatrical business." Woodrum's words and actions paid off handsomely: he was rewarded with more publicity in the months that followed than at any time in his congressional career, and when he ran for reelection in 1940 he trounced his more conservative opponent.

The last firewall was the Senate. Flanagan, now recognizing that her superiors in the WPA were prepared to abandon her controversial project, no longer kept silent. She appealed to influential voices in the theater and movie worlds, and their response was overwhelmingly supportive. Organizations that had once fought or undermined the Federal Theatre, including Actors' Equity and the League of New York Theatres, now rallied behind it. *Variety* called on its readers to write to their senators in protest. The Senate felt the pressure, especially when, as *The Washington Post* put it, the "glamorous eyes of Tallulah Bankhead, golden-haired heroine of the movies and stage, were turned on a Senate Appropriations sub-committee yesterday in an effort to rescue the Federal Theater Project from threatened destruction." It helped that she was also the daughter of the Speaker of the House and niece of Senator Bankhead of Alabama (and persuaded him to change his vote on the Federal Theatre). Many other stars weighed in as well, including Al Jolson, James Cagney, Henry Fonda, Claudette Colbert, and Tyrone Power. On radio, Orson Welles, despite his rocky relationship with the Federal Theatre, fiercely defended it in a debate with several members of Congress, reminding them that they were "legislating against one of the most important things that ever happened in a democratic government," pointedly adding: "You forget that you have an art form that you are legislating against. This seems to mean nothing to you."

The extended deliberations in the House meant that the Senate had only ten days to arrive at its own version of the relief bill, a crammed schedule that had to include hearings of a subcommittee of the Senate Appropriations Committee, followed by a vote of that entire committee, before the full Senate had a chance to debate and vote on its recommendations. Time also had to be reserved for conferees representing the House and Senate to reconcile differences in their proposed legislation before it could be forwarded to the president and signed into law by midnight on June 30. If that deadline was missed, two and a half million Americans would be thrown off relief. With only four days to go, the press reported the surprising news that the subcommittee of the Senate Appropriations Committee had recommended restoring funding for Flanagan's project. But the Federal Theatre still had to survive the onslaught of a pair of Southern senators bent on its elimination, Robert Reynolds of North Carolina and Rush Holt of West Virginia. Reynolds had turned sharply against Roosevelt and was using the hearings to undermine the president and secure his own political future. It was ideological for Reynolds, who had tarred his opponent as a Communist to win his Senate seat in 1932, was part owner of the antisemitic newspaper *The Defender*, and had recently founded the Vindicators Association, an ultra-nationalist, anti-immigrant, and isolationist group that denied membership to Jews and Blacks. The Federal Theatre, that hotbed of Jews, Blacks,

Reds, and un-American activity, embodied pretty much everything he loathed.

Reynolds kept close to the path marked out by Dies, condemning "the damage done and the danger to America from the 'red' propaganda being broadcast by the majority of the plays and the presentations of the theater project," and opposing funding for those who "are bent upon either changing our form of government or overthrowing the present Government of the United States." The "control of the WPA theater project and most of its plays," he declared, "is in the hand of Communism," which "should compel us to condemn the WPA Theatre Project to the ashcan of oblivion." Even conservatives were growing weary of this rhetoric, and Senator Pat McCarran of Nevada surprised many when he chastised Reynolds, saying that the "trouble is that there are those who are forever using the bugbear of communism to scare somebody in order that they themselves may rise up and thus be held up as the champions against the so-called danger of communism."

Reynolds, unchecked, was so over-the-top that he risked sounding like a parody of Martin Dies: he attacked Flanagan's writing and even her suitability as a professor to run the project, and twice reminded his fellow senators of the Sally Saunders incident and how the Federal Theatre had encouraged interracial dating, before taking his turn at reciting and mocking salacious-sounding play titles. He described "the tripe being served across the footlights by the WPA" as "putrid." And he decried how "the cardinal keystone of Communism—free love and racial equality—is being spread at the expense of the God-fearing, home-loving American taxpayer who must pay the bills for all this dangerous business." Senators rose to the defense of both Flanagan and her project, but Reynolds's rant was more effective than the pieties offered by those like Henry Ashurst of Arizona, who urged that "the Senate not go on record as censoring art. The stage is art. Art is truth, and in the final sum of worldly things, only art endures."

It would be hard to outdo Reynolds in sheer nastiness. But Rush Holt, the youngest member of the Senate, bent on self-promotion, tried his best. He was another Southern Democrat who had turned against the New Deal. Holt's attacks were directed as much at the liberal senators he detested as against Flanagan, whose work he read aloud, then smeared as Communist. When Senator James E. Murray of Montana lambasted Holt for devoting "his time constantly to nothing else but an attempt to discredit the administration of the WPA," and called his attacks "absolutely unfair, dishonest, and corrupt," tempers flared, and the Senate's presiding officer had to intervene, admonishing Holt. But Holt wouldn't be stopped, and sneeringly read the review in the *New Masses* of Flanagan's *Can You Hear Their Voices?*—which wasn't, others pointed out, even a Federal Theatre play. Undeterred, Holt then pivoted to criticizing one that was, W. H. Auden's *The Dance of Death*, before offering a by now stale rendition, greeted with laughter, of obscene-sounding play titles. More experienced legislators let these attacks play out, before asking the exhausted Senate to vote upon a consensus amendment, put forward by Robert Wagner of New York, preserving (though trimming) arts funding. It passed. The Federal Theatre had won a last-minute reprieve. One final hurdle had to be cleared as June 30 fast approached: the conference between representatives of the House and Senate to iron out their differences.

Woodrum had closely followed the debate in the Senate and prepared his delegation for the ensuing conference on June 29: they would bend on other issues, but when it came to the Federal Theatre they must remain obdurate—it had to go. He must have been encouraged that even the liberal press was turning against the Federal Theatre. When Mayor La Guardia called for saving the Theatre Project ("I have 3,000 of those people" in New York City, and they "have to eat"), *The New York Times*, questioning the premise of work relief for artists, replied that the point is "not whether they have to eat but whether they have to act." *The Washington Post* reported on June 30 that to strengthen his case Woodrum brought to the conference "the manuscript of a WPA play containing an allegedly incestuous episode." We don't know which playscript he introduced as evidence; it could just as well have been *Hamlet*. Woodrum, hoping to erode support for the Arts Project, had, according to *The Daily Worker*, also brought along "two books of nudes which they said had been used by WPA artists"—photographs of professional models, a standard practice in the field—and that it "was understood that the conferees poured over the picture[s] during their discussion." Woodrum knew well enough (*The Daily Worker* also reported) that five of the seven conferees from the Senate leaned right, so that "the conferees representing both Houses were almost equally reactionary."

The last issue the conferees negotiated was the fate of the Federal Theatre. House members held firm, senators caved, and they agreed to eliminate the program entirely (with Woodrum offering a concession that all the employees to be laid off July 1 be paid for an additional three months). The other arts projects were spared, though in the future they would have to be subsidized in part with local funding. To prevent any last-minute protests, the conferees agreed to remain tight-lipped until the House and Senate gave their final approval, *The New York Times* reported, due "to fear that opponents of the changes would besiege Congress in force this morning." President Roosevelt was handed the legislation with only a few hours to spare before midnight on June 30. He grudgingly signed it, then released a brief statement calling the legislation's abolition of the Federal Theatre "discrimination of the worst type," for it "singles out a special group of professional people." He then wrote privately to Flanagan, thanking her for providing "work for those who follow a particular calling" and for having made theater "available to large numbers of our people who otherwise might not have had such advantages."

When news reached the actors performing the Federal Theatre's latest hit, *Pinocchio*, on Broadway, they decided to change the ending of the play in what was now their final performance: instead of the puppet becoming a living boy, he dies. As stagehands knocked down the sets in full view of the packed house, the cast stood around the lifeless Pinocchio, now a symbol of the Federal Theatre itself, and recited fresh lines: "So let the bells proclaim our grief / That his small life was all too brief." "Thus passed Pinocchio," they added, who "died June 30, 1939. Killed by act of Congress." A defeated Flanagan acknowledged what she had not until now felt free to say, writing in an op-ed in *The New York Times* that her congressional adversaries "were afraid of the Federal Theatre because it was educating the people to know more about government and politics and such vital issues of the day as housing, power, agriculture and labor. . . . They are afraid, and rightly so, of thinking people." And they were also afraid of the Federal Theatre "because it gave Negro actors as well as white actors a chance."

A week after her program was terminated, Flanagan wrote to her husband that she had spoken with Florida senator Claude Pepper, who told her that "there are still fights in the Senate and House cloak rooms every day on the Federal Theatre," and that it had become "the focal point of the whole power issue, housing issue, and socialized medicine issue." Flanagan pitched to Pepper a plan to salvage what could be preserved under the guise of a federal department of arts, subsidized by taxing amusements. But nothing came of that. When Flanagan addressed the National Theatre Conference in November 1939, she acknowledged that while the Federal Theatre was "dead," not even an "act of Congress can kill an idea"; while conceding that any reincarnation of it would have to be broader based, she believed that "a national theater of some sort was inevitable." Calls by Actors' Equity and the WPA for funding theater projects in the 1940 and 1941 budgets fell on deaf ears at the House Appropriations Committee.

Reflecting in 1941 on the demise of the Federal Theatre, Malcolm Cowley, literary editor of *The New Republic*, located the "principal blame" for its elimination not "with the newspapers and magazines that attacked it," or with the "congressmen who hated it so much that they refused to be told the truth about it," or even with "the bureaucrats in Washington who were quite willing to sacrifice the project so long as their own jobs were saved," but rather "with you the reader, and me the writer, in so far as we represent progressive opinion in the United States." Progressives "liked the idea of the Federal Theatre," went to "some of the plays," and "at the very end, when it was too late, we perhaps signed protests against its suppression. . . . But during the four preceding years, when we might have helped to build up a sentiment for the Federal Theatre so strong that Congress would not have dared to abolish it; when we might have proved to Mr. Roosevelt that his always good intentions were receiving wide popular approval, we had done, well, not exactly nothing, but not really enough to matter."

For Cowley, the fate of the Federal Theatre embodied the failure of progressives to secure what they had briefly and too complacently achieved in the 1930s:

> This failure is typical of the whole decade that has just ended. In 1933, progressive opinion in America received a chance that it was never given before—a President in sympathy with its aims and a business community so frightened that for once it was willing to accept liberal measures. Brave things were done in the following years, but not enough of them; and some of the bravest attempts were permitted to fail through lack of intelligent support. The progressives had their chance and most of them lost it—sometimes because they failed to see it, sometimes because they saw but failed to grasp it, and sometimes because they were so busy quarreling among themselves that after grasping it they let it slip from their hands. The story would have been different if more of us had been as imaginative and hard-working and self-forgetful as Hallie Flanagan.

Not long after writing this, having joined the War Department as an information analyst as part of the war effort, Cowley would be attacked by Martin Dies, who publicly accused him of membership in seventy-two Communist or Communist-front organizations. Cowley, a leftist, though not a member of the Communist Party, was forced to resign, an outcome celebrated in the Hearst-owned *Chicago Tribune* under the headline "Dies Denounces New Campaign to Destroy U.S.: Exposes Spearhead of Totalitarianism." The article goes on to describe a special report produced by Dies's committee that named many other names, even impugning Dies's new House Un-American Activities Committee member, fellow Democrat Jerry Voorhis of California, who had refused to sign on to this defamatory report (unsurprisingly, since Voorhis was allegedly "an intimate friend of many of the Communists named in the report"), and flagged as well *Time* magazine and *The New Republic* as part of a Communist inspired movement "aimed at destroying our representative form of government." Dies would go on to target and accuse hundreds of government workers, none of whom were ever tried or found guilty of anything, though that didn't much matter.

Federal Theatre storage crates,
George Mason University, 1974.

Epilogue

mmet Lavery believed that had the Federal Theatre managed to survive for another six months, the outbreak of World War II might have secured a future for it "as a necessary arm of entertainment, with the army." But the war brought only a brief respite for the other Federal One projects, and in 1943 the entire WPA came to an end. By then, the now defunct Federal Theatre's playbooks, set designs, posters, programs, and photographs—nine hundred cubic feet of government property—had been packed up in wooden crates and put in storage, though exactly where nobody seemed to recall. For decades, this trove was believed lost, until 1974, when a pair of intrepid scholars from George Mason University, Lorraine Brown and John O'Connor, found it, unceremoniously dumped and covered in pigeon droppings, in an old airplane hangar in Middle River, Maryland.

Following the closure of the Federal Theatre, Hallie Flanagan returned to Vassar, her world once more contracted to the confines of a college campus. A few months later tragedy struck again when her husband died suddenly of a heart attack. It was a terrible blow, as his support had carried her through her work on the project; "without it," she noted in her unpublished memoir, "the hard days of the Dies attack etc. would have been impossible." "I feel and always have," she added, "that Phil's early and unaccountable death was bound up with the violent end of the Federal Theatre." Flanagan published *Arena* and in 1942 accepted a position as dean of Smith College, where she continued to oversee campus productions and write plays, none to the acclaim with which her work had once been met. In 1946 she was diagnosed with Parkinson's disease, and not long after that retired and moved back to Poughkeepsie, telling a friend, "My whole life has been a failure. Nothing that I cared about has turned out as I hoped it would." In the early 1950s, when Columbia University envisioned building a major arts center, her son-in-law Eric Bentley, who taught there, recalls that Flanagan "was our first idea of who should head it up. And slight overtures were made to her" before it became clear that she was not up to it. Around then Flanagan stopped attending plays, as "she was self-conscious and didn't like her old friends to see her in a semi-crippled condition." By 1960, Bentley further recalled, "she could no longer concentrate. She'd watch a little TV, a thing you don't have to concentrate on, and that was about all she could muster. That was an effect of the Parkinson's, and she would get into very bad states of mind." In a nursing home in Beacon, New York, in 1963, Flanagan, her stepdaughter writes, "was not just fighting a battle against failing health. She was haunted by memories of the Dies Committee hearings. In moments of self-doubt she would wonder if the voices she heard in the corridor outside her room were accusing her of being a Communist." Hallie Flanagan died on July 23, 1969, and was buried in Grinnell, Iowa, not far from the grave of Harry Hopkins, who had died in 1946.

Martin Dies outlived her by just a few years, dying on November 14, 1972. After the war broke out, Dies stopped holding regular public hearings; his popularity slowly waned and his committee's grip on the nation slackened, though Congress continued to reauthorize it, then made the special Un-American Activities Committee a more permanent standing one. Dies's attempt to win a Senate seat in 1941 failed badly (he finished last in a four-way race), and he left Congress in 1944, for personal reasons, probably a health scare. He returned to the House in 1952, winning an at-large seat, but was rebuffed in his efforts to rejoin his old committee. He failed again in a Senate bid in 1957 and retired from Congress two years later, though not before signing the so-called Southern Manifesto opposing the desegregation of America's public schools. He continued to give speeches, mostly on "The Communist Threat to America" and on how he was victimized, themes repeated in his 1963 autobiography, *Martin Dies' Story*, for which he struggled to find a publisher. From 1964 to 1967 Dies wrote monthly for the John Birch Society's right-wing publication *American Opinion*, until a stroke put an end to his public life; another killed him five years later. By then J. Parnell Thomas, who had so hounded Flanagan, was dead as well; he had left Washington, D.C., in 1950 for federal prison in Danbury, Connecticut, after his conviction for defrauding the U.S. government, his criminal activity dating back to 1940.

Lyndon Johnson was in his late twenties in 1939 when as a member of the House he voted to defund the Federal Theatre. In 1965, as president, he signed into law the creation of the National Endowment for the Arts (NEA) under the rubric of the National Foundation on the Arts and the Humanities, the first major federal investment in the performing arts in the United States since the New Deal (during the Cold War, as part of its propaganda effort, the government had paid American artists to perform abroad, though not at home). Its budget, adjusted for inflation, has never been more than a fraction of what was spent on Federal One. Those running the NEA had learned a valuable lesson from the fate of the Federal Theatre and did their best to ensure that its reach would extend to every congressional district. It has helped the NEA withstand repeated attempts to defund it, first in 1981, under Ronald Reagan; then again in 1989 and 1990, in response to controversial visual art; next in 1995, when House Speaker Newt Gingrich called for its elimination; and again in 2018, when Donald Trump's proposed budget called for its termination. Republicans in the House are committed to reducing the NEA budget in 2024, and a bill to reduce its funding to zero dollars has already been submitted by Andy Biggs of Arizona, a leading member of the far-right House Freedom Caucus. The conservative Heritage Foundation's list of reasons for eliminating this federal arts program shows how little the right-wing playbook has changed since 1938: taxpayer support of the arts is "welfare for culture elitists," promotes "the worst excess of multiculturalism and political correctness," and "demeans the values of ordinary Americans." The vehemence of these recycled arguments may stem in part from how a Federal Theatre had once offered (and might again) a viable model for a network of regional theaters and touring companies that connected Americans, sitting cheek by jowl, across long-standing political, economic, and racial divides. For some, apparently, such an outcome remains a frightening prospect.

It's hard to imagine what America would be like today had support for the Federal Theatre continued and the Dies Committee not been renewed. Counterfactual history is best left to novelists. But a more vibrant theatrical culture extending across the land might well have led to a more informed citizenry, and by extension, a more equitable and resilient democracy. What happened instead was that Martin Dies begat Senator Joseph McCarthy, who begat Roy Cohn, who begat Donald Trump, who begat the horned "QAnon Shaman," who from the dais of the Senate on January 6, 2021, thanked his fellow insurrectionists at the Capitol "for allowing us to get rid of the Communists, the globalists, and the traitors within our government."

In the aftermath of that attack on the Capitol, in the midst of the COVID-19 pandemic that shuttered theaters and put many actors and writers out of work, there was talk of resurrecting the federal writers' and theater projects. On the eighty-sixth anniversary of the establishment of the WPA, Democrats Ted W. Lieu of California and Teresa Leger Fernández of New Mexico urged fellow members of the House to pass a "21st Century Federal Writers' Project Act." At much the same time, hopeful articles—with *American Theatre* optimistically asking, "So What Could a 'New Federal Theatre Project' Actually Look Like?"—began calling for the return of a Federal Theatre as well. But these efforts have found no traction. Their timing could not have been worse, for culture warriors in Congress, in state legislatures, even in once-benign community schoolboards, were turning time and again to the Dies playbook to secure power and challenge progressive initiatives, including anything having to do with the arts or America's racial reckoning.

Of late, the Dies playbook has once again been employed in culture-war attacks on theater, this time in America's schools. *The New York Times* reported in July 2023 that productions of such popular high school plays as the musical *Oklahoma!* (in which a character says the word "damn") and August Wilson's *Fences* (objectionable because it has no White characters), as well as plays that explore same-sex love, have been attacked and censored from Florida to Oregon, with objections "coming largely from right-leaning parents and school officials." Staging Chekhov's *Three Sisters* has been nixed in Chattanooga, Tennessee (since it deals with adultery), while in Lansing, Kansas, students are not even allowed to study, let alone stage, *The Laramie Project*, a play about the murder of a gay student, Matthew Shepard. In a 2023 Education Theatre Association survey, 85 percent of American theater teachers expressed concern about censorship. In Florida, a newly minted law has led to *A Midsummer Night's Dream* being pulled from middle school libraries and classrooms, while *Romeo and Juliet* will now be taught in snippets, to avoid falling afoul of legislation targeting "sexual conduct." The clash between the playbooks of Martin Dies and Hallie Flanagan continues to resonate across the land, with lessons for both the right and the left, and consequences for us all.

Acknowledgments

I am deeply grateful to the friends and expert readers who challenged me to make this a better book: Mary Cregan, Anne Edelstein, Jessica Friedman, David Scott Kastan, Ira Katznelson, Fintan O'Toole, Daniel Pollack-Pelzner, Alvin Snider, Daniel Swift, and Sean Wilentz. I am once again indebted to ongoing conversations with James Bednarz, Richard McCoy, Michael Shapiro, and H. Aram Veeser. I am fortunate in my publishers, as well as my extraordinary editors—William Heyward and Ann Godoff at Penguin Press and Alex Bowler at Faber—and to my longtime friend and agent, Anne Edelstein. I owe much to my superb production editor, Randee Marullo. I am also indebted to the American Academy in Berlin, which awarded me a fellowship that allowed me to finish the book, as well as to Columbia University for its ongoing support of my scholarship over the past four decades. I am also grateful to Catriona Crowe at the Galway International Arts Festival as well as to Tulane University, for invitations to share this work in progress. I have learned about the extraordinary impact that free theater can have from my work for the past decade at the Public Theater in New York City, where I serve as a scholar in residence; through offering free Shakespeare in Central Park since 1962, and through its touring Mobile Unit, which brings free productions to prisons, community centers, libraries, and homeless shelters, the Public Theater has also helped sustain the vision of the Federal Theatre.

This book could not have been written without access to the rich archival material that informs almost every page. It was challenging accessing archives during COVID-19 (when much of the book was researched), and my heartfelt thanks goes to the devoted archivists who made this possible, at the National Archives and Records Administration (NARA) at College Park, Maryland; the Center for Legislative Archives (a part of the NARA) in Washington, D.C.; the George Mason University Libraries, including their invaluable oral history collection "Voices of the WPA"; the Library of Congress; the New York Public Library (both the Billie Rose Theatre Division and the Schomburg Center for Research in Black Culture); Vassar College's Archives and Special Collections Library; the Wisconsin Center for Film and Theater Research at the University of Wisconsin–Madison; the Hoover Institution Library and Archives at Stanford University; Yale Library; the Sam Houston Regional Library and Research Center, part of the Texas State Library and Archives Commission; and Columbia University Libraries. Newspaper databases also made this research possible, and I have relied on three in particular: Chronicling America; Newspapers .com; and ProQuest. I have also relied on the online *Congressional*

Record (https://www.congress.gov/congressional-record), as well as a link to the Dies Committee hearings (https://onlinebooks .library.upenn.edu/webbin/metabook?id=diescommittee).

In capitalizing both "Black" and "White" (except in quotations) I am following the style guide of the American Psychological Association, and am persuaded by Kwame Anthony Appiah's argument in "The Case for Capitalizing the *B* in Black" that "Black" *and* "White," both social constructs, ought to be capitalized (*The Atlantic*, June 18, 2020).

PHOTOGRAPH ACKNOWLEDGMENTS

The photographs heading the preface and chapters 1, 2, 3, 4, 5, 6, 8, and 9 are from the Library of Congress. The photographs heading chapters 7 and 10 are by permission of the Billy Rose Theatre Division, the New York Public Library for the Performing Arts. The photograph heading the epilogue is by permission of the Broadside Collection from the Special Collections & Archives of the George Mason University Libraries.

Bibliographical Essay

The bibliographical essay that follows is intended to serve the needs of those searching for a specific source as well as those seeking a broader guide to the stories explored in this book. For those interested in the history of the Federal Theatre, two books are indispensable, and I have drawn on them extensively: Hallie Flanagan, *Arena* (New York: Duell, Sloan and Pearce, 1940), and Jane De Hart (Mathews), *The Federal Theatre, 1935–1939: Plays, Relief, and Politics* (Princeton, NJ: Princeton University Press, 1967). Also invaluable are the two hundred or so interviews conducted in the late 1970s and early 1980s of those involved in the Federal Theatre, "Voices of the WPA: Oral Histories of the Works Progress Administration," in the George Mason University Libraries collections, most of them accessible online at https://vwpa.gmu.edu/audiocollection. For those interested in Martin Dies and his committee, Dennis Kay McDaniel, "Martin Dies of Un-American Activities: Life and Times" (diss., University of Houston, 1988), is unsurpassed; I have relied as well on August Raymond Ogden, *The Dies Committee: A Study of the Special House Committee for the Investigation of Un-American Activities, 1938–1944*, rev. ed. (Washington, D.C.: Catholic University of America Press, 1945).

PREFACE

For the seven surviving New Deal programs, see www.thoughtco .com/new-deal-programs-still-in-effect-today-4154043. For John Steinbeck on the Federal Writers' Project, see *Travels with Charley: In Search of America* (New York: Viking, 1962), p. 121. For a helpful overview of the New Deal, democracy, and the arts, see Jane De Hart (Mathews), "Arts and the People: The New Deal Quest for a Cultural Democracy," *The Journal of American History* 62, no. 2 (September 1975), pp. 316–39. For the radio division, see Alan Kreizenbeck, "The Radio Division of the Federal Theatre Project," *New England Theatre Journal* 2, no. 1 (1991), pp. 27–37, as well as David Goodman and Joy Elizabeth Hayes, *New Deal Radio: The Educational Radio Project* (New Brunswick, NJ: Rutgers University Press, 2022). For the Federal Theatre's performances in orphanages, hospitals, and elsewhere, see "The Federal Theatre Project," for "Harry Hopkins' report to Senate, May 1, 1937," in Hallie Flanagan Papers, New York Public Library (NYPL), Series 2, Federal Theatre Project Correspondence, box 6, folder 11. For the Federal Theatre's work with mental patients, see, for example, "Mental Patients Find Aid in Drama," *The New York Times*, April 7, 1937. For plays in production when the Federal Theatre closed, see Stuart Cosgrove, "The Living Newspaper: History, Production and Form" (diss., University of Hull, 1982), p. 138.

For the culture wars, see James Davison Hunter, *Culture Wars: The Struggle to Define America* (New York: Basic Books, 1991), especially pp. 67–106 on their origins; Edward P. Lazear, *Culture Wars in America* (Stanford, CA: Hoover Institution on War, Revolution and Peace, 1996); Todd Gitlin, *The Twilight of Common Dreams: Why America Is Wracked by Culture Wars* (New York: Henry Holt, 1995); Andrew Hartman, *A War for the Soul of America: A History of the Culture Wars* (Chicago: University of Chicago Press, 2015); Michael Mark Cohen, *The Conspiracy of Capital: Law, Violence, and American Popular Radicalism in the Age of Monopoly* (Amherst: University of Massachusetts Press, 2019); Bill O'Reilly, *Culture Warrior* (New York: Broadway Books, 2006); and Irene Taviss Thomson, *Culture Wars and Enduring American Dilemmas* (Ann Arbor: University of Michigan Press, 2010), who confirms that "participants and observers alike contend that the culture wars originated in the late 1960s" (p. 3). For a text of Patrick Buchanan's "cultural war" speech of 1992, see voicesofdemocracy.umd.edu/buchanan-culture -war-speech-speech-text.

For Alexis de Tocqueville, see his "Some Observations on the Drama Amongst Democratic Nations," section 1, chapter 19, trans. Henry Reeve, vol. 2 (New York: Adlard and Saunders, 1838). For statistics on high school and college graduates in 1930, see nces.ed .gov/programs/digest/d15/tables/dt15_104.10.asp.

For more on the Dies playbook, see chapter 8, and for that threat to punch a Black congressman, see *The Chicago Defender*, July 26, 1930. For an overview of what Hallie Flanagan thought the Federal Theatre had accomplished by early 1938, see "A Brief Delivered by Hallie Flanagan, Director, Federal Theatre Project,

Works Progress Administration, before the Committee on Patents, House of Representatives, Washington, D.C., February 8, 1938," in the Library of Congress (loc.gov/item/farbf.00040002).

CHAPTER ONE: IS MARLOWE A COMMUNIST?

Most of the material in this chapter comes from the testimony preserved in the *Congressional Record, Investigation of Un-American Propaganda Activities in the United States: Hearings before a Special Committee on Un-American Activities, Seventy-fifth Congress, Third Session, on H. Res. 282*, vol. 4, November 19–December 14, 1938, especially pp. 2720–85. The quotation from the *Washington Star*, October 29, 1939, is cited from McDaniel, "Martin Dies," pp. 390–91. I have also relied on newspaper accounts in *The New York Times, New York Herald Tribune, Chicago Tribune*, and *The Baltimore Sun*, all from December 7, 1938, from which I take details about Flanagan's reactions during her testimony. See too Flanagan's own account in her *Arena*, especially p. 346, as well as Kate Dossett, "Gender and the Dies Committee Hearings on the Federal Theatre Project," *Journal of American Studies* 47, no. 4, "Special Issue: The 'Un-American'" (November 2013), pp. 993–1017. On Dies's speeches in New York, see the *New York Herald Tribune*, December 4, 1938; *The New York Times*, December 5, 1938; the *Los Angeles Times*, December 4, 1938; and *The Boston Globe*, December 4, 1938.

For "federal" rather than "national" theater, see *The New York Times*, June 30 and July 5, 1935; and Flanagan, *Arena*, pp. 23, 313–14, and 323, where Burns in quoted. For Starnes's obituary mentioning the Marlowe incident, see *The New York Times*, January 10, 1962. On Euripides and *Trojan Incident*, see Robert Davis, "Is Mr.

Euripides a Communist? The Federal Theatre Project's 1938 *Trojan Incident*," *Comparative Drama* 44, no. 4 (Winter 2010), and 45, no. 1 (Spring 2011), special double issue "Translation, Performance, and Reception of Greek Drama, 1900–1960: International Dialogues," pp. 457–76; and Elizabeth Cooper, "Dances about Spain: Censorship at the Federal Theatre Project," *Theatre Research International* 29, no. 3 (2004), pp. 232–46. For the number of Communists in the United States in the 1930s, see https://depts.washington.edu/moves/CP_intro.shtml. For their influence on the Federal Theatre, see Flanagan, *Arena*, pp. 36–37 and 57ff., as well as De Hart, *Federal Theatre*, pp. 228–32, from which I quote Flanagan's letter and which cites Communist Party tactics from Irving Howe and Lewis Coser, *The American Communist Party: A Critical History, 1919–1957* (Boston: Beacon Press, 1957), chapter 8. For "Mother Goose Marx," see *The New York Times*, May 21, 1937.

The reporter from *Variety* awarded "the first round" in this "preliminary skirmish" between Flanagan and the Dies Committee to Flanagan, noting that she "succeeded in tying up committee members on numerous points in the testimony" (December 7, 1938), p. 47. See too Clarence J. Wittler's rarely cited "Some Social Trends in WPA Drama" (diss., Catholic University of America Press, 1939), which offers a contemporary and conservative study of the moral positions espoused by the plays themselves and concludes that the Federal Theatre had a "slight but definite anti-Fascist-Nazi, pro-Communist trend," was strongly pro-labor and keen on fostering better race relations, and was also pro-family and neutral on religion, though sanctioned immorality and endorsed blasphemy.

CHAPTER TWO: THE CREATION OF
THE FEDERAL THEATRE

For Cather's early reviews, see the Willa Cather Archive (cather
.unl.edu) and Nebraska Newspapers (nebnewspapers.unl.edu). I
have quoted from her reviews in the *Nebraska State Journal* of February 11 and 25, April 8, November 22, and December 16, 1894,
and consulted the April 7, 1894, issue of the *Lincoln Courier*. See
too the two-volume *The World and the Parish: Willa Cather's Articles
and Reviews, 1893–1902*, ed. William M. Curtin (Lincoln: University of Nebraska Press, 1970); and Hermione Lee, *Willa Cather:
Double Lives* (New York: Pantheon, 1989). See as well "Willa
Cather Mourns Old Opera House," *Omaha World-Herald*, October
27, 1929, p. 9, which is available online in the Willa Cather Archive. For the great actors of the land touring through Lincoln, see
E. P. Brown, *Seventy-Five Years in the Prairie Capital* (Lincoln: Miller
and Paine, 1955). I have consulted the 1897–98 2nd edition as well
as the 1905 10th edition of *Julius Cahn's Official Theatrical Guide:
Containing Information of the Leading Theatres and Attractions in
America* (New York: Empire Theatre Building, 1897 and 1905).
For demographics on Nebraska in the late nineteenth century, I
have relied on census reports; *Nebraska Historical Population* (un
omaha.edu/college-of-public-affairs-and-community-service/cen
ter-for-public-affairs-research/documents/nebraska-historical
-population-report-2018.pdf); and *Immigrant Nebraska* (unomaha
.edu/college-of-arts-and-sciences/ollas/research/immigrant
-nebraska.php). For the Federal Theatre in Nebraska, including
newspaper reports, see Flanagan, *Arena*, pp. 176–79.

For the decline of theater and the rise of film in the early twentieth century, see William Winter, *Wallet of Time: Containing Personal, Biographical, and Critical Reminiscences of the American Theatre,* 2 vols. (New York: Moffat, Yard, 1913); Alfred L. Bernheim, *The Business of the Theatre: An Economic History of the American Theatre, 1750–1932* (New York: Actors' Equity Association, 1932); Jack Poggi, *Theater in America: The Impact of Economic Forces, 1870–1967* (Ithaca, NY: Cornell University Press, 1968); Thomas Gale Moore, *The Economics of the American Theater* (Durham, NC: Duke University Press, 1968); and Felicia Hardison Londré and Daniel J. Watermeier, *The History of North American Theater: From Pre-Columbian Times to the Present* (New York: Continuum, 1998). See too Robert D. Leiter, *The Musicians and Petrillo* (New York: Bookman Associates, 1953), pp. 54–57; Oliver Reed and Walter L. Welch, *From Tin Foil to Stereo: Evolution of the Phonograph* (New York: H. W. Sams, 1959), pp. 286–87; and De Hart (Mathews), "Arts and the People," pp. 316–39.

For the U.S. Census and other employment figures from the early twentieth century, see www2.census.gov/library/publications /decennial/1920/volume-4/41084484v4ch02.pdf; www2.census.gov /library/publications/decennial/1930/labor-volume-2 /03453339v2ch1.pdf; www2.census.gov/library/publications/decennial/1940/population-volume-3/33973538v3p1ch2.pdf; thebalance money.com/unemployment-rate-by-year-3305506; thebalancemoney .com/unemployment-rate-by-year-3305506; U.S. Bureau of the Census, *Historical Statistics of the United States, Colonial Times to 1957* (Washington, D.C.: Government Printing Office, 1960), p. 70; and russellsage.org/research/chartbook/unemployment-rate-year-and -gender-1900-to-2011.

For the number of theatrical unions, see Bernheim, *The Business of the Theatre*, p. 214; and for the dire situation of theaters in New York City, see William Grange, *The Business of American Theatre* (New York: Routledge, 2021). For actor charities in New York, see Burns Mantle, *The Best Plays of 1933–34* (New York: Dodd, Mead, 1933), p. 4. For actors signing up with Hollywood agencies in 1932, see Flanagan, *Arena*, p. 14. And for FERA and its support of artists, see *The Emergency Work Relief Program of the F.E.R.A. April 1, 1934–July 1, 1935: Submitted by the Work Division*, report compiled by Jacob Baker for Harry Hopkins, pp. 108, 111, and 130. See too Richard D. McKinzie, *The New Deal for Artists* (Princeton, NJ: Princeton University Press, 1973), pp. 75–89. For a helpful overview of relief efforts in the theater before the creation of the Federal Theatre, see William F. McDonald, *Federal Relief Administration and the Arts* (Columbus: Ohio State University Press, 1969), pp. 483–95; McDonald's account of the ever-changing and byzantine nature of the Federal Theatre bureaucracy (pp. 496–543) is invaluable.

For earlier reflections on an American national theater, see William Dunlap, *History of American Theater*, vol. 1 (London: Richard Bentley, 1833), pp. 132–33 and 406ff. See too Edith J. R. Isaacs, "The Irresistible Theatre: A National Playhouse for America," *Theatre Arts Monthly* 18 (August 1934), pp. 577–90. For Hallie Flanagan's view of a federal theater's potential, see her "Theatre and Geography," *Magazine of Art* 31 (August 1938), p. 468; "Federal Theatre: Tomorrow," *Federal Theatre* 2, no. 1 (1936), pp. 5–6; "The People's Theatre Grows Stronger," *Federal Theatre* 1, no. 6 (May 1936), p. 6; and "Project to Continue on National Basis," *Equity* 21 (May 1936), pp. 8 and 10. For the state of the theater in the 1930s, see Edith J. R. Isaacs, "Portrait of a Theatre: America—1935,"

Theatre Arts Monthly 17 (January 1933), pp. 32–42. For Hollywood's bankrolling of plays, see Elmer Rice, "The Federal Theatre Hereabouts," *The New York Times*, January 5, 1936.

For Harry Hopkins, see Henry H. Adams, *Harry Hopkins: A Biography* (New York: Putnam, 1977); George T. McJimsey, *Harry Hopkins: Ally of the Poor and Defender of Democracy* (Cambridge, MA: Harvard University Press, 1987); June Hopkins, *Harry Hopkins: Sudden Hero, Brash Reformer* (New York: St. Martin's Press, 1999), especially p. 190, and her "The Road Not Taken: Harry Hopkins and New Deal Work Relief," *Presidential Studies Quarterly* 29, no. 2 (1999), pp. 306–16; Searle F. Charles, *Minister of Relief: Harry Hopkins and the Depression* (Syracuse, NY: Syracuse University Press, 1963), pp. 223–43; Donald S. Howard, *The WPA and Federal Relief Policy* (New York: Russell Sage Foundation, 1943); William W. Bremer, "Along the American Way: The New Deal's Work Relief Programs for the Unemployed," *The Journal of American History* 62 (December 1975), pp. 636–52; and Hopkins's own *Spending to Save: The Complete Story of Relief* (New York: W. W. Norton, 1936). For a helpful overview, see William E. Leuchtenburg, *Franklin D. Roosevelt and the New Deal* (New York: Harper and Row, 1963). For Hopkins's sense that Americans were tiring of relief, see his "The Future of Relief," *The New Republic* 90 (1937), pp. 8–9.

For Hopkins and the various candidates to direct the Federal Theatre, as well as his "now or never" speech to his staff, see De Hart, *Federal Theatre*, p. 8. For Flanagan's first meeting with Hopkins, see Flanagan, *Arena*, pp. 3–12. See too Eva Le Gallienne, "The Government and Art: Miss Le Gallienne Makes a Suggestion for a National Theatre," *The New York Times*, December 8, 1935;

and Helen Sheehy, *Eva Le Gallienne: A Biography* (New York: Knopf, 1996). For an abridged version of Elmer Rice's letter to Hopkins, see Elmer Rice, *The Living Theatre* (New York: Harper and Bros., 1959), pp. 150–53; and his essay in *The New York Times*, January 5, 1936. For how Flanagan was offered the job, see her *Arena*, pp. 1–24; and De Hart, *Federal Theatre*, pp. 4–29. For the CWA pilot program in New York City, see woc.gov/collections /federal-theatre-project-1935-to-1939/articles-and-essays/wpa -federal-theatre-project. For the challenge of persuading others to work for low wages for the Federal Theatre, see Flanagan, *Arena*, p. 41, as well as Flanagan's letters to her husband, "Correspon-dence, Personal, from HDF to Philip Davis," Hallie Flanagan Papers, Vassar College, September 6 and 9, 1935.

For other challenges facing Flanagan, see her *Arena*, pp. 19–47; and De Hart, *Federal Theatre*, pp. 44–88, from whom I quote from pp. 45 and 60. For Hopkins's remark about censorship, see De Hart, *Federal Theatre*, p. 33; and for his impatience, see Charles, *Minister of Relief*, p. 138. See too "Red Tape Stymies WPA," *Variety* (December 11, 1935), pp. 59 and 61. For Mabie, see, in addition to Flanagan, *Arena*, pp. 22–24 and 131–33, lib.uiowa.edu/exhibits/ previous/mabie. For a critique from the left of how the Federal Theatre was being run, see Walter Pell, "Which Way the Federal Theatre?," *New Theatre and Film*, April 1937, p. 7ff. For Flanagan's letter to her husband about the first meeting of her regional direc-tors, see "Correspondence, Personal, from HDF to Philip Davis," Hallie Flanagan Papers, Vassar College, October 8, 1935.

My account of Flanagan's early life draws heavily on Joanne Bentley, *Hallie Flanagan: A Life in the American Theatre* (New York:

Knopf, 1988), which in turn draws upon Flanagan's unpublished autobiography, "Notes on My Life" (c. 1948), in the Vassar College archives (see especially pp. 29, 47, and 86 in Bentley's biography, from which I quote). I draw as well on Flanagan's own accounts in her three books: *Arena, Shifting Scenes of the Modern European Theatre* (New York: Coward-McCann, 1928), and *Dynamo* (New York: Duell, Sloan and Pearce, 1943), especially pp. 107–10, as well as her essay "A Theatre Is Born," *Theatre Arts Monthly*, November 15, 1931, pp. 908–15. I have also drawn on Rania Karoula, *The Federal Theatre Project, 1935–1939: Engagement and Experimentation* (Edinburgh: Edinburgh University Press, 2021). For her most famous play, see Hallie Flanagan and Margaret Ellen Clifford, *Can You Hear Their Voices? A Play of Our Time* (Poughkeepsie, NY: Experimental Theatre of Vassar College, 1931); for reviews of it, see *Theatre Guild Magazine*, July 1931; *The New York Times*, May 10, 1931; and *Workers' Theatre*, January 1932; and for its New York staging, see the *Amsterdam News*, October 6, 1934. See too the entry on "The Experimental Theatre of Vassar College" in the *Vassar Encyclopedia*, vcencyclopedia.vassar.edu.

For congressional hearings on relief, see Hearing before the House Committee in Charge of Deficiency Appropriations: *First Deficiency Appropriation Bill for 1936, Part 2, Emergency Relief*, Seventy-fourth Congress, Second Session (1936), pp. 206–10. See too De Hart, *Federal Theatre*, p. 78. For statistics about relief, see Federal Works Agency, *Final Report on the WPA Program, 1935–43* (Washington, D.C.: U.S. Government Printing Office, 1946), pp. 63 and 122. For Flanagan's words at McClean Mansion, see Hallie Flanagan, "First Meeting of Regional Directors, Federal Theatre

Project, delivered at the McClean Mansion in Washington D.C."
(FTP 1 LAC 222, folder 1). And for her sense of the short- and
long-term goals, see Hallie Flanagan, *Instruction: Federal Theatre
Projects* (Works Progress Administration, October 1935), p. 1.

For *Ethiopia*, in addition to Flanagan's account in *Arena*, pp.
65ff., and De Hart, *Federal Theatre*, pp. 62–68, see Arent's own
recollections in Arthur Arent, "*Ethiopia*: The First 'Living Newspaper,'" introduced by Dan Isaac, *Educational Theatre Journal* 20,
no. 1 (March 1968), pp. 15–31. For the radical roots of the Living
Newspaper, see, for example, Douglas McDermott, "The Living
Newspaper as a Dramatic Form," *Modern Drama* 8 (May 1965).
And for Flanagan's defensiveness, see Cosgrove, "The Living Newspaper," p. 83; and De Hart, *Federal Theatre*, p. 78. For Brooks Atkinson's review, see *The New York Times*, January 25, 1936. For a
broader discussion of political censorship of American drama at
this time, see John Houchin, *Censorship of the American Theatre
in the Twentieth Century* (Cambridge: Cambridge University Press,
2003); and Bruce McConachie, *American Theater in the Culture of the
Cold War: Producing and Contesting Containment, 1947–1962* (Iowa
City: University of Iowa Press, 2003). For John McGee's *Jefferson
Davis*, see *The New York Times*, January 14, 1936; the *New York
Herald Tribune*, February 19, 1936; and *The Daily Worker*, February
24, 1936. For Arthur Miller on the Living Newspaper, see "Reminiscences of Arthur Miller: Oral History, 1959," pp. 923–28, Columbia University Special Collections.

For Asadata Dafora, see Maureen Needham, "*Kykunkor, or The
Witch Woman*: An African Opera in America, 1934," in Thomas F.
DeFrantz's *Dancing Many Drums: Excavations in African American
Dance* (Madison: University of Wisconsin Press, 2002), pp. 233–66;

Pamyla A. Stiehl, "The Curious Case of *Kykunkor*: A 'Dansical'/ Musical Exploration and Reclamation of Asadata Dafora's *Kykunkor, or the Witch Woman* (1934)," *Studies in Musical Theatre* 3, no. 2 (2009), pp. 143–56; as well as *Time*, June 4, 1934; Rebekah J. Kowal, "Staging Diaspora: Asadata Dafora and Black Cultural Diplomacy," chapter 3 in *Dancing the World Smaller: Staging Globalism in Mid-Century America* (New York: Oxford University Press, 2020), pp. 121–63; the *Amsterdam News*, June 23, 1934, and February 9, 1935; *The New Journal and Guide*, July 24, 1934; *The Wall Street Journal*, June 16, 1934; and *The New York Times*, May 13, 1934; John Martin, in *The New York Times*, January 13, 1935, notes that some of the performers in the Shogola Oloba troupe were African Americans. For Flanagan's letter about Jefferson Davis, see Hallie Flanagan Papers, Vassar College, HFD to Philip Davis, February 18, 1936, and March 3, 1936.

CHAPTER THREE: *MACBETH*

For extended accounts of *Macbeth* in Harlem, see John Houseman, *Run-Through: A Memoir* (New York: Simon & Schuster, 1972), pp. 188–205; Kate Dossett, *Radical Black Theatre in the New Deal* (Chapel Hill: University of North Carolina Press, 2020), pp. 204–16; Susan Quinn, *Furious Improvisation: How the WPA and a Cast of Thousands Made High Art out of Desperate Times* (New York: Walker, 2008), pp. 196–211; and Karoula, *The Federal Theatre Project*, pp. 93–104. For a link to the playbill, see michianamemory.sjcpl.org /digital/collection/p16827coll4/id/2135.

For accounts of the alleged voodoo curse, see Houseman's *Run-Through*, pp. 202–3; Welles's *Sketchbook Transcripts*, episode 2, April 30, 1955, www.wellesnet.com/Sketchbook%20episode2.htm; and

Barry B. Witham's superb essay, "Percy Hammond and the Fable of the Scottish Play," *New England Theatre Journal* 18 (2007), pp. 1–12, which separates myth from fact, and which I rely on heavily. For Hammond's review, see the *New York Herald Tribune*, April 15, 1936. And for *Kykunkor*, see *The New York Times*, May 13, 1934, and January 13, 1935. On what would be seen as the controversial use of voodoo in the production, see Benjamin Hilb, "Afro-Haitian-American Ritual Power: Vodou in the Welles-FTP Voodoo *Macbeth*," *Shakespeare Bulletin* 32, no. 4 (Winter 2014), pp. 649–81, and the responses to his essay by Marguerite Rippy, "Welles's 'Voodoo' *Macbeth*: Neither Vodou nor Welles?," *Shakespeare Bulletin* 32 (Winter 2014), pp. 687–92; and Ayanna Thompson, "Racial Authenticity: The Tension between Production and Reception in the Shakespeare Archive," *Shakespeare Bulletin* 32, no. 4 (Winter 2014), pp. 683–86. See too Rippy's "The Death of the Auteur: Orson Welles, Asadata Dafora, and the 1936 *Macbeth*," in *Orson Welles in Focus*, ed. James N. Gilmore and Stanley Gottlieb (Bloomington: Indiana University Press, 2018), pp. 11–33. Hallie Flanagan's plans for the Negro Unit were reported in the *New York Herald Tribune*, September 22, 1935, and *The New York Times*, March 15, 1936.

For the state of Black theater in the early 1930s and the Lafayette Theatre in 1935, see *The Chicago Defender*, November 26, 1932, and the *Pittsburgh Courier*, March 23, 1935. On *Sailor, Beware!*, see *The New York Times*, May 7, 1935; *Baltimore Afro-American*, April 27, 1935; and McClendon's letter in *The New York Times*, June 30, 1935, where she speaks of how the company that played there in May "gave up." On the White owners of the Lafayette, see

www.americansforthearts.org/blog-feed/breaking-barriers-and
-embracing-change-a-history-of-the-apollo-theater-0.

On Flanagan's choice of McClendon, see Flanagan to McClure,
September 1–18, 1935, WPA Central Files 211.2 NA, as well as
published accounts in Flanagan, *Arena*, pp. 62–63; and Houseman, *Run-Through*, p. 175. For McClendon's career, see Cheryl
Black, "Abject No More: Authority and Authenticity in the Theatrical Career of Rose McClendon," *Theatre History Studies* 30 (2010),
pp. 42–64; Jay Plum, "Rose McClendon and the Black Units of
the Federal Theatre Project: A Lost Contribution," *Theatre Survey*
33, no. 2 (1992), pp. 144–53; "Final Services Held for Rose McClendon," *Amsterdam News*, July 18, 1936; Regina Andrews, "Three
Years with the Harlem Experimental Theatre—Its Purpose," *New
York Age*, April 11, 1931; and Rose McClendon, "As to a New Negro
Stage," *The New York Times*, June 30, 1935. For the *Waiting for Lefty*
benefit, see *The Chicago Defender*, June 15, 1935. With the support of
Communist groups, the Negro People's Theatre was able to perform
Sharecropper and *Exhibit A* at "Camp Unity" before 1,500 left-wing
workers, where McClendon told the audience, "We believe in the
left-wing theater and only in the left-wing movement can we build
and maintain such a theatre," *The Daily Worker*, August 16, 1935. For
Mulatto, see the *New York Herald Tribune*, October 24, 1935.

For the account of the Negro Unit leadership, see the *Amsterdam
News*, November 23, 1935. For criticism of Houseman and other
Whites in leadership roles, see the *Baltimore Afro-American*, March
14, 1936. See too J. F. McDougald, "The Federal Government and
the Negro Theatre," *Opportunity: Journal of Negro Life* 14 (May
1936), pp. 135–37, for an overview of the various Negro Units and

their locations in Harlem. For Houseman's career leading up to his joining the Federal Theatre, see, in addition to his memoir, the *Amsterdam News*, March 17, 1934; and the *New York Times* reviews on February 21 and 25, 1934. For his role in the Phoenix Theatre, see *The New York Times*, July 22, 1934; and the *New York Herald Tribune*, March 3 and 10, 1935; as well as Houseman's obituary in the *Los Angeles Times*, November 1, 1988. For *Medea*, see the *New York Herald Tribune*, August 5, 1934. And for Houseman's work on *Hamlet*, see *The Boston Globe*, October 20, 1836; the *New York Herald Tribune*, July 17, 1935; and *The New York Times*, July 17, 1935. Barbara Leaming reports in her *Orson Welles: A Biography* (New York: Viking, 1985) that he had planned to cast McClendon as Lady Macbeth, though it is unclear whether that would have conflicted with her performing in *Mulatto* (p. 102). For the all-Black Boston production of *Macbeth* in September and October 1935, see Lisa Simmons, "Before Welles: A 1935 Boston Production," in *Weyward Macbeth*, ed. Scott Newstock and Ayanna Thompson (New York: Palgrave, 2010), pp. 79–82. Hallie Flanagan, "Report of Federal Theatre Project as released to various theatrical publications, December 23, 1935," notes that by late December Houseman was the sole director of the Negro Unit.

Sterling A. Brown's reflections on *Macbeth* appear in "The Federal Theatre," in *Anthology of the American Negro in the Theatre*, ed. Lindsay Patterson (New York: Publishers Company, 1967), p. 103. For *Macbeth* in production, see Matthew J. Kinservik, "A Sinister *Macbeth*: The Macklin Production of 1773," *Harvard Library Bulletin* 6, no. 1 (Spring 1995), pp. 51–76; Atkinson's review in *The New York Times*, October 8, 1935; "*Macbeth* in Khaki: Sir Barry Jackson's Experiment," *Manchester Guardian*, February 7, 1928; Gareth

Lloyd Evans, "Macbeth in the Twentieth Century," *Theatre Quarterly* 1 (1971), pp. 36–39; Michael Mullin, *"Macbeth* in Modern Dress: Royal Court Theatre, 1928," *Educational Theatre Journal* 30, no. 2 (May 1978), pp. 176–85; and Heather S. Nathans, "'Blood Will Have Blood': Violence, Slavery, and Macbeth in the Antebellum American Imagination," in Newstock and Thompson, *Weyward Macbeth*, pp. 23–33. On the politics of the production, see France, "Voodoo," p. 67, as well as Willson Whitman, reviewing it in *Stage*, July 1936, who thought that Maurice Ellis's Macduff bore an uncanny physical resemblance to Hailie Selassie. For a review of *Voodoo Fire in Haiti*, from which I quote, see *Los Angeles Times*, August 4, 1935. For an analysis of how the Negro Unit production of *Macbeth* was haunted by *The Emperor Jones*, see Kate Dossett, "Commemorating Haiti on the Harlem Stage," *Journal of American Drama and Theatre* 22, no. 1 (Winter 2010), pp. 83–119. For the fraught early months of 1936 for the Federal Theatre, see De Hart, *Federal Theatre*, pp. 70–74. See too Ira Katznelson, *Fear Itself: The New Deal and the Origins of Our Time* (New York: Liveright, 2013), which has powerfully shaped my argument.

For Orson Welles and *Macbeth*, see Richard France, "The 'Voodoo' *Macbeth* of Orson Welles," *Yale Theatre* 5, no. 3 (1974), pp. 66–78; Richard France, ed., *Orson Welles on Shakespeare: The W.P.A. and Mercury Theatre Playscripts*, forward by Simon Callow (New York: Routledge, 2001); Simon Callow, *Orson Welles: The Road to Xanadu* (New York: Viking, 1996), pp. 216–45; Leaming, *Orson Welles*; Michael Anderegg, *Orson Welles, Shakespeare, and Popular Culture* (New York: Columbia University Press, 1999); Susan McCloskey, "Shakespeare, Orson Welles, and the Voodoo *Macbeth*," *Shakespeare Quarterly* 36, no. 4 (Winter 1985), pp. 406–16; Alva

Johnston and Fred Smith, "How to Raise a Child: The Education of Orson Welles, Who Didn't Need It," *The Saturday Evening Post*, part 1, January 20, 1940; part 2, January 27, 1940; part 3, February 3, 1940; Kenneth Tynan, "Orson Welles," Ronald Gottesman, ed., in *Focus on Orson Welles* (Englewood Cliffs, NJ: Prentice Hall, 1976), pp. 8–27; Robert Sawyer, "'All's Well That Ends Welles': Orson Welles and the 'Voodoo' *Macbeth*," *Multicultural Shakespeare: Translation, Appropriation and Performance* 1 (2016), pp. 87–103; Marguerite Rippy, "Black Cast Conjures White Genius: Unraveling the Mystique of Orson Welles's 'Voodoo' *Macbeth*," pp. 83–90; and Scott L. Newstok, "After Welles: Re-do Voodoo Macbeths," in Newstock and Thompson, *Weyward Macbeth*, pp. 91–100. For Welles's politics (and the leftist politics of artists at this time), see Michael Denning, *The Cultural Front: The Laboring of American Culture in the Twentieth Century* (New York: Verso, 1996).

For accounts of the Negro Units of the Federal Theatre, see Federal Theatre Project, "Report of the Activities and Accomplishments of Negro Dramatists Laboratory" (Washington, D.C.: National Archives, Record Group 69); Edith Isaacs, *The Negro in American Theatre* (New York: Theatre Arts, 1947); Anne Powell, "The Negro and the Federal Theatre," *The Crisis* 43 (November 1936), pp. 340–42; Dossett, *Radical Black Theatre*; Rena Fraden, *Blueprints for a Black Federal Theatre, 1935–1939* (Cambridge: Cambridge University Press, 1994); E. Quita Craig, *Black Drama of the Federal Theatre Era* (Amherst: University of Massachusetts Press, 1980); Glenda Eloise Gill, "Six Black Performers in Relation to the Federal Theatre" (diss., University of Iowa, 1981); Zanthe Taylor, "Singing for Their Supper: The Negro Units of the Federal Theater Project and Their Plays," *Theatre* 27 (1997), pp. 42–59; Ronald

Ross, "The Role of Blacks in the Federal Theatre, 1935–1939," *The Journal of Negro History* 59, no. 1 (January 1974), pp. 38–50, as well as his dissertation, "Black Drama in the Federal Theatre, 1935–1939" (University of Southern California, 1972); Robert Adubato, "A History of the WPA's Negro Theatre Project in New York City, 1935–1939" (diss., New York University, 1978); Lorraine Brown, "A Story Yet to Be Told: The Federal Theatre Research Project," *The Black Scholar: Journal of Black Studies and Research* (July–August 1979), pp. 70–78; Jo A. Tanner, "Classical Black Theatre: Federal Theatre's All-Black 'Voodoo *Macbeth*,'" *Journal of American Drama and Theatre* 7, no. 1 (1995), pp. 50–63; Adrienne Macki Braconi, *Harlem's Theaters: A Staging Ground for Community, Class, and Contradiction, 1923–1939* (Evanston, IL: Northwestern University Press, 2015); and Clifford Mason, *Macbeth in Harlem: Black Theater in America from the Beginning to Raisin in the Sun* (New Brunswick, NJ: Rutgers University Press, 2020).

For contemporary reviews of *Macbeth* in Harlem, see Brooks Atkinson, *The New York Times*, April 15, 1936; John Mason Brown, the *New York Post*, April 18, 1936; Percy Hammond, the *New York Herald Tribune*, April 16, 1936; Roi Ottley, the *Amsterdam News*, April 18, 1936; Burns Mantle, the *New York Daily News*, April 15, 1936; Arthur Pollack, the *Brooklyn Daily Eagle*, April 16, 1936; Ralph Matthews, the *Afro-American*, April 15, 1936; the *Pittsburgh Courier*, April 25, 1936; the *New York Age*, April 15, 1936; *The Hartford Courant*, July 29, 1936; and Willson Whitman, "Uncle Sam Presents," *Stage*, July 1936, p. 2. No company would attempt to stage *Macbeth* again in New York City until 1941, when Margaret Webster's traditional production starring Judith Anderson and Maurice Evans ran for 131 performances.

For the cuts and changes that Welles made to the text, see Susan McCloskey, "Shakespeare, Orson Welles, and the Voodoo *Macbeth*," as well as John S. O'Connor, "But Was It 'Shakespeare'?: Welles's *Macbeth* and *Julius Caesar*," *Theatre Journal* 32, no. 3 (October 1980), pp. 336–48; and Bernice W. Kilman, *Macbeth*, 2nd ed. (Manchester: Manchester University Press, 2004), pp. 120–21. Several drafts of Welles's scripts survive—in the New York Public Library as well as several in the Library of Congress. For Burroughs's training, see, in addition to his Wikipedia entry, the *Amsterdam News*, April 25, 1936. I have found no evidence to support the oft-repeated claim that Burroughs attended the Royal Academy of Dramatic Arts in London.

For the various myths and facts concerning Welles's early experience of Shakespeare, see Callow, *Orson Welles*, pp. 67–68; and Johnston and Smith, "How to Raise a Child: The Education of Orson Welles, Who Didn't Need It"; and Robert Sawyer, "'All's Well That Ends Welles.'" For what took place in rehearsals I rely on France, "Voodoo *Macbeth*," who interviewed some of those in the room in 1971–72 (including Samuel Leve, who spoke of "pandemonium"), and to a lesser extent Houseman—banished by Welles from rehearsals—as well as Callow, *Orson Welles*, pp. 229–34, who draws on their accounts. See too Leaming, *Orson Welles*, p. 103. For Mary McCarthy, see her "Versions of Shakespeare," *Partisan Review* 43 (1938), pp. 34–38.

For the Harlem riot of March 1935, see Mayor's Commission on Conditions in Harlem, *The Negro in Harlem: A Report on Social and Economic Conditions Responsible for the Outbreak of March 19, 1935* (New York, [1936]). See too Cheryl Greenberg's *"Or Does It Explode?" Black Harlem in the Great Depression* (New York: Oxford

University Press, 1997); Alain Locke, "Harlem: Dark Weather-Vane," *Survey Graphic* 25 (August 1936), pp. 439ff.; the *Amsterdam News*, April 4, 1936; Houseman, *Run-Through*, p. 197; *The New York Times*, May 19, 1935; and Raymond Wolters, *Negroes and the Great Depression: The Problem of Economic Recovery* (Westport, CT: Greenwood, 1970). In its July 18, 1936, issue the *Amsterdam News* published the suppressed report in full ("Complete Riot Report Bared," pp. 6ff., including the original conclusions in chapter 9, "considered too hot, too caustic, too critical, too unfavorable by the Mayor, and was allegedly revamped by the commission to make it more to his liking." The riot drew many "curious white visitors [who] thronged Harlem's sidewalks," the *Chicago Tribune*, March 21, 1935.

For *Walk Together, Chillun* and *Conjur Man Dies*, see Houseman, *Run-Through*; and Jo A. Tanner, "Classical Black Theatre: Federal Theatre's All-Black 'Voodoo *Macbeth*,'" *Journal of American Drama and Theatre* 7, no. 1 (1995), pp. 50–63; Herbert Kline, "Drama of Negro Life," *New Theatre*, February 1936, pp. 26–27; and "A Survey of the WPA Negro Theatre in New York City," in "Press Releases of the Department of Information," box 533, RG 69, National Archives (NA).

For opening night of *Macbeth* in Harlem and what led up to it, see www.loc.gov/collections/federal-theatre-project-1935-to-1939/articles-and-essays/play-that-electrified-harlem; Clifford Mason, *Macbeth in Harlem: Black Theater in America from the Beginning to Raisin in the Sun* (New Brunswick, NJ: Rutgers University Press, 2020); Clare Corbould, "Streets, Sounds and Identity in Interwar Harlem," *Journal of Social History* 40, no. 4 (Summer, 2007), pp. 859–94. For the Tree of Hope, see ephemeralnewyork.wordpress

.com/2009/11/12/the-tree-of-hope-of-the-harlem-renaissance; and *The New York Times*, July 5, 1936. See too *The New York Times*, April 15, 1936; and the *Norfolk New Journal and Guide*, July 18, 1936; the *Chicago Tribune*, March 21, 1935; and the *Atlanta Daily World*, April 27, 1936. For Welles on the curtain call, see Leslie Megahey, "Interview from the Orson Welles Story," in *Orson Welles Interviews*, ed. Mark W. Estrin (Jackson: University of Mississippi, 2002), pp. 180–81. See too Martha Gellhorn, "The Federal Theatre," *The Spectator*, July 10, 1936, pp. 51–52; Robert Littell, "Everyone Likes Chocolate," *Vogue*, November 1, 1936, pp. 66–67; and "Macbeth in Chocolate," reprinted in *Reader's Digest* 30 (January 1937), pp. 88–89. Littell followed that up with a piece in *The Baltimore Sun*, February 27, 1937. Edward R. Murrow is quoted in France, "The 'Voodoo' *Macbeth*," p. 70, from *Stage* (July 1936).

For Black responses to *Macbeth*, see the *Norfolk New Journal and Guide*, July 18, 1936; and the *Baltimore Afro-American*, May 2, 1936. For Amster, see the *Sunday Worker*, July 5, 1936; for Wright, see *The Daily Worker*, October 15, 1937; for Hughes, see *Remember Me to Harlem: The Letters of Langston Hughes and Carl Van Vechten, 1925–1964*, ed. Emily Bernard (New York: Knopf, 2001), p. 137; as well as the interview in the *Pittsburgh Courier*, October 17, 1936; *The Collected Poems of Langston Hughes*, ed. Arnold Rampersad (New York: Knopf, 1994); and *Shakespeare in Harlem* (New York: Knopf, 1942). For Roi Ottley, see "The Negro Theatre *Macbeth*," *New Theatre*, May 1936, p. 24; and the *Amsterdam News*, April 4 and July 11, 1936. When the show moved down to Broadway, Ottley was quick to note that the "ofays didn't receive the production downtown with the same gusto exhibited in the Harlem environs."

For the *Macbeth* tour, see the *Norfolk New Journal and Guide*,

September 19, 1936; the *Baltimore Afro-American*, July 18, 1936; and *The Philadelphia Tribune*, September 3, 1936. For Cincinnati, see www.loc.gov/ghe/cascade/index.html?appid=8f8d1416f3234d dc8addc42880f25a4b&bookmark=On%20Tour. For Detroit, see the *Detroit Tribune*, September 19, 1936. For Dallas, see Jesse O. Thomas, *Negro Participation in the Texas Centennial Exhibition* (Boston: Christopher Publishing House, 1938), p. 83; and Rosenfeld's pieces in *The Dallas Morning News*, August 5 and 14, 1936, and October 29, 1941. See too the admiring and detailed account of this production in the *Tennessean*, September 20, 1936. For the incident on the train leaving Dallas, see the *Amsterdam News*, September 5, 1936, and the *Baltimore Afro-American*, September 5, 1936. There seems to have been talk of continuing the tour, and a story ran that some of the professional members of the cast wanted to get rid of less trained ones—"and when done it is believed that *Macbeth* will continue to run in different sections of the country for at least another year unless a decision comes to undertake some other play in a similar manner," the *Cleveland Call and Post*, October 8, 1936.

For life after *Macbeth*, see Houseman, *Run-Through*, pp. 211–81; Callow, *Orson Welles*, 243ff.; Leaming, *Orson Welles*, p. 244; and Mona Z. Smith, *Becoming Something: The Story of Canada Lee* (New York: Farrar, Straus and Giroux, 2004). For Welles's interview with Leslie Megahey, see "Interview from the Orson Welles Story," in Estrin, *Orson Welles Interviews*. On the painfully slow progress of Black stagehands to gain membership in the all-White Local No. 1 of Theatrical Stage Employees, see Kathy Anne Perkins, "Black Backstage Workers, 1900–1969," Black American Literature Forum, Black Theatre Issue, *African American Review* 16, no. 4

(Winter 1982), pp. 160–63. For brief footage of *Macbeth*, likely filmed during the run at the Adelphi Theatre, that miraculously survives from the contemporary film *We Work Again* (1937), see https://www.filmpreservation.org/preserved-films/screening-room /voodoo-macbeth#.

CHAPTER FOUR: *IT CAN'T HAPPEN HERE*

For texts of the novel, see Sinclair Lewis, *It Can't Happen Here* (New York: Doubleday, Doran, 1935), as well as Sinclair Lewis, *It Can't Happen Here*, with an introduction by Michael Meyer and an afterword by Gary Scharnhorst, rev. ed. (2014; New York: Signet, 1970). The official Federal Theatre Project playtext, which varied from production to production and continued to be revised after this date, is *It Can't Happen Here: A Play* by John C. Moffitt and Sinclair Lewis, rev. ed. (Federal Theatre Playscript Publication No. 1, September 18, 1936). See too the various drafts in the Sinclair Lewis Papers housed at Yale Library. For biographies of Lewis that deal extensively with his involvement with the play, see Mark Schorer, *Sinclair Lewis: An American Life* (New York: McGraw Hill, 1961); and Richard Lingeman, *Sinclair Lewis: Rebel from Main Street* (New York: Random House, 2002). See too Gary Scharnhorst and Matthew Hofer, eds., *Sinclair Lewis Remembered* (Tuscaloosa: University of Alabama Press, 2012). I have also drawn upon S. J. Woolf, "It Won't Happen Here, Lewis Believes: The Author Holds That Liberalism Can Save Our System from Left or Right Dictators," *The New York Times*, October 4, 1936, as well as the following reviews of the novel: Benjamin Stolberg, the *New York Herald Tribune*, October 20, 1935; and J. Donald Adams, *The New York Times*, October 20, 1935. And for Lewis's defense of the politics of the play, see, for example, Department of Information News Release, September 14, 1936, RG 69, FTP.

For the influence of Dorothy Thompson on the novel and play, see Peter Kurth, *American Cassandra: The Life of Dorothy Thompson* (Boston: Little, Brown, 1990); as well as Dorothy Thompson, *"I Saw Hitler!"* (New York: Farrar and Rinehart, 1932). For the alarm over fascism in America in the 1930s, I have drawn on Raymond Gram Swing, *Forerunners of American Fascism* (New York: Julian Messner, 1935); Stephen L. Tanner, "Sinclair Lewis and Fascism," *Studies in the Novel* 22, no. 1 (Spring 1990), pp. 57–66; Benjamin Leontif Alpers, *Dictators, Democracy, and American Public Culture: Envisioning the Totalitarian Enemy, 1920s–1940s* (Chapel Hill: North Carolina University Press, 2003); Alan Brinkley, *Voices of Protest: Huey Long, Father Coughlin, and the Great Depression* (New York: Knopf, 1969); and Michael Mark Cohen, "Buzz Can Happen Here: Sinclair Lewis and the New American Fascism," *New Ohio Review*, Winter 2020. On reports about concentration camps, see, for example, "Mass Internment of Jews Reported from Germany: Returning Exiles Being Herded into Concentration Camps," the *New York Herald Tribune*, March 5, 1935.

On the banning of *It Can't Happen Here* in Hollywood, see Ben Urwand's illuminating *The Collaboration: Hollywood's Pact with Hitler* (Cambridge, MA: Harvard University Press, 2013). Thomas Doherty, *Hollywood and Hitler, 1933–1939* (New York: Columbia University Press, 2013), is also useful. See too David Platt, to whom the filmscript was leaked, "The Case of *It Can't Happen Here*: A First-Hand Discussion of the Suppressed Lewis-Howard Script," *The Daily Worker*, May 11, 1936. See as well "Hays Gets Blame for Book Ban," *Publishers Weekly*, February 29, 1936, p. 988;

and *"It Can't Happen Here* Storm Continues Unabated," *Publishers Weekly*, March 14, 1936, p. 1174.

On the self-censorship of the stage production, see Macy Donyce Jones, "Precarious Democracy: *It Can't Happen Here* as the Federal Theatre's Site of Mass Resistance" (diss., Louisiana State University, 2017), which includes a reproduction of the opposition newsletter, Windrip's "Fifteen Points" (Underground Newspaper, box 308, series 29, subgroup 867, record group 69, NACP, College Park, MD). She also cites Flanagan's concerns in her letter to Morris Watson, October 20, 1936, box 116, series 29, subgroup 867, record group 69, NACP, College Park, MD. I am especially indebted to her account of E. E. McCleish and his "Instructions Governing Exploitation Concerning *It Can't Happen Here*," October 27, 1936, box 116, series 29, subgroup 867, record group 69, NACP, College Park, MD. See too "Legitimate: Ban of Negro WPA Play Has Loop in Turmoil; *Happen* Also Worries," *Variety*, October 21, 1936. For the Hearst paper threat against the Federal Theatre Project at this time, see the letter of J. Howard Miller to W. P. Farnsworth, October 25, 1936, RG 69, FTP Records, NOC, 1936–1939.

For many details about the specific productions across the country, I have drawn on the excellent account in Marjorie S. Korn, *"It Can't Happen Here*: Federal Theatre's Bold Adventure" (diss., University of Missouri, 1978). Flanagan's own account in *Arena*, including her reconstruction of long conversations with Sinclair Lewis, is also helpful. For other illuminating accounts of the productions, see De Hart; Willson Whitman, *Bread and Circuses: A Study of Federal Theatre* (New York: Oxford University Press,

1937); Quinn, *Furious Improvisation*; Bonnie Nelson Schwartz, *Voices from the Federal Theatre* (Madison: University of Wisconsin Press, 2003); and Barbara Melosh, *Engendering Culture: Manhood and Womanhood in New Deal Public Art and Theater* (Washington, D.C.: Smithsonian Institution Press, 1991).

For more on the making of *It Can't Happen Here*, see as well "Visit with 'Red,'" *The New Yorker*, November 21, 1936, pp. 13–14; "Multiple 'Can't Happen' Performances Due Next Week—Much Temperament," *Variety*, October 21, 1936, p. 60; Pierre de Rohan, "It IS Happening Here—and Everywhere!," *Federal Theatre Bulletin* 2, no. 2 (1936); and Hallie Flanagan, "Papa's Got a Job," *Virginia Quarterly Review* 15, no. 2 (Spring 1939), pp. 249–58, as well as her "Why Not Here?," *Federal Theatre Bulletin* 2, no. 2 (1936). See too William Farnsworth's interview by John O'Connor, March 16, 1977, "WPA Oral Histories," George Mason University Libraries.

For productions in translation, see, for the Spanish one in Tampa, Kenya C. Dworkin y Méndez, "When a 'New Deal' Became a Raw Deal: Depression-Era, 'Latin' Federal Theatre," *Transmodernity: Journal of Peripheral Cultural Production of the Luso-Hispanic World* 1, no. 1 (2011); and for Yiddish ones in New York and Los Angeles, see Joel Schechter, *Messiahs of 1933: How American Yiddish Theatre Survived Adversity through Satire* (Philadelphia: Temple University Press, 2008). On the play's critical reception, see especially "'Can't Happen Here' Is Disappointing in Treatment as Play," *The Hollywood Reporter* 36, no. 9 (1936); "WPA Finds 'New Audience,'" *Variety*, November 4, 1936, pp. 53–54; the *New York Herald Tribune*, October 28, 1936; *The New York Times*, October 28 and November 8, 1936; and *The Chicago Daily Tribune*, November 8, 1936. For Lewis acting the part of Jessup, see *Time*, August 8, 1938, p. 33.

CHAPTER FIVE: *HOW LONG, BRETHREN?*

For Huffman's testimony, see *Investigation of Un-American Propaganda Activities in the United States: Hearings before a Special Committee on Un-American Activities, House of Representatives, Seventy-fifth Congress, Third Session–Seventy-eighth Congress, Second Session, on H. Res. 282*, vol. 1, especially pp. 784–85; and for Flanagan on *How Long, Brethren?* and *Professor Mamlock*, see her *Arena*, pp. 198–99.

For the history of the African American spiritual, I have relied heavily on John Lovell, Jr.'s comprehensive *Black Song: The Forge and the Flame; The Story of How the Afro-American Spiritual Was Hammered Out* (New York: Macmillan, 1972); and Eileen Guenther, *In Their Own Words: Slave Life and the Power of Spirituals* (St. Louis: MorningStar Music Publishers, 2016). See too Sterling A. Brown, "Negro Folk Expression: Spirituals, Seculars, Ballads and Work Songs," *Phylon* 14 (1953), pp. 45–61, as well as his "Negro Songs of Protest in America," *Music Vanguard* (March–April 1935), pp. 3–14. I quote Du Bois from Guenther, p. 335, and Douglass from Lovell, p. 493.

For Gellert's *Negro Songs of Protest*, see Bruce M. Conforth, *African American Folksong and American Cultural Politics: The Lawrence Gellert Story* (Lanham, MD: Scarecrow Press, 2013), from which I quote (on the charge that he was a "dupe") from p. 159. And for Steven Garabedian's repudiation of Conforth's claims, see his "Forgotten Manuscripts: Lawrence Gellert, *Negro Songs of Protest*," *African American Review* 49, no. 4 (Winter 2016), pp. 297–31, and his

A Sound History: Lawrence Gellert, Black Musical Protest, and White Denial (Amherst: University of Massachusetts Press, 2020), from which I quote from pp. 9 and 302. I have also found valuable Alex Lichtenstein's judicious review of Garabedian's book, "A Sound Archive," *Reviews in American History* 49, no. 4 (2021), pp. 583–89. The Bancroft Library at the University of California, Berkeley, has a collection of Gellert papers, including Langston Hughes's correspondence with him and a draft of the introduction. Yale University digitized its holdings of Gellert's writings from the Federal Writers' Project Negro Group papers, including the essay "Negro Songs of Protest" (collections.library.yale.edu/catalog/10589567) and an outline on "American negro folk music" (collections.library .yale.edu/catalog/10589203). Conforth writes that Mike Gold came up with the label "Negro Songs of Protest" (p. 61). See *Time*, June 15, 1936, for the early description of Gellert. For an early account of *Negro Songs of Protest*, see H. Howard Taubman, "Negro Folksongs: New Genre Dealing with Everyday Life Produced, Particularly in South," *The New York Times*, July 5, 1936. For the review in *The New Republic*, see December 30, 1936, pp. 280–81. For quotations from an interview with Gellert, see Laura Brown's interview with him, "Voices of the WPA," George Mason University Libraries, October 22, 1976, tape 1. I am greatly indebted to Robin Reeder for providing a transcription of this interview. Gellert says in the interview that he knew Tamiris and apparently wanted to contribute to *How Long, Brethren?*, but Flanagan told him that they already had the rights to the music and that "there's nothing you can do" on the production. Langston Hughes's introduction was not published in the American edition; I have drawn upon Arnold Rampersad, *The Life of Langston Hughes*, 2nd ed. (New York: Oxford

University Press, 2002), vol. 1, p. 252, for this background and for the circumstances surrounding the publication of "Good Morning Revolution." See too David E. Chinitz, "Behind Closed Doors," *The Langston Hughes Review* 25, no. 1 (2019), pp. 95–104.

For Tamiris's life and career, I draw extensively on Christena L. Schlundt, *Tamiris: A Chronicle of Her Dance Career, 1927–1955* (New York: New York Public Library, 1972). For her unfinished autobiography, see "Tamiris in Her Own Voice: Draft of an Autobiography," ed. Daniel Nagrin, *Studies in Dance History* 1, no. 1 (Fall 1989), pp. 1–64, including her comments on race, pp. 40–52, from which I quote. Tamiris's archives are in the New York Public Library, including the manuscript of her unfinished autobiography and interviews with her, circa 1950 and 1965; a brief unpublished biography of her by Katharine A. Wolfe; the text of *How Long, Brethren?*; as well as clippings, programs, and scrapbooks. See too Pauline Tish's invaluable "Remembering Helen Tamiris," *Dance Chronicle* 17, no. 3 (1994), pp. 327–60; Maude Babcock Urtell, "The Dancer Who Stages Herself," *Dance Magazine*, July 1928, p. 61; and Tamiris's obituary in *The New York Times*, August 5, 1966. For Tamiris's performance with the Bahama Negro Dancers, see *The New York Times*, August 19, 1933, as well as the *New York Herald Tribune*, August 18 and 19, 1933. For Martin's reflection on Tamiris and race, see *The New York Times*, August 27, 1933. On Tamiris as "the Harlem savage," see Schlundt, *Tamiris*, p. 71. For Lillian Shapero performing to Hughes's "Good Morning Revolution," see the *Amsterdam News*, October 6, 1934. See too, for rare film footage of Tamiris, the 1959 film *Negro Spirituals*, produced by the William Skipper Corporation with an introduction by John Martin, and the 1977 *Trailblazers of Modern Dance*, directed by

Emile Ardolini for the PBS series *Dance in America*. For Tamiris's blacklisting and her FBI file, I quote from Carol A. Stabile, Jeremiah Favara, and Laura Strait, The Broadcast 41, "Tamiris, Helen: Biography," broadcast41.uoregon.edu/biography/tamiris-helen; as well as Milly S. Barranger, *Unfriendly Witnesses: Gender, Theater, and Film in the McCarthy Era* (Carbondale: Southern Illinois University Press, 2008), p. 147.

For contemporary reviews of *How Long, Brethren?*, see *The Daily Worker*, May 2, 1937; and the *New York Herald Tribune*, May 7, 1937; as well as reviews of its revivals in the *Afro-American*, June 19, 1937; *The New York Times*, December 22, 1937; "Tamiris–Charles Weidman," *Dance Observer* 4 (June–July 1937), p. 68; *The Brooklyn Daily Eagle*, May 7, 1937, from which I quote on the audience's exuberant response; Margaret Lloyd in *The Christian Science Monitor*, February 15, 1938, and especially her earlier review of the revival, in *The Christian Science Monitor*, January 4, 1938, where she speaks of "artistic miscegenation." See as well the *Federal Theatre Magazine* 2, no. 5 (1937). See too Audience Survey, *Candide* and *How Long, Brethren?*, audience survey files, May 6–13, 1937, Federal Theatre Project, National Archives. For fifty-five photographs of the dances, see www.loc.gov/item/musftpnegatives.12170123. For the change of "Nigger" to "Darkie," see Ellen Graff, *Stepping Left: Dance and Politics in New York City, 1928–1942* (Durham, NC: Duke University Press, 1997), p. 213, note 75, and for the music's adaptation, see Margaret Lloyd, *The Christian Science Monitor*, February 15, 1938, from which I quote. There were revivals of *Brethren* in 1991 at George Mason University and in 1993 at the American Dance Festival. For representative reviews of these, see Alan Kriegsman, "*The Washington Post*, May 4, 1991, and Anna

Kisselgoff, *The New York Times*, July 14, 1993. For the warm response of the audiences who saw it, see Schlundt, *Tamiris*, pp. 46–47. For contemporary accounts of the sit-in strike after the performance on May 19, see the *New York Herald Tribune* and the *New York Post*, May 20, 1937. For the responses of Black newspapers, see "Talbert Choir on Broadway: Group Shines in WPA Dance Drama," the *Amsterdam News*, May 15, 1937; the *Pittsburgh Courier*, January 15, 1938; and the *Baltimore Afro-American*, January 29, 1938. For Tamiris's radio remarks, see the transcript to "Backstage Interviews," December 25, 1937, Tamiris Clippings 1936–1939, folder 3, Jerome Robbins Dance Collection, NYPL for the Performing Arts. For a 1995 videorecording of *How Long, Brethren?*, see the American Dance Festival Video, presented by the Cleo Parker Robinson Dance Ensemble, reconstructed by Dianne McIntyre, which can be viewed at the Jerome Robbins Dance Division of the NYPL.

For the history and politics of modern dance in the 1930s, I have drawn especially on Graff, *Stepping Left*; Helen Thomas, *Dance, Modernity and Culture* (New York: Routledge, 1995); Julia L. Foulkes, *Modern Bodies: Dance and American Modernism from Martha Graham to Alvin Ailey* (Chapel Hill: University of North Carolina Press, 2002), as well as her "Angels 'Rewolt!': Jewish Women in Modern Dance in the 1930s," *American Jewish History* 88, no. 2 (2000), pp. 233–52; and Mark Franko, *The Work of Dance: Labor, Movement, and Identity in the 1930s* (Middletown, CT: Wesleyan University Press, 2002). See too John Martin, *America Dancing: The Background and Personalities of the Modern Dance* (New York: Dodge, 1936); and the *Christian Science Monitor* dance critic Margaret Lloyd, *The Borzoi Book of Modern Dance* (New York: Knopf, 1949), from which I quote from pp. 138 and 141–42. For Jewish modern dancers, see Joanna Gewertz, "From Tenement to Theater: Jewish Women as Dance Pioneers: Helen Becker (Tamiris), Anna Sokolow, Sophie Maslow," *Judaism* 45, no. 3 (Summer 1996), pp. 259–76; Josh Perelman, "Choreographing Identity: Modern Dance and American Jewish Life, 1924–1954" (diss., New York University, 2008); and Naomi M. Jackson, *Converging Movements: Modern Dance and Jewish Culture at the 92nd Street Y* (Hanover, NH: University Press of New England, 2000), especially pp. 173–77 and 185–87, from which I quote.

And for Black modern dance, see Richard Long, *The Black Tradition in Modern Dance* (New York: Rizzoli, 1989); John O. Perpener III, *African-American Concert Dance: The Harlem Renaissance and Beyond* (Urbana: University of Illinois Press, 2001); and A. Kaye, "Reviews—Negro Dance Evening," *Dance* (May 1937), pp. 32–33, as well as the *Y.M.H.A. Bulletin* 38 (March 5, 1937), which notes that ticket prices were as low as fifty cents for members and seventy-five cents for nonmembers.

For the history of the Federal Dance Theatre, see the contemporary account by Grant Code, "Dance Theatre of the WPA: A Record of National Accomplishment," *Dance Observer* (October 1939), pp. 264–65, 274; (November 1939), pp. 280–81, 290, 302; and (February 1940), pp. 34–35. For John Martin on Becque's plan and its sluggish start, see *The New York Times*, March 15 and November 22, 1936; and for the failure of Becque's *Young Tramps*, see *The Daily Worker*, November 16, 1936. See as well Tony Buttitta, "The Dance Comes Back to the Theatre," *Federal Theatre Magazine* 1, no. 5 (April 1936), p. 9; Elizabeth Cooper, "Tamiris and the Federal Dance Theatre 1936–1939: Socially Relevant Dance Amidst the Policies and Politics of the New Deal Era," *Dance Research Journal* 29, no. 2 (1997), pp. 23–48; Kathleen Ann Lally, "A History of the Federal Dance Theatre of the Works Progress Administration, 1935–1939" (diss., Texas Women's University, 1978); Luba Markoff, "Dance in the Political Arena: The Federal Dance Project and Helen Tamiris" (MA thesis, San Jose State University, 1992); and Kim C. Friedman, "The Federal Dance Theatre in New York City: Legislative and Administrative Obstacles" (MA thesis, American University, 1992). Flanagan spoke of the dancers as "volcanic" in *Arena*, p. 76; I quote Flanagan on the triumph of *How Long, Brethren?*, from Susan Manning, *Modern Dance, Negro Dance: Race in Motion* (Minneapolis: University of Minnesota Press, 2004), p. 109. And see Hallie Flanagan, "The Dance and the Modern Theatre," typescript dated May 14, 1937, Federal Theatre Collection, National Archives.

For Flanagan's view of what theater directors could learn from dancers, see *New Theatre*, February 1936, p. 5. I quote Susan Manning's criticism of Tamiris from her "Black Voices, White Bodies: The Performance of Race and Gender in *How Long Brethren*," *American Quarterly* 50, no. 1 (1998), pp. 24–46, where her argument is influenced by Michael Rogin, *Blackface, White Noise: Jewish Immigrants in the Hollywood Melting Pot* (Berkeley: University of California Press, 1996). When, six years later, Manning reworked her account of *How Long, Brethren?* in her book *Modern Dance, Negro Dance*, she would return to "Tamiris's metaphorical minstrelsy," though make much less of the argument (pp. 85 and 113). For Beryl Banfield's remarks, see her interview of May 22, 1978, conducted by Lorraine Brown, as well as Anne Lief Barlin's of October 25, 1977, interviewed by Karen Wickre, "Voices of the WPA,"

George Mason University Libraries. For the situation of the twenty-two Black modern dancers at the Lafayette Theatre, see "The Negro and Federal Project No. 1 (WPA Arts Projects) for New York City: A Brief," prepared by the Negro Arts Committee Federal Arts Council, entry 21, box 1, file "Miscellaneous," 2, RG 69, pp. 10–11. For a critique of the all-White Los Angeles Dance Unit performing *Let My People Go*, which "mirrored some of the very patterns of inequality it was critiquing," see Margaret F. Savilonis, "Choreographing Diversity and American Experience: Myra Kinch and Group, Federal Theatre Project (1937–39)," in *Experiments in Democracy: Interracial and Cross-Cultural Exchange in American Theatre, 1912–1945*, ed. Cheryl Black and Jonathan Shandell (Carbondale: Southern Illinois University Press, 2016), pp. 147–71. For the performance of Tamiris's Black spirituals alongside Alvin Ailey's at the 92NY, see the program for the April 21, 1974, "A Gala Evening of Dance" at the Theresa L. Kaufmann Concert Hall (my thanks to dance historian Jessica Friedman for sharing a copy of this with me). For Martha Graham and the politics of her dance, see Victoria Phillips, *Martha Graham's Cold War: The Dance of American Diplomacy* (New York: Oxford University Press, 2020), from which I quote from pp. 11 and 15.

CHAPTER SIX: *ONE THIRD OF A NATION*

For the backstory to *One Third of a Nation*, see Flanagan, *Arena*, pp. 185ff. For the background of *Injunction Granted*, see Arnold Goldman's introduction to Arthur Arent, Joe Losey, Hjalmar Hermanson, and Virgil Thomson, *"Injunction Granted," Minnesota Review* 1 (Fall 1973), pp. 46–50. For more on Losey, as well as the press response to his *Triple-A Plowed Under*, see David Caute, *Joseph Losey:*

A Revenge on Life (London: Faber, 1994), p. 55; and the *New York Evening Journal*, October 24, 1936. For Flanagan's journal entry on her differences with Losey and Watson, see De Hart, p. 111; see too Losey's introduction to *"Injunction Granted"* in the *Minnesota Review*, pp. 51–53. Arent spoke of "Young Turks" who changed the play in a November 1961 interview (see De Hart, *Federal Theatre*, pp. 109–10). For Langdon Post, see his *The Challenge of Housing* (New York: Farrar and Rinehart, 1938), and *The New York Times Book Review*, July 3, 1938. For quotations from the play, see *Injunction Granted* (Federal Theatre Project Play Bureau, 1936). And for the announcement of cuts to the Theatre Project, see the *New York Herald Tribune*, November 23, 1936.

Arthur Arent and his collaborators drew upon the *Congressional Record*, vol. 81, part 7, for the first week of August 1937 for the scene. For a detailed account of the Housing Act, see Timothy L. McDonnell, *The Wagner Housing Act: A Case Study of the Legislative Process* (Chicago: Loyola University Press, 1957). For President Roosevelt on the ill-housed in the nation, see his State of the Union speech of January 6, 1937, factba.se/sotu/transcript/fdr-sotu-19370106, as well as his second inaugural address on January 20, 1937, politic alrhetoricarchive.wcu.edu/speech/second-inaugural-address -by-franklin-d-roosevelt. See too D. Bradford Hunt, "Was the 1937 U.S. Housing Act a Pyrrhic Victory?," *Journal of Planning History* 4, no. 3 (2005), pp. 195–221; Mark Gelfand, *A Nation of Cities: The Federal Government and Urban America, 1933–1975* (New York: Oxford University Press, 1975); Lawrence M. Friedman, "Public Housing and the Poor: An Overview," *California Law Review* 54, no. 2 (May 1966), pp. 642–69; Gwendolyn Wright, *Building the Dream: A Social History of Housing in America* (Cambridge,

MA: MIT Press, 1981); Gail Radford, *Modern Housing for America: Policy Struggles in the New Deal Era* (Chicago: University of Chicago Press, 1995); and Cory Pillen, *WPA Posters in an Aesthetic, Social, and Political Context: A New Deal for Design* (New York: Routledge, 2020). For Wagner's threat to appeal directly to Southern voters about anti-lynching legislation, see the *Congressional Record*, vol. 83, part 2, February 21, 1938, pp. 2204–6; and for Andrews, see the *Congressional Record*, vol. 82, part 1, for November 22, 1937, as well as Keith M. Finley, *Delaying the Dream: Southern Senators and the Fight against Civil Rights, 1938–1965* (Baton Rouge: Louisiana State University Press, 2008), p. 31. For the editorials attacking Wagner on his anti-lynching bill, see the *Congressional Record*, vol. 82, part 1, for February 22, 1938. For the threatened investigation of the Federal Theatre, see, for example, *The Hartford Courant*, February 7, 1938.

For Bailey's performance and Minton's response, see the *Congressional Record*, vol. 83, part 2, for February 22, 1938, pp. 2304ff. For information about Bailey, I have drawn on John Robert Moore, "Senator Josiah W. Bailey and the 'Conservative Manifesto' of 1937," *The Journal of Southern History* 31, no. 1 (February 1965), pp. 21–29, as well as his biography: *Senator Josiah William Bailey of North Carolina: A Political Biography* (Durham, NC: Duke University Press, 1968), including his account of Bailey's solitary vote against funding relief. For the conservative coalition emerging in the Senate, see Douglas Carl Abrams, *Conservative Constraints: North Carolina and the New Deal* (Jackson: University Press of Mississippi, 1992), from which I draw on Daniel's harsh view of Bailey (p. 242). For Bailey's views of the anti-lynching bill, see the *Congressional Record*, vol. 82, part 1, for November 18, 1937; and for

Andrews's, see the *Congressional Record*, vol. 82, part 1, for November 22, 1937. For background on Senator Minton, I have drawn on Linda C. Gugin and James E. St. Clair, *Sherman Minton: New Deal Senator, Cold War Justice* (Indianapolis: Indiana Historical Society, 1997); and William Franklin Radcliff, *Sherman Minton: Indiana's Supreme Court Justice* (Indianapolis: Guild Press of Indiana, 1996). For reactions in the press to their exchange and for accounts of the laughter that greeted Bailey's performance, see the stories that ran in the *New York Herald Tribune*, *The Baltimore Sun* (from which I quote), and the *Chicago Tribune* on February 23, 1938; the *Congressional Record*, vol. 83, part 2, for February 22, 1938, notes some of the moments where he was interrupted by laughter. For Ernest L. Meyer's sense of the danger of the Senate confrontation over *One Third of a Nation*, as well as his quotation from Maverick, see the *Capital Times* of Madison, Wisconsin, February 4, 1938.

For the correspondence between Byrd and Andrews and various WPA administrators, see Carol Anne Highsaw, "A Theatre of Action: The Living Newspapers of the Federal Theatre Project" (diss., Princeton University, 1988); and De Hart, *Federal Theatre*, p. 174; for specific correspondence, see Andrews to Hopkins, February 10, 1938, RG 69, FTP Records, NOGSF; Byrd to Hopkins, February 10, 1938, RG GSS-211.2; Flanagan to Andrews, March 7, 1938, RG 69, FTP Records, NOGSF; and Memorandum, Flanagan to Ellen Woodward and Lawrence Morris, March 5, 1938, RD 69, FTP Records, NOGSF. For the close questioning of Aubrey Williams by the Senate, see *Hearings before the Senate Committee on Appropriations on H.J. Res. 596: Supplemental Appropriation; Relief and Work Relief, Fiscal Year 1938, Seventy-fifth Congress, Third Session*

(1938), especially pp. 43–46. For Arent's insistence that the play did not ridicule anyone, see *The New York Times*, February 8, 1938, and the *New York Herald Tribune*, February 10, 1938. For Andrews's suggestion that there was a foreign element behind the play, see the *Motion Picture Herald*, February 12, 1938, p. 21. I am also indebted to Adam Flores's "A Director's Approach to Arthur Arent's *One Third of a Nation*" (MFA thesis, Baylor University, 2015).

Much has been written about the Federal Theatre's Living Newspapers. Arthur Arent was one of the first to do so, in "The Technique of the Living Newspaper," *Theatre Arts Monthly* 22, no. 11 (1938), pp. 820–25; followed by Morris Watson, "'Writing the Living Newspaper,' Report for the National Service Bureau," 1938, Library of Congress Federal Theatre Project Collection, Washington, D.C., container 133; and Flanagan, in her introductions to the two-volume Random House edition of Living Newspapers, *Federal Theater Plays* (New York: Random House, 1938). See too Marjorie Louise Platt Dycke, "The Living Newspaper: A Study of the Nature of the Form and Its Place in Modern Social Drama" (diss., New York University, 1948); Jordana Cox, "'Propaganda for Democracy': Dialogue and Dissemination in the Federal Theatre Project's Living Newspapers, 1936–1939" (Evanston, IL: Northwestern University, 2015), as well as her "The Phantom Public, the Living Newspaper: Reanimating the Public in the Federal Theatre Project's *1935* (New York, 1936)," *Theatre Survey* 58, no. 3 (September 2017), pp. 300–325; as well as Cosgrove, "The Living Newspaper." Also useful are Gerry Cobb, "*Injunction Granted* in Its Times: A Living Newspaper Reappraised," *New Theatre Quarterly* 6, no. 23 (1990), pp. 279–96; Morgan Y. Himelstein, *Drama Was a*

Weapon: The Left-Wing Theatre in New York, 1929–1941 (New Brunswick, NJ: Rutgers University Press, 1963); Arnold Goldman, "Life and Death of the Living Newspaper Unit," *Theatre Quarterly* 3, no. 9 (1973), pp. 69–89; Ilka Saal, *New Deal Theater: The Vernacular Tradition in American Political Theater* (New York: Palgrave Macmillan, 2007); Douglas McDermott, "The Living Newspaper as a Dramatic Form," *Modern Drama* 8 (May 1965), pp. 82–94; Highsaw, "A Theatre of Action"; and John W. Casson, "Newspaper: Theatre and Therapy," *TDR/The Drama Review* 4, no. 2 (2000), pp. 107–22. For Mary McCarthy's incisive reflections on the Living Newspaper, see "The Federal Theatre Settles Down," *Partisan Review* 4, no. 6 (May 1938), pp. 43–47, reprinted as "The Federal Theatre," in *Sights and Spectacles, 1937–58* (New York: Farrar, Straus and Cudahy, 1956), pp. 30–38.

The summer workshop at Vassar is well documented in Pierre de Rohan, *The First Federal Summer Theatre: A Report / Works Progress Administration* (New York: Federal Theatre National Publication, 1937). For the *Variety* review of the Vassar performance of *One Third of a Nation*, see "Summer Theatres: 1/3 of the Nation," August 4, 1937, p. 56. Flanagan quotes Hopkins's remarks about *Power* in *Arena*, p. 185; for her definition of the Living Newspaper, see "Not in Despair," *Federal Theatre Magazine* 2, no. 4 (1937), p. 5. For national productions of *One Third of a Nation*, see Federal Theatre Project Collection, box 1181, 1932–1943, Music Division, Library of Congress, as well as Flores's and Highsaw's excellent accounts. For reviews of *One Third of a Nation* quoted here, see the *New York Post*, January 8, 1938; *The Nation*, January 29, 1938; *The New York Times*, January 30, 1938; *The Wall Street Journal*, January 19, 1938; and *The Christian Science Monitor*, January 25, 1938. See too, for the crowds of young people who came to see it, Walter Winchell's account in the *New York Daily Mirror,* October 21, 1938.

The Philadelphia production is richly illuminated by Arthur R. Jarvis, Jr., "The Living Newspaper in Philadelphia, 1938–1939," *Pennsylvania History: A Journal of Mid-Atlantic Studies* 61, no. 3 (July 1994), pp. 332–55, on which I draw extensively. Amy Brady, "Staging the Depression: The Federal Theatre Project's Dramas of Poverty, 1935–1939" (diss., University of Massachusetts, Amherst, 2013), is also helpful. See too the Philadelphia File, box 1051, Federal Theatre Project Collection, 1932–1943, Music Division, Library of Congress. See Jarvis, "The Living Newspaper in Philadelphia," p. 341, for how some cast members lived in substandard housing, as well as "Houses Creak but Don't Fall: 'One-Third' Stage Too Weak," *The Philadelphia Record,* October 18, 1938, for the sad state of the Walnut Street Theatre. See too Jonathan Shandell, "Caricatured, Marginalized, and Erased: African American Artists and Philadelphia's Negro Unit of the FTP, 1936–1939," in *Theatre History Studies* 40 (2021), pp. 31–49.

The film version of *One Third of a Nation* can be viewed at www .youtube.com/watch?app=desktop&v=bl2gZKrL-k4. I have relied heavily in my account of the film's making and reception on two excellent studies: Richard Kozarski, *Hollywood on the Hudson: Film and Television in New York from Griffith to Sarnoff* (New Brunswick, NJ: Rutgers University Press, 2008); and Laura Browder, *Rousing the Nation: Radical Culture in Depression America* (Amherst: University of Massachusetts Press, 1998). Vincent L. Barnett, "Cutting Koerners: Floyd Odlum, the Atlas Corporation and the Dismissal of Orson Welles from RKO," *Film History* 22, no. 2 (2010), pp. 182–98, is also useful, and includes an account of Odlum's role in removing Welles from RKO. Sylvia Sidney's recollections about Odlum, quoted in Kozarski, were recorded in an interview with film historian Robert Sklar on February 12, 1985. On the director Dudley Murphy, see Susan Delson, *Dudley Murphy, Hollywood Wild Card* (Minneapolis: University of Minnesota Press, 2006). For the Paramount ad and theater owner responses to the box office disaster, see the *Motion Picture Herald*, February 18, April 8 and 29, and March 25, 1939, especially the column on "What the Picture Did for Me."

See as well, for more background information, and for reviews, *The New York Times*, June 15 and 19, 1938, and February 11, 1939; the *New York Herald Tribune*, October 23, 1938, and February 13, 1939; the *New York World-Telegram*, November 22, 1938; *The Hollywood Reporter*, January 11, 1939; *Variety*, February 10, 1939; and *The Christian Science Monitor*, December 19, 1938—where Orlob is quoted as saying, "We have options on all Living Newspaper Productions," though none but *One Third of a Nation* was ever filmed. The $5,000 fee was given to the Guild Committee for Federal Writers' Publications. At an early preview screening on the West Coast "many of the puzzled audience left before the finale." Feedback from movie theater owners across the country was withering: the owner of the Palace Theatre in Eufaula, Oklahoma, wrote that "no one liked it." The response was much the same at the Rialto Theatre in Paynesville, Minnesota: "Am very sorry I played this. It has an interesting story but it leaves a very bad taste in the mouths of the few who will come out for a picture of this type." Mrs. W. A. Wright, owner of Rex Theatre in Konawa, Oklahoma, stopped showing the film after two days, noting that "Sylvia Sidney's suffering in this picture was almost as bad as mine. Poor picture; no business" (for this and other responses, see the *Motion Picture Herald*, February 18, March 25, April 8, and April 29, 1939).

CHAPTER SEVEN: *LIBERTY DEFERRED*

For *Ethiopia*, see Flanagan, *Arena*, pp. 65–66; De Hart, *Federal Theatre*, pp. 60–69; Arthur Arent, "'Ethiopia': The First 'Living Newspaper,'" *Educational Theatre Journal* 20, no. 1 (1968), pp. 15–31; Elmer Rice, "Statement of Resignation," *New Theatre*, February 1936; and *The New York Times*, "Rice Quits in Row over W.P.A. Drama," January 24, 1936. Hopkins spoke of a "free, adult, uncensored theatre" at the National Theatre Conference at Iowa University in July 1935 (quoted in Flanagan, *Arena*, p. 28). For Baker's letter to Park Trammell, see De Hart, *Federal Theatre*, p. 68; and for Baker's letter to Trammell of February 21, 1936, see RG 69, FTP Records, NOC-State. I have relied on Cosgrove, "The Living Newspaper," pp. 54–55, for an account of, and quotations from, *The South*. On Elmer Rice's resignation, see his "Statement of Resignation," published in *New Theatre*, February 1936, p. 2, as well as "Politics Charged to the WPA by Rice," *The New York Times*, January 25, 1936. For *Stars and Bars*, see the superb scholarship of Dossett's *Radical Black Theatre*, pp. 81–84 and 89–101, which I draw on extensively. For quotations from *Stars and Bars*, see the Library of Congress copy, S19896 (2).

Four typed early drafts of *Liberty Deferred* survive, though given how closely three of them resemble one another and date from a fairly narrow time span in 1938, it is likely that several earlier and later drafts are lost, making it next to impossible to track the changes made from the earliest submission in November 1937 through the spring of 1939, when the play was still being considered for production. A pair of the surviving drafts can be found in the Library of Congress; a third, slightly revised, can be found at George Mason University. A later draft, an outlier, is housed at the New York Public Library. I quote from the strongest of the three early drafts—the first of the two copies in the Library of Congress—on the last page of which someone scribbled, in pencil, "ROUGH COPY!!!" Insofar as it depicts the first National Negro Congress of 1936, rather than the second one of 1937, as in the other early drafts, this is also likely the earliest (and least watered-down) version. For these original scripts, see Library of Congress, box 694, S1092 (1), which is missing pp. 111 and 124, and S1092 (2), which is missing pp. 47–51; George Mason University, which has photocopies of the two scripts in the Library of Congress, as well as a third photocopy (Federal Theatre Project Collection, Playscripts, box 191, folders 8 and 9; and box 192, folder 1); and the NYPL's Performing Arts Research Collection, from which I quote. A heavily edited version of the first half of the play was anthologized in James V. Hatch and Ted Shine, *Black Theatre U.S.A.: Plays by African Americans; The Recent Period, 1935–Today*, rev. and expanded ed. (New York: Free Press, 1996). A version of the full play—though likely from after 1945, since it introduces television, and in which Jimmy turns out to be Jewish and Mary Lou is Catholic—has been printed in Lorraine Brown, ed., and Tamara Liller and Barbara Jones Smith, coeditors, *Liberty Deferred and Other Living Newspapers of the 1930s: Federal Theatre Project*, with an introduction by Stuart Cosgrove (Fairfax, VA: George Mason University Press, 1989). Hill seems to have continued revising the play. A typed note appended to the back of the second copy in the Library of Congress reads: "*Liberty Deferred* by Abram Hill and John Silvera was revised circa 1980 by Abe Hill, now deceased. The revised (and shortened) version needs permission from Mrs. Hill to be produced. Contact Lorraine Brown for further information." No scholar has cited this version, and if it still exists its location is unknown. For Hill's four-page bibliography, see the Library of Congress, Federal Theatre Project, Administrative Records 1935–1942, Background File, 1935–1940, box 1031, dated August 30 to September 5, 1938.

This chapter draws extensively on interviews conducted in the 1970s for "Voices of the WPA" with many of those involved with *Liberty Deferred*, including Emmet Lavery interviewed by Mae Mallory Krulak and John O'Connor, January 5, 1976, and again by O'Connor, October 17, 1977; Ben Russak, interviewed by Lorraine Brown, February 19, 1976; Halsted Welles, by John O'Connor, November 17, 1975; Abram Hill, by Lorraine Brown, February 2, 1977, and again by Brown on March 30, 1978; Carlton Moss, by Lorraine Brown, August 6, 1976; and John Silvera, by Lorraine Brown, July 11, 1977. Apparently, in addition to Knaster and McGee, a pair of Black playwrights, Augustus Smith and Maurice Clark, were also asked to help out in "whipping it into shape," *The Philadelphia Tribune*, July 7, 1938. See too the interview with Abram Hill by Mischell Wallace on January 19, 1974, in the Hatch-Billops collection at the Schomburg Center for Research in Black Culture at the NYPL.

For Federal Theatre correspondence about *Liberty Deferred*, see Lavery to Silvera, December 21, 1937, Series E879, box 182, RG 69, NA; Lavery to Knaster, December 21, 1937, Series E879, box 182, RG 69, NA; Lavery to Silvera and Knaster, December 22, 1937, Series E879, box 182, RG 69, NA; Lavery to Silvera and

Knaster, April 15, 1938, Series E879, box 182, RG 69, NA; Lavery to Silvera, July 6, 1938, Series E879, box 182, RG 69, NA; Lavery to Kondulf, July 13, 1938, Series E879, box 182, RG 69, NA; Hill and Silvera to Lavery, July 27, 1938, Series E879, box 182, RG 69, NA; Lavery to Gibbs, October 3, 1938, Series E879, box 182, RG 69, NA; Lavery to Knaster, November 10, 1938, Series E879, box 182, RG 69, NA; Hill to Flanagan, September 23, 1938, E839, box 19, RG 69, NA; Hill to Flanagan, December 11, 1938, and Flanagan to Hill, December 19, 1938, in NDABA, reel 24. For Lavery's complaint to Russak about his difficult identifying with the play, see his letter of September 30, 1938, RG 69, NA, box 178, cited by Tina Redd, "The Struggle for Administrative and Artistic Control of the Federal Theatre Negro Units" (diss., University of Washington, 1996), p. 175, n. 18. For Silvera's leaked letter to Alfred E. Smith of May 17, 1938, about "discrimination," see Redd, "The Struggle," pp. 171ff.

For biographical details on Abram Hill, see, in addition to interviews, Glenda Eloise Gill, "Six Black Performers in Relation to the Federal Theatre" (diss., University of Iowa, 1981); Ethel Louise Pitts, "The American Negro Theatre: 1940–1949" (diss., University of Missouri-Columbia, 1975); www.nypl.org/blog/2015/11/12/legacy-abram-hill; "Harlem on My Mind: Abram Hill," *Into America* (www.msnbc.com/podcast/harlem-my-mind-abram-hill-n1258783); and E. Quitta Craig, *Black Drama of the Federal Theatre Era: Beyond the Formal Horizons* (Amherst: University of Massachusetts Press, 1980), who notes that "there are also among the Federal Theatre papers a separate first scene, which was reworked by the authors in response to a suggestion by Mr. McGee, Director of the Federal Theatre's Southern Region, and a memorandum which contains constructive suggestions for the play's development" (p. 65, n. 32—Memorandum, suggestions for improvement of *Liberty Deferred*, Federal Theatre Project Collection, George Mason University); I have not been able to locate these, nor are they cataloged. Fascinatingly, Hill's and Knaster's names show up in a news item in *Broadcasting Magazine* on July 14, 1946, p. 44, announcing, "All-Negro Opera Group Starts Series on WNEW," produced "in association with Abram Hill, director of the American Negro Theatre, the programs will be directed by Jack Grogan, WNEW production manager, with Ira Knaster adapting the librettors [*sic*]." See too Abram Hill, *Hell's Half Acre*, Subseries 3.1, Playscripts box 170, folder 6, George Mason University. John D. Silvera's life has been more difficult to track, but see Pam Platt's helpful profile, "John Silvera: Giving History a Nudge," *Florida Today*, February 18, 1997, as well as the *New York Age*, April 16, 1938, for his time at Lincoln University.

The manuscript of Lavery's unpublished book, "The Flexible Stage: The Federal Theatre in Profile" (1940), is located in Emmet Lavery Papers, 1925–1962, Wisconsin Center for Film and Theater Research, University of Wisconsin–Madison, box 3, folder 3. For more on Lavery's Catholic plays and commitment to Catholic theater, see Mary Michael Keefe, "The National Catholic Theatre Conference: Its Aims and Its Achievements" (diss., Northwestern University, 1965), p. 7.

For major scholarship on *Liberty Deferred*, I have drawn on Dossett's superb discussion in *Radical Black Theatre*, and quote from p. 111; as well as the insights in Paul Nadler, "Liberty Censored: Black Living Newspapers of the Federal Theatre Project," *African American Review* 29, no. 4 (Winter 1995), pp. 615–22; Rena Fraden,

Blueprints for a Black Federal Theatre, 1935–1939 (Cambridge: Cambridge University Press, 1994); Ronald Ross, "The Role of Blacks in the Federal Theatre, 1935–1939," *The Journal of Negro History* 59, no. 1 (January 1974), pp. 38–50; Lorraine Brown, "A Story Yet to Be Told: The Federal Theatre Research Project," *The Black Scholar* 10, no. 10 (July–August 1979), pp. 70–78; Zanthe Taylor, "Singing for Their Supper: The Negro Units of the Federal Theater Project and Their Plays," *Theatre* 27 (1997), pp. 42–59. See too Kate Dossett's "Black Theatre Archives and the Making of a Black Dramatic Tradition," in *African American Literature in Transition*, vol. 10, *1930–1940*, ed. Eve Dunbar and Ayesha K. Hardison (Cambridge: Cambridge University Press, 2022), pp. 170–208; and Tina Redd, who cites Hill's letter to Flanagan of September 23, 1938, NARA RG 69, where he claims that he and Silvera have been working on the play for eighteen months (as quoted in "The Struggle," pp. 178–79). See too Catherine A. Stewart, *Long Past Slavery: Representing Race in the Federal Writers' Project* (Chapel Hill: University of North Carolina Press, 2016). See as well John D. Silvera, "Still in Blackface," *Crisis* 46 (March 1, 1939), p. 76. For the quotation from Martin Dies on the Negro National Congress, see his *The Trojan Horse in America* (New York: Dodd, 1940), p. 125.

For a valuable conversation about *Liberty Deferred*, including a reading from *Liberty Deferred* (directed by Kimille Howard), see "A Past Becomes a Heritage: The Negro Units of the Federal Theatre Project," arts.princeton.edu/events/play-readings-and-panel-discussion-on-federal-theatre-project-negro-unit, which took place at Princeton University on March 30, 2021. For evidence that Hill and Lavery had begun working on the play as early as April 1937, see Redd, "The Struggle," p. 191, n. 12, which cites Hill's letter to

Flanagan of September 23, 1938 (NARA RG 69). See too Jordana Cox, "The Keeper of Records," ch. 4 in *Staged News: The Federal Theatre Project's Living Newspapers in New York* (Amherst: University of Massachusetts Press, 2023), from which I quote from Morris Surofsky's reader report (p. 128).

For background on Lynchotopia, see Robert L. Zangrando, "The NAACP and a Federal Antilynching Bill, 1934–1940," *The Journal of Negro History* 50, no. 2 (April 1965), pp. 106–17; Koritha Mitchell, *Living with Lynching: African American Lynching Plays, Performance, and Citizenship, 1890–1930* (Urbana: University of Illinois Press, 2011); and Amy Louise Wood, *Lynching and Spectacle: Witnessing Racial Violence in America, 1890–1940* (Chapel Hill: University of North Carolina Press, 2009). And for the National Negro Congress, see Erik Gellman, *Death Blow to Jim Crow: The National Negro Congress and the Rise of Militant Civil Rights* (Chapel Hill: University of North Carolina Press, 2012).

For Burley's account of the play, see his *"Liberty Deferred* Living Newspaper: Silvera-Hill Dramatic Offering Is Called Unique by Reviewer," *Amsterdam News*, December 10, 1938. For the Negro Arts Committee brief, see "The Negro and Federal Project No. 1 (WPA Arts Projects) for New York City: A Brief," 1939, E839, box 16, RG 69, NA, as well as Lavery's reply, c/o John Rimassa, March 31, 1939, E878, box 166, RG 69, NA. Also useful is Catherine A. Stewart, *Long Past Slavery*. For the Black community's criticism of the WPA, including the possibility of reaching out to the Dies Committee, see Memorandum from White to Marshall, April 3, 1939, referring to a letter from C. T. Williams of March 28, 1939, and Memorandum from Marshall to White, April 13, 1939, Records of the NAACP, Series I, C Administrative File, box 286, folder "June–Dec. 1939," MD-LC, quoted in Stewart's *Long Past Slavery*, p. 233.

On Allison's *Panyared*, see Lavery's unpublished "The Flexible Stage" (1940), from which I quote. Lavery wrote on May 9, 1938, to Irwin A. Rubenstein in his "weekly round-up" that he had "conferred with Hughes Allison, Negro author of *Trial of Dr. Beck*, who would like to write a trilogy of Negro plays. I like the idea very much" (Series E879, box 178, RG 69, NA). See too Fraden, *Blueprints for a Black Federal Theatre*, p. 109, on which I draw; and Dossett, who is pathbreaking on this play as well in *Radical Black Theatre*. Dossett's account, on which I draw, cites these additional sources for Lavery's enthusiastic support of the play (in her notes on p. 310): Flanagan's handwritten comments on Lavery to Flanagan, Interdepartmental Memorandum, March 17, 1939; Flanagan's comments are typed up in a document dated March 28, 1939, and both are in the correspondence of Hallie Flanagan, June 1937–1939, E841, box 43, RG 69, NA; Lavery's letter to Flanagan, March 29, 1939, E841, box 43, RG 69, NA; Abram Hill, Reader's Report on *Panyared*, April 7, 1939, E879, box 174, RG 69, NA; and Lavery's Interdepartmental Memo to Flanagan, April 11, 1939, E839, box 19, RG 69, NA. Langston Hughes's reflections in his 1951 poem "Harlem" on that which is deferred—where the speaker asks, "What happens to a dream deferred?"—feel relevant here.

For a critique of the New Theatre League, which a frustrated Abram Hill had approached in the hopes of seeing *Liberty Deferred* staged, see Lynn Mally, "Inside a Communist Front: A Post-Cold War Analysis of the New Theatre League," *American Communist History* 6, no. 1 (2007), pp. 65–95; she quotes the theater historian Morgan Himelstein, who concludes in *Drama Was a Weapon*, p. 73, that the "Federal Theatre helped to ruin its Marxist competitors" (p. 89).

CHAPTER EIGHT: THE CREATION
OF THE DIES COMMITTEE

My main and indispensable source for Dies's career here is Dennis Kay McDaniel's superb and deeply researched dissertation, "Martin Dies." For Dies's exaggerations and fabrications, see McDaniel, "Martin Dies," pp. 62ff. For the life of Martin Dies, Sr., I quote from p. 50; see too McDaniel's "The First Congressman Martin Dies of Texas," *The Southwestern Historical Quarterly* 102 (October 1998), pp. 131–61.

For Dies's 1930 campaign, in addition to McDaniel, "Martin Dies," pp. 104ff., see Dies's "Opening Speech to Be Delivered at Center, Texas, on the Court House Square, 2 O'clock, March 29, 1930," p. 32, folder, speeches—political, Drawer H DP, Martin Dies Papers, Sam Houston Regional Library and Research Center; and "Many Hear Address of Martin Dies," *The Marshall News Messenger*, June 29, 1930; for his unscripted remarks about De Priest, see "This Ought to Get Him Some Votes," *The Chicago Defender*, July 26, 1930. See too "Box Defeated in Texas Race," the *Los Angeles Times*, July 29, 1930; and "Martin Dies in the Picture," the *Austin Statesman*, July 30, 1930. On De Priest, see as well McDaniel, "Martin Dies," p. 124. For Blease—who also recited from the Senate floor the anonymous poem "Niggers in the White House," see www.washingtonpost.com/nation/2019/06/27/julian-castro-beto -orourke-section-immigration-illegal-coleman-livingstone-blease.

On voting rights in Texas, see Darlene Clark Hine, "The Elusive Ballot: The Black Struggle against the Texas Democratic

White Primary, 1932–1945," *Southwestern Historical Quarterly* 81, no. 4 (April 1978), pp. 371–92; and John Egerton, *Speak Now Against the Day: The Generation before the Civil Rights Movement in the South* (New York: Knopf, 1994). For the poll tax, see Donald S. Strong, "American Government and Politics: The Poll Tax; The Case of Texas," *American Political Science Review* 38, no. 4 (August 1944), pp. 693–709.

On Dies and Swank visiting President Hoover, see the *New York Herald Tribune*, September 25, 1931. For Dies's shelved plan to run for the Senate in 1936, see McDaniel, "Martin Dies," pp. 224–66; and the *Beaumont Enterprise*, December 31, 1935. For the backlash to Dies's anti-alien campaign, see the *New York Herald Tribune*, July 11, 1935. For Dies's early journalism, see his "Nationalism Spells Safety," the *National Republic* 21 (March 1934), pp. 1–2, 32; and "The Immigration Crisis," *The Saturday Evening Post* 207 (April 20, 1935), pp. 27, 105–14. For more on Dies and anti-immigration, see *The New York Times*, February 1 and June 23, 1935; February 16, 1936; and March 21, 1937.

On lynching in Beaumont, and Texas, see *The Crisis* 16, no. 3 (July 1918), p. 141; www.abhmuseum.org/sacrificing-black-lives -for-the-american-lie; and www.lynchingintexas.org/files/show/395. See too *Anti-Black Violence in Twentieth-Century Texas*, ed. Bruce A. Glasrud (College Station: Texas A&M University Press, 2015), as well as his article "Child or Beast? White Texas' View of Blacks, 1900–1910," *East Texas Historical Journal* 15, no. 2 (1977), pp. 38–44; Mary Elizabeth Estes, "An Historical Survey of Lynchings in Oklahoma and Texas" (MA thesis, University of Oklahoma, 1942); and David William Livingston, "The Lynching of Negroes in Texas, 1900–1925" (MA thesis, East Texas State University, 1972).

For early profiles of Dies in Congress, see Frederick R. Barkley, "Martin Dies of Texas," *Current History* 51, no. 4 (December 1939), pp. 29–30; Allan A. Michie and Frank Ryhlick, *Dixie Demagogues* (New York: Vanguard, 1938); Willson Whitman, "Background of a Demagogue," in *Martin Dies and His Committee on "Un-Americanism,"* a special supplement published by *The Nation* 155 (October 3, 1942), pp. 311–13; Marquis Childs, *I Write from Washington* (New York: Harper and Brothers, 1942), pp. 91ff.; and William Gellermann, *Martin Dies* (New York: John Day, 1944), from which I take the quotation about Dies taking every position once (p. 33). For Dies's first bill and first major speech in the House, see First Session, 72nd Congress, *Congressional Record*, vol. 75, part 1, for December 8, 1931 (p. 159) and December 17, 1931 (pp. 736ff.). For Dies and the media, see Joy Elizabeth Hayes, "Populist Conservatism on the Air: The Dies Committee and Network Radio," *Journal of Broadcasting and Electronic Media* 66, no. 3 (2022), pp. 484–503; and Joseph Alsop and Robert Kinter, "Behind the Headlines," as it appears in the *Spokane Spokesman-Review*, August 22, 1938.

On the decline of the New Deal during Roosevelt's second term and the newly forged coalition between Republicans and Southern Democrats, see Basil Rauch, *The History of the New Deal, 1933–1938* (New York: Creative Age Press, 1944); James T. Patterson, "A Conservative Coalition Forms in Congress, 1933–1939," *The Journal of American History* 52, no. 4 (1966), pp. 757–72, as well as his *Congressional Conservatism and the New Deal* (Lexington: University Press of Kentucky, 1967); Alan Brinkley, *The End of Reform: New Deal Liberalism in Recession and War* (New York: Knopf, 1995); Jason Scott Smith, *A Concise History of the New Deal* (Cambridge: Cambridge University Press, 2014); Steven Attewell, *People Must*

Live by Work: Direct Job Creation from FDR to Reagan (Philadelphia: University of Pennsylvania Press, 2018); and Lionel V. Patenaude, *Texans, Politics and the New Deal* (New York: Garland, 1983). For more on Congress at this time, see Keith T. Poole and Howard Rosenthal, *Ideology and Congress*, 2nd rev. ed. (New Brunswick, NJ: Transaction Publishers, 2007); V. O. Kay, *Southern Politics in State and Nation* (New York: Vintage Books, 1949); David A. Bateman, Ira Katznelson, and John S. Lapinski, *Southern Nation: Congress and White Supremacy after Reconstruction* (Princeton, NJ: Princeton University Press, 2018); and Alan D. Monroe, *Public Opinion in America* (New York: Harper and Row, 1975). In his biography of Dies, McDaniel notes that Senator Joseph McCarthy followed a similar political trajectory, initially failing to win authorization to investigate "housing, education, executive branch reorganization and five percenters," before at last being appointed chair of the Senate committee to investigate un-American activities ("Martin Dies," p. 279, n. 50).

For histories of the House Un-American Activities Committee, see August Raymond Ogden, *The Dies Committee*; Robert K. Carr, *The House Committee on Un-American Activities* (Ithaca, NY: Cornell University Press, 1952); Walter Goodman, *The Committee: The Extraordinary Career on Un-American Activities* (New York: Farrar, Straus and Giroux, 1968); William F. Buckley, Jr., *The Committee and Its Critics: A Calm Review of the House Committee on Un-American Activities* (New York: Putnam, 1962); and Michael Wreszin's excellent "The Dies Committee 1938," in *Congress Investigates: A Documented History, 1792–1974*, vol. 4, ed. Arthur M. Schlesinger and Roger Bruns (New York: Chelsea House, 1975), pp. 2923–3112. For the history of special committees in general, see Marshall Edward Dimock, *Congressional Investigating Committees* (Baltimore: Johns Hopkins Press, 1929).

For the Fish and McCormack-Dickstein committees, in addition to Goodman, see Ernest Volkman, *A Legacy of Hate: Anti-Semitism in America* (New York: F. Watts, 1982), p. 42; Hamilton Fish, Jr., "The Menace of Communism," *The Annals of the American Academy of Political and Social Science* 156 (1931), p. 54; and *The New York Times*, November 18, 1930. McCormack would complain on January 26, 1937, in support of Dickstein's proposal for a new committee, that the $30,000 given to their previous committee had been insufficient (*Congressional Record*, vol. 81, part 1, p. 434). For the Dies Committee in particular, see Kenneth O'Reilly, "The Dies Committee v. the New Deal Real Americans and the Unending Search for Un-Americans," in *Little "Red Scares": Anti-Communism and Political Repression in the United States, 1921–1946*, ed. Robert Justin Goldstein (London: Routledge, 2014); and a contemporary puff piece by Wesley Price, "We Investigate Dies," *American Magazine* 129 (1940), pp. 72ff.

For Samuel Dickstein, see Nancy Lynn Lopez's excellent "'Allowing Fears to Overwhelm Us': A Re-examination of the House Special Committee on Un-American Activities, 1938–1944" (diss., Rice University, 2002); and Dorothy Wang's celebratory *Samuel Dickstein: American Defender* (New York: Robert Speller, 1935). For press coverage of Dickstein's attacks on Hitler, see, for example, *The Boston Globe*, March 3, 1938. For the revelations about his spying for the Soviet Union, see Allen Weinstein and Alexander Vassiliev, *The Haunted Wood: Soviet Espionage in America—the Stalin*

Era (New York: Random House, 1999), pp. 140ff.; Sam Roberts, "A Soviet Spy in Congress Still Has His Street," *The New York Times*, May 22, 2013; and Peter Duffy, "The Congressman Who Spied for Russia," *Politico*, October 6, 2014. After retiring from Congress in 1945, Dickstein served as a Supreme Court justice in New York. In his oral "Reminiscences of Samuel Dickstein, 1950," for the Columbia University Oral History Collection, Dickstein criticizes Dies but makes no mention of working for the Soviet Union (dx.doi.org/10.7916/d8-jn05-sg62).

On John Nance Garner, see Bascom Timmons, *Garner of Texas* (New York: Harper, 1948), p. 220; George Rothwell Brown, *The Speaker of the House: The Romantic Story of John N. Garner* (New York: Brewer, Warren and Putnam, 1932); O. C. Fisher, *Cactus Jack* (Waco: Texian Press, 1978); Thomas T. Spencer's invaluable "For the Good of the Party: John Nance Garner, FDR, and New Deal Politics, 1933–1940," *Southwestern Historical Quarterly* 121, no. 3 (January 2018), pp. 254–82; and Lionel V. Patenaude, *Texans, Politics and the New Deal* (New York: Garland, 1983), especially pp. 43ff., and his "Garner, Sumner, and Connally: The Defeat of the Roosevelt Court Bill in 1937," *Southwestern Historical Quarterly* 74 (July 1970), pp. 36–51. Also useful are Patrick Cox, "John Nance Garner," in *Profiles in Power: Twentieth Century Texans in Washington*, ed. Kenneth E. Hendrickson, Jr., and Michael L. Collins (Arlington Heights, IL: Harlan Davidson, 1993), 43–59; Norman Brown, "Garnering Votes for Cactus Jack: John Nance Garner, Franklin D. Roosevelt and the 1932 Democratic Presidential Nomination," *Southwestern Historical Quarterly* 104 (July 2000), pp. 149–86; Anthony Champagne, "John Nance Garner," in *Masters of the House: Congressional Leadership over Two Centuries*, ed. Raymond Smock and Susan Hannah (Boulder, CO: Westview Press, 1998); and Ted Morgan, *Reds: McCarthyism in Twentieth-Century America* (New York: Random House, 2003), from which I draw on in my account of Garner's fake populism, p. 185.

For Roosevelt's purge and Dies, see *The Baltimore Sun*, June 30, 1938. For Dies's recounting of his conversation with Garner, see Martin Dies, *Martin Dies' Story* (New York: Bookmailer, 1963), pp. 140–41, and on how the House leadership asked him to put forward the resolution, see pp. 59–60. McDaniel interviewed Dies's son, Judge Martin Dies, in June 1987, who told McDaniel that his father had told him that Garner had urged him to submit this resolution; see McDaniel, "Martin Dies," p. 353, n. 9. For Stokes's article that connects the dots between Garner and the Dies Committee, see Richard L. Stokes, "Un-American Probe Epochal: Turn of Events Makes Dies International Figure," in the *Washington Evening Star*, October 29, 1939, where it also ran. Dies had a copy of Stokes's article pasted in his scrapbook, preserved in the National Archives. For Roosevelt's list of congressmen—including Dies— he was hoping to purge, see *Chicago Tribune*, October 9, 1938. For Garner's claim in 1938 about the likely influence of the Dies Committee on the future of American politics, see Harry S. Truman, *Memoirs*, 2 vols. (Garden City, NY: Doubleday, 1955–56), vol. 2, p. 275.

For a transcript of the debate on May 26, 1938, over Dies's resolution HR 282, see *Congressional Record*, vol. 83, part 7, pp. 7568–87. Dies admits he has never heard of the Fish Committee on p. 7570. On Rankin's vote, see Robert E. Stripling, *The Red Plot against America* (Drexel Hill, PA: Bell Publishing, 1949), p. 21. On Thomas's earlier claims about WPA propaganda, see *The New York Times*,

March 9, 1938. Rankin's slur is quoted in *Time*, February 14, 1944. For Speaker of the House Bankhead, see Walter J. Heacock, "William B. Bankhead and the New Deal," *The Journal of Southern History* 21, no. 3 (1955), pp. 347–59. M. E. Hennessey would later report in *The Boston Globe* that Dies, before he "began the investigation," traveled to Garner's home in Uvalde, Texas, and "conferred" there with Garner (October 31, 1938).

CHAPTER NINE: THE DIES COMMITTEE
V. THE FEDERAL THEATRE

This chapter, like the previous one, draws heavily on the foundational works on Dies and his committee by Dennis Kay McDaniel, Nancy Lynn Lopez, Ted Morgan, August Raymond Ogden, Robert K. Carr, Walter Goodman, and Michael Wreszin. I also rely heavily on De Hart's informative account of the Federal Theatre's responses to the Dies hearings, *Federal Theatre*, pp. 199ff. Also valuable are D. A. Saunders, "The Dies Committee: First Phase," *Public Opinion Quarterly* 3, no. 2 (April 1939), pp. 222–28; Stewart Henderson Britt and Selden C. Menefee, "Did the Publicity of the Dies Committee in 1938 Influence Public Opinion?," *Public Opinion Quarterly* 3, no. 3 (July 1939), pp. 449–57, who ran tests on psychology students that showed that hearing stories in the press about Dies drove up their anti-Communist sentiment; Raymond Brandt, "The Dies Committee: An Appraisal," *Atlantic Monthly* 165 (February 1940), pp. 232–37; Raymond Clapp, "The Dies Committee: A Necessary Job, Badly Done," *Forum* 103 (March 1940), pp. 155–57; and Willson Whitman, Background of a Demagogue." See too Robert E. Stripling, *The Red Plot against America* (Drexel Hill, PA: Bell Publishing, 1949); and Dies, *Martin Dies'*

Story. For Dies taking payoffs from Jewish organizations, see Mc-Daniel, "Martin Dies," on his interview with Stripling, pp. 429–30. For a transcript of the testimony, see volume 1 of the *Investigation of Un-American Propaganda Activities in the United States: Hearings before a Special Committee on Un-American Activities, House of Representatives, Seventy-fifth Congress, Third Session–Seventy-eighth Congress, Second Session, on H. Res. 282.* For earlier congressional attacks on the Federal Theatre, see Hearing before the House Committee in Charge of Deficiency Appropriations: *First Deficiency Appropriation Bill for 1936, Part 2, Emergency Relief,* Seventy-fourth Congress, Second Session (1936), pp. 208–10. And for a report on Senator Davis's attack in April 1936 on Flanagan, see *The New York Times,* April 27, 1936.

For J. Parnell Thomas, see Lewis Herbert Carlson, "J. Parnell Thomas and the House Committee on Un-American Activities, 1938–1948" (diss., Michigan State University, 1967), which includes Thomas's request to Snell, which he told Carlson about in an interview, p. 13. For Parnell's attack on the New Deal before joining the committee, see, for example, *The New York Times,* March 9, 1938. For Stripling's interview in March 1988 with McDaniel about how Dies initially didn't know what he was doing, see McDaniel, "Martin Dies," p. 611. For Dies's response to Bankhead regarding McCormack's concerns, see McDaniel, "Martin Dies," p. 362. I also quote from reports in *The New York Times,* June 19, July 28, August 10, and August 12, 1938; the *Austin Statesman,* July 1, 1938; *The Hartford Courant,* July 30, 1938; the *New York Herald Tribune,* July 30, 1938; and the *Chicago Tribune,* August 12, 1938. For Flanagan's announcement that she was still waiting to be heard, see *The New York Times,* September 2, 1938.

And for Thomas's radio attack on Flanagan in September, see RG FTP Records, NOOSF, September 12, 1938. For Birmingham, see National Archives, RG 233 box 5, which includes his letter to Dies as well as his résumé. Birmingham must have been steered his way early on, for he was hired on June 5, before the rest of the committee was named.

For more on Viereck, see *The New York Times*, August 4, 1938; *The Baltimore Sun*, August 4, 1938; *The Washington Post*, February 18, 1942, and on the Hamilton Fish connection; Tom Reiss, *The Orientalist: Solving the Mystery of a Strange and a Dangerous Life* (New York: Random House, 2005), pp. 288–89; Phyllis Keller, "George Sylvester Viereck: The Psychology of a German-American Militant," *Journal of Interdisciplinary History* 2, no. 1 (1971), pp. 59–108; "Nazis, Seditionists, and Gay Vampire Porn: Rachel Maddow Reveals Her New Podcast 'Ultra,'" *Rolling Stone*, October 3, 2022, from which I quote; and especially "Episode 4: A Bad Angle," of Maddow's podcast series *Ultra*, www.msnbc.com/msnbc-podcast/rachel-maddow-presents-ultra/episode-4-bad-angle-n1300105.

For the survey of reporters covering the hearings, see the *New York Daily News*, October 31, 1938. See too Kenneth Heineman, "Media Bias in Coverage of the Dies Committee on Un-American Activities 1938–1940," *The Historian* 55, no. 1 (1992), pp. 37–52, who quotes Ickes's claim that 85 percent of the media was against the New Deal, and notes that others place that figure closer to 60 percent, and that by June 1938, 72 percent of Americans "wanted the Roosevelt administration to become more conservative." For Paul Y. Anderson's attacks on Dies, see, for example, "Behind the Dies Intrigue," *The Nation* 147 (November 12, 1938), pp. 499–500;

and "Fascism Hits Washington," *The Nation* 147 (August 27, 1938), pp. 198–99. See too Heywood Broun, "Uriah Comes to Judgment: Dies Committee," *The New Republic* 96 (September 7, 1938), pp. 129–30; and the only attack in 1938 on Dies by a Federal Theatre administrator: Emmet Lavery, "Communism and the Federal Theatre," *Commonweal* 28 (October 7, 1938), pp. 610–12. For the consequential poll of Dies's committee in December 1938, see George H. Gallup, *The Gallup Poll: Public Opinion, 1937–1971* (New York: Random House, 1972), vol. 1, December 11, 1938.

For Hazel Huffman, see Kate Dossett's outstanding "Gender and the Dies Committee Hearings on the Federal Theatre Project," *Journal of American Studies* 47, no. 4, "Special Issue: The 'Un-American'" (November 2013), pp. 993–1017, as well as De Hart. For Huffman's "Why Throw the Baby Out the Window," see too K. Kevyne Baar, *Broadway and the Blacklist* (Jefferson, NC: McFarland, 2019), p. 40. For Huffman's reflections on her role in shutting down the Federal Theatre, see the two copies (one twenty pages, the other forty-five pages) of her unpublished "Why Throw the Baby Out the Window," National Republic Records, box 769, Collection #60006, Hazel Huffman Office Records, reel 625, Hoover Institution Library and Archives. For Flanagan's letter to her husband about Huffman, see Hallie Flanagan Papers, Vassar College, Correspondence, personal, HFD to Philip Davis, March 17, 1936. For Barber's recollections of Huffman, see his November 1975 interview for George Mason University's "Voices of the WPA." On Equity's view of Huffman's competing so-called organization, see "Notice to H. Huffman & Co. 'Keep Out!,'" *Equity* 22 (December 1937), p. 12, and "Authorization Spokesman," *Equity*

23 (October 1938), p. 15. For Sally Saunders, see the Birmingham files in the National Archives, RG 233, box 5. While researching *Arena*, Flanagan wrote to E. C. Mabie on March 13, 1940, having heard that Saunders had studied at the University of Iowa, where he taught; Mabie wrote back on March 16, 1940, saying that Saunders had studied there, that she had changed her name from Helen Ligart, that her "work here was very poor," and that she had transferred to Carnegie Institute of Technology (Hallie Flanagan Papers, NYPL, Series I, Correspondence, box 2, folder 25).

For Roosevelt and Dies, see Albert Alexander, "The President and the Investigator: Roosevelt and Dies," *Antioch Review* 15 (1955), pp. 106–16; Kenneth O'Reilly, "The Dies Committee v. the New Deal: Real Americans and the Unending Search for Un-Americans," in *Little "Red Scares,"* ed. Robert Justin Goldstein (London: Routledge, 2016), pp. 237–59; Richard Polenberg, "Franklin Roosevelt and Civil Liberties: The Case of the Dies Committee," *The Historian* 30 (February 1968), pp. 165–78; George Wolfskill and John A. Hudson, *All but the People: Franklin D. Roosevelt and His Critics, 1933–1939* (London: Macmillan, 1969); and Landon R. Y. Storrs, *The Second Red Scare and the Unmaking of the New Deal Left* (Princeton, NJ: Princeton University Press, 2012). For Roosevelt's attack on Dies, and Dies's riposte, I quote from *The New York Times*, October 27 and 30, 1938; the *New York Herald Tribune*, October 27, 1938; and *The Washington Post*, October 30, 1938. For Ickes's undelivered attack on Dies, see Harold L. Ickes, *The Secret Diary*, 3 vols. (New York: Simon & Schuster, 1954), vol. 2, pp. 455, 501, 507, 528–29, 546–47, 573–74, and 654–55. Secretary of Labor Frances Perkins thought that Dies, a son of the South and the Confederacy, was still "cherishing those strange hidden feelings of the defeated," cited in Bella Dodd, *School of Darkness* (New York: P. J. Kenedy, 1954), pp. 188–89. See too Jeanne Nienaber Clarke, *Roosevelt's Warrior: Harold L. Ickes and the New Deal* (Baltimore: Johns Hopkins University Press, 1996). For Sam Rayburn on Dies's popularity, see McDaniel, "Martin Dies," p. 301. For Jeane J. Kirkpatrick, see her "Politics and the New Class," *Society* 16, no. 2 (1979), pp. 42–48, from which I quote.

For Flanagan being awarded the first round in her encounter with the Dies committee, see *Variety*, December 7, 1938, p. 47. For where Dies was when Huffman testified again on November 8, 1938, see "The '400' Fete Dies; Nazi Is Among Sponsors," *The Daily Worker*, December 9, 1938; and for the Nazi rally at Madison Square Garden, where Dies was praised, see *The Baltimore Sun*, February 21, 1939. See too Henry F. Pringle, "The Education of Martin Dies," *Scribner's Commentator*, February 1940, pp. 15–21. The playhouse to which Dempsey refers is the New Brighton Theater, or Brighton Beach Theater, near Coney Island, which was built in 1909 and renamed the Brighton Theater in 1936. Before moving to Santa Fe in 1920, Dempsey had lived in New York City. The sparse press coverage of Dempsey's remarks focused on his explanation that the committee had gone "astray" because of inadequate funding: "Had we been better financed, we could have boiled it down before the witnesses came into the hearings" (*Tacoma News Tribune*, December 10, 1938).

CHAPTER TEN: THE END OF
THE FEDERAL THEATRE

My account of the demise of the Federal Theatre is indebted to both Flanagan, *Arena*, pp. 347–73, and De Hart, *Federal Theatre*, pp. 236–95. For the Dies Committee report of January 3, 1939, see *Investigation of Un-American Activities and Propaganda: Report of the Special Committee on Un-American Activities Pursuant to H. Res. 282*, Seventy-fifth Congress (Washington, D.C.: Government Printing Office, 1939), especially p. 31. For Dies's popular support, see George Gallup's article in *The Washington Post*, December 11, 1938, on the results of his recent poll; and for Dies's public campaign, see, for example, the *Chicago Tribune*, December 22, 1938. For Roosevelt's failure to pressure congressional leaders to prevent Dies from continuing his investigations, see the *Chicago Tribune*, January 5, 1939. For the response in the House to the Dies report, see *Congressional Record*, vol. 84, part 1 (January 3, 1939), pp. 1100ff. And for the pivot, in pursuing WPA cuts, to the House Appropriations Committee, see *The New York Times*, January 13, 1939.

For Woodrum and his committee's investigation of the WPA and especially the Federal Theatre, see *Further Additional Appropriation for Work Relief and Relief, Fiscal Year 1939: Hearings before the House Subcommittee of the Committee on Appropriations, Work Relief, and Relief for Fiscal Year 1940, Seventy-sixth Congress, First Session (1939)* and *Congressional Record*, vol. 84, part 3 (March 27, 1939), pp. 3368ff. For an incisive account of Woodrum's political life and his turn against the New Deal, see James E. Sargent, "Clifton A. Woodrum of Virginia: A Southern Progressive in Congress, 1923–1945," *The Virginia Magazine of History and Biography* 89, no. 3

(July 1981), pp. 341–64; and James E. Sargent, "Woodrum's Economy Bloc: The Attack on Roosevelt's WPA, 1937–1939," *The Virginia Magazine of History and Biography* 93, no. 2 (1985), pp. 175–207. And for Woodrum's growing popularity, see (in addition to Sargent), "Relief: Indelible Red," *Time*, May 1, 1939, which noted that Woodrum had succeeded where Dies had failed, for Woodrum had gotten Herbert Benjamin, the organizational secretary of the Workers Alliance, to admit that he was a Communist, while in "all his Red-hunting, Texas' Representative Martin ('Un-American') Dies never put on the stand a real, live, current Communist." See too Allan A. Fletcher, "Poll-Tax Politics," *The New Republic*, May 20, 1940. For Flanagan's letter to Woodrum shared with the press, see *The New York Times*, June 12, 1939, pp. 191–92. For Woodrum's concern about the interracial casting of Federal Theatre productions, see *U.S. House Committee on Appropriations (Hearings under H. Res. 130), Investigation and Study of the Works Progress Administration, 76th Congress, 1st Session, 1939*, pp. 191–92, as cited in Donald S. Howard, *The WPA and Federal Relief Policy* (New York: Russell Sage Foundation, 1943), pp. 294–95. For the photographs of models from the Arts Project passed around by Woodrum, see Richard D. McKinzie, *The New Deal for Artists* (Princeton, NJ: Princeton University Press, 1973), p. 160.

For announcements in June 1939 of further cuts to the WPA, see, for example, *The New York Times*, June 14, 1939. *The Baltimore Sun*, June 15, 1939, called for the end of the Federal Theatre. Eleanor Roosevelt was quoted on the Federal Theatre possibly harboring Communists in the *Atlanta Constitution*, June 21, 1939. For the description of Flanagan watching the congressional debate, see *The Baltimore Sun*, June 17, 1939. For Dirksen's performance, the "gaffaws" that Mary Norton's amendment was met with, and Flanagan's departure from the gallery, see the *Chicago Tribune*, June 17, 1939, as well as the *Richmond Times-Dispatch*, June 17, 1939. For Reynolds, see northcarolinahistory.org/encyclopedia/robert-rice-reynolds -1884-1963.

For the last-minute campaign in support of the Federal Theatre by leading actors and theater organizations, see Flanagan, *Arena*, pp. 358–59; De Hart, *Federal Theatre*, pp. 285–87; *The Washington Post*, June 21 and 26, 1939; *The New York Times*, June 27, 1939; and *Variety*, June 21, 1939. For *The New York Times* questioning work relief for actors, see its editorial "Federal Theatre Project," June 26, 1939. For a transcript of the radio program in which Welles rebuked members of Congress, see "Panel Discussion, American Forum of the Air, WOR-Mutual Broadcasting Company, on 'Relief Program,'" Hallie Flanagan Papers, NYPL, Federal Theatre Project, Closing, Radio Campaigns, box 13, folder 6.

For debates over WPA and especially Federal Theatre funding in the House and Senate, I rely heavily on the *Congressional Record*, vol. 84, part 7 (June 10–27, 1939), and *Congressional Record*, vol. 84, part 8 (June 28–July 13, 1939), especially pp. 8084ff. See too *House of Representatives, Investigation and Study of the Works Progress Administration Hearings before the Subcommittee of the Committee on Appropriations, Seventy-sixth Congress, First Session* (1939); and *Hearings before the House Subcommittee of the Committee on Appropriations, Work Relief, and Relief for Fiscal Year 1940, Seventy-sixth Congress, First Session* (1939). For reports in the press on the debate in the House and Senate leading to the elimination of the Federal Theatre, see the almost daily reports in *The New York Times*, the *New York Herald*

Tribune, The Washington Post, and other national newspapers. For Roosevelt's statement on the termination of the Federal Theatre, see *The Public Papers of Franklin D. Roosevelt,* ed. Samuel Rosenbaum (New York: Macmillan, 1941), pp. 376–77. For the final performance of *Pinocchio,* see *The New York Times,* July 1, 1939; *The Washington Post,* July 2, 1939; and the *New York Herald Tribune,* July 2, 1939. For Roosevelt's private letter to Flanagan of July 19, 1939, see the Hallie Flanagan Papers, NYPL Series 2, Federal Theatre Project, Closing, box 3, folder 3.

For Flanagan's op-ed, see *The New York Times,* August 29, 1939. For Flanagan's letter to Philip Davis about meeting with Senator Pepper, see the Hallie Flanagan Papers, NYPL, Series I, Personal Papers, box 4, folder 7. For the proposed plans for a federal department of arts in the summer of 1939, see Hallie Flanagan Papers, NYPL, Series I correspondence, "Fine Arts Bill," box 2, folder 4. See too her address of November 25, 1939, "Theatre Intermission," *National Theatre Conference Quarterly Bulletin* 1, no. 4 (December 1939), pp. 3–8, as well as *The New York Times,* November 26, 1939; and the *New York Herald Tribune,* November 26, 1936, from which I quote. For failed efforts to secure new funding for theater projects, see William F. McDonald, *Federal Relief Administration and the Arts,* pp. 539–41. For Malcolm Cowley on the Federal Theatre, see his "The People's Theatre," *The New Republic* 104, no. 2 (January 13, 1941), pp. 57–58. See too the *Chicago Tribune,* January 16 and January 24, 1942; and Christopher Benfey, "Review of *The Long Voyage: Selected Letters of Malcolm Cowley, 1915–1917,*" *The New Republic,* February 28, 2014.

EPILOGUE

For Lavery on the survival of the Federal Theatre as part of the war effort, see his 1976 interview in George Mason University's "Voices of the WPA." And for the rediscovery of the Federal Theatre's scripts, programs, posters, and designs, see *The Washington Post*, September 17, 1974. See too the "Voices of the WPA" interview with Julius Davidson about how the records ended up in Middle River, Maryland.

For Flanagan's life after the Federal Theatre closed, see Joanne Bentley, *Hallie Flanagan*, from which I quote from pp. 398–99 and 403. See too Eric Bentley's 1976 interview in "Voices of the WPA." For where Flanagan and Hopkins are buried, see George T. McJimsey, *Harry Hopkins: Ally of the Poor and Defender of Democracy*, p. 1. For Dies's life after leaving Congress, see McDaniel, "Martin Dies," pp. 517ff. For Thomas, see Lewis Herbert Carlson, "J. Parnell Thomas and the House Committee on Un-American Activities, 1938–1948" (diss., Michigan State University, 1967), pp. 221ff.

For Lyndon Johnson's vote to defund the Federal Theatre, see *Congressional Record*, vol. 84, part 7 (June 16, 1939), p. 7385. Only a small percentage of the NEA's modest investment in the arts trickles into national theater programs, primarily through politically inoffensive programs like the Musical Theater Songwriting Challenge for high school students and Shakespeare in American Communities, which focuses on schools and the juvenile justice system. See too www.arts.gov/sites/default/files/NEA-FY24-Congressional-Budget-Request.pdf. And for the most recent efforts to defund the NEA, see Andy Biggs's bill, www.congress.gov/bill

/118th-congress/house-bill/2223/text, as well as news.artnet.com /art-world/smithsonian-museum-american-latino-funding-2024 -2340880. For the cost of a battleship today, the measure Flanagan used for estimating the cost of her program, see news.usni.org /2022/11/10/ddgx-destroyer-could-cost-up-to-3-4b-a-hull-ssnx -attack-boat-up-to-7-2b-says-cbo-report. And for the Heritage Foundation's 1997 report, see www.heritage.org/report/ten-good-reasons -eliminate-funding-the-national-endowment-orthe-arts as well as its 2020 reiteration of that position: www.heritage.org/budget-and -spending/commentary/9-wasteful-programs-massive-spending -bill-can-and-should-be-reversed. See too William J. Baumol and William G. Bowen, *Performing Arts: The Economic Dilemma; A Study of Problems Common to Theater, Opera, Music, and Dance* (New York: Twentieth Century Fund, 1966); and Gary O. Larson, *The Reluctant Patron: The United States Government and the Arts, 1943–1965* (Philadelphia: University of Pennsylvania Press, 1983). For a conservative perspective, see James T. Bennett, *Subsidizing Culture: Taxpayer Enrichment of the Creative Class* (New Brunswick, NJ: Transaction, 2016).

For the words of the QAnon Shaman, Jacob Chansley, see www .newyorker.com/news/video-dept/a-reporters-footage-from-inside -the-capitol-siege. For Dies and McCarthyism, see *Little "Red Scares": Anti-Communism and Political Repression in the United States, 1921–1946*, ed. Robert Justin Goldstein (Farnham, UK: Routledge, 2014), especially Kenneth O'Reilly, "The Dies Committee v. the New Deal: Real Americans and the Unending Search for Un-Americans," pp. 237–59. Senator McCarthy called Dies "the greatest Communist hunter of all" (McDaniel, "Martin Dies," p. 574).

For the legislative effort in 2021 to resurrect a Federal Writers' Project, see lieu.house.gov/media-center/press-releases/reps-lieu-and -leger-fernandez-introduce-21st-century-federal-writers. For calls for a new Federal Theatre Project, see newyorktheater.me/2020/09/26 /we-need-a-new-federal-theater-project; www.americantheatre.org /2021/02/03/so-what-could-a-new-federal-theatre-project-actually -look-like; and Elizabeth A. Osborne, "The Promise of the Green New Deal: A 21st-Century Federal Theatre Project," *TDR: The Drama Review* 65, no. 4 (December 2021), pp. 11–28. See too, for a version less dependent on a single governmental funding source, "Echoing Federal Theater Project, 18 Towns Plan Simultaneous Events," *The New York Times*, September 12, 2023; and www.arts foreverybody.org.

For culture-war attacks on plays in American schools, see "It's Getting Hard to Stage a School Play without Political Drama," *The New York Times*, July 4, 2023, as well as "High School Theater Attendance Is Up—as Are Concerns about Censorship, Survey Finds," NPR, June 5, 2023. For censorship of Shakespeare in Florida's schools, under the state's new book-banning laws, see, for example, the *Orlando Sentinel*, July 3, 2023. Pen America reported in 2023 that the banning of books in schools is rising sharply (pen .org/report/banned-in-the-usa-state-laws-supercharge-book -suppression-in-schools).

Index

Italicized page numbers indicate material in photographs.

INDEX